MAR 5 1988

1974

Call No. 792.09   M583f

JUL 7 1989
JUL 1 0 1990

WITHDRAWN

DULUTH PUBLIC LIBRARY
DULUTH, MINNESOTA

Main Library Phone 722-5803

Footlights
on the
Prairie

THE STORY OF THE REPERTORY
TENT PLAYERS IN THE MIDWEST

Jere C. Mickel

FOOTLIGHTS
ON THE
PRAIRIE

NORTH STAR PRESS

ST. CLOUD   MINNESOTA

The International Standard Book Number: 0-87839-018-9.

Picture Credits: Sources for illustrations in this book are as follows: Mrs. Evelyn Wilson Barrick: 1, 37, 38, 39, 40, 41, 44, 45, 47, 63, 71, 72, 79, 80, 81, 86, 88, 89, 93, 94, 95, 96; Mrs. Chick Boyes: 34, 62; Mrs. Neva Brasfield: 85; Choate Family: 4; William Chagnon: 32, 61, 90; Jimmy Davis: 33; Paul A. Dwyer: 59; Crawford and Grace Eagle: 16, 17; John McIvor: 14; Arch Marshall: 53; Jere C. Mickel: 64, 91, 92; Minnesota Historical Society: 6, 49, 55, 57, 58, 67, 68, 69, 70; William Oliver: 15, 35, 48; Leroy Overstreet: 54, 76, 77, 78; Pitcaithley Collection: 3, 10, 11, 12, 13, 20, 21, 25, 26, 27, 50, 56; Rogers Tent & Awning Company: 73, 74; Mrs. Walter Savidge: 30, 31, 51, 52; Caroline Schaffner: 82, 83; Slout Collection: 5, 7, 8, 9, 18, 19, 22, 23, 24, 75, 87; Joy Swift: 2; Charles Worthan: 28, 29, 36, 43, 46, 60, 84; End Paper and jacket illustrations: Mrs. Walter Savidge.

Copyright © 1974 by Jere C. Mickel. All rights in this book are reserved. No part of this book may be used or reproduced in any manner whatsoever without written permission except in the case of brief quotations embodied in critical articles or book reviews.

Printed in the United States of America by Sentinel Printing Company, St. Cloud, Minnesota. This book was bound by Midwest Editions, Minneapolis, Minnesota.

For further information address: North Star Press, P.O. Box 451, St. Cloud, Minnesota 56301.

792.09
M583f   Copy 1

In Memory Of

Fred Wilson

[1879 - 1952]

Who with his audiences created

TOBY

The One Folk Character Of The

American Theater

Fred Wilson as The Man from Pike
County.

Preface

During a leave from Millikin University, in 1965, I followed the trail of the shows from the wide expanses of central and western Texas, to the pinewoods of east Texas, and the hills of Arkansas, from the Flint Hills of Kansas, to the high plateau of the North and West, through the woods of Missouri, and the cornfields of Iowa, up the beautiful Elkhorn valley of Nebraska, to the steep, bare hills of southern South Dakota. In the spring, I travelled over the melting snows, and flooding rivers of northern Iowa, a country still forbidding at that time of the year. The eight years, and many thousands of miles both literally and figuratively, spent with the old rep shows, has been a rewarding experience. I was awed at the boldness and courage of the showmen who played these remote areas, year after year.

Today, the real story of the shows is extant only in the copies of the old show business magazines like *Bill Bruno's Bulletin*, and *The Billboard*; and in the memories and records of the few people who owned the shows, and those who participated in them.

To all those who have helped me re-create the life and times of the shows, I owe an unpayable debt:

To Mrs. Evelyn Wilson Barrick of Portland, Oregon, for lively letters, full of valuable details concerning the several shows which her father, Fred Wilson worked on, and the principal events of his life, and for many pictures from the old days.

To James (Jim) Parsons of Philadelphia, for extended and detailed correspondence about every aspect of the shows.

To Mr. and Mrs. James V. Davis, of Quincy, Illinois, for allowing me to visit their show, the Schaffner Players, whenever I wished to familiarize myself with the workings of a tent show.

To Mr. and Mrs. Alex Pitcaithley of Carlsbad, New Mexico, for their wonderful hospitality, which gave me the opportunity to study, at leisure, Mr. Pitcaithley's theater collection of memorabilia from the old rep show days.

To Mr. William Sachs, Executive Editor of the Billboard Publishing Company, of Cincinnati, Ohio, for an uninterrupted study of the files of the old *Billboard*, and a place to read, and take notes.

To Mrs. Walter Savidge of Wayne, Nebraska, for many valuable pictures.

To Mr. and Mrs. Robert LaThey Johnson of Texarkana, Texas, for their kind hospitality.

To Mr. and Mrs. Wallace Bruce of Hutchinson, Kansas, Charles Worthan of Perry, Oklahoma, and Alex Pitcaithley, for many copies of *Bill Bruno's Bulletin*.

To Mrs. Chick Boyes of Hebron, Nebraska, Mrs. Amber Rebein of Great Bend, Kansas, and Dr. William Slout of San Bernardino, California, for copies of many of the old scripts.

To all of these, and many others who have talked to me, and written to me about the theatre of yesterday, to the Pioneer Heritage Center, of Monticello, Illinois, which gave me financial backing, and facilities for producing many of the old plays in the summer of 1967, I extend my heartfelt thanks and appreciation.

Jere Mickel

Contents

IV Life on the Show

V When Toby Came to Town

VI Obit

Appendix

*Footlights
on the
Prairie*

Tent set-up Salem, Nebraska, August 1898.

This is the story of the rep shows and tent repertoire, the small town theater. It is the history of rep theater, from the time when the first dramatic show was given in a tent. This is an account of how the show worked, what kind of organization it had, and how it differed from the metropolitan theater. This is the story of how people lived and worked on the show. It is the tale of their daily lives, full of adventure and humdrum.

Rep shows brought laughter and tears to the country towns and villages during the last half of the nineteenth, and the first half of the twentieth century. These were the shows to which entertainment starved people drove a horse and buggy forty miles over the wide prairie to see.

I   PROLOGUE

1. Niobrara, Nebraska, June, 1915

Niobrara is a small town in northeastern Nebraska just emerging from the frontier. Two miles outside the town, the Niobrara River pours its waters, full of silt brought across the wild river bottoms from Wyoming, into the bigger and rougher waters of the muddy Missouri.

The town sits on the first rise above the bottom lands, surrounded by steep hills of sand and shale. Sparse grass, prickly pear, and spider-wort are all that grow on these barren hills. At the foot of these hills, houses are set in wide lots beneath drought-stunted trees.

There is a main street two blocks long, with wooden buildings on either side. Many of them have square false fronts hiding the gable of the roofs. Hotels face each other across the main street. Two saloons at either end of the street do a lively business. The one at the north end, toward the depot of the Northwestern Railroad, is set in a well-cared-for yard, full of shade trees. A drug store and a square bank building make up the rest of the main street. Up a side street from the bank is the opera house.

1

One morning posters in lurid colors appear in the windows of the stores. The posters announce: *Red Feather and His Squaw*. Beneath the huge letters is a picture of a feathered Indian, and a white girl. Below the picture, in bright red lettering, is the play date.

A few days later on the empty lot at the end of the business section, right across the street from the principal hotel, the Koster House, the tents of a show appear. Circuses are the kind of shows that usually come in tents, but this is not a circus. It is a different type of show.

The right side of the lot is filled with a huge, circular wooden structure, called a motordrome. Inside the motordrome, a wooden floor gradually ascends to the top. A barker announces that a man, defying gravity, will ride a motorcycle at great speed, round and round, until he reaches the top of the structure.

Behind the motordrome, making a small alley down the lot, are the side shows, and rides. There is a ride called the giggler. It has small boatlike vehicles attached to a revolving floor, in which the rider sits to be whirled around in different directions. There may have been other rides not remembered, but there is nothing so simple, and civilized as a carnival merry-go-round.

Near the giggler is the tent which contains Hai-Kai, the human fish. On the other side of the alley are various similar attractions, including the Venetian glass blower.

At the end of the alley is the main tent, in which the plays are to be given. When the play is about to start, all the carnival attractions close down. Inside the tent, benches and canvas chairs front a stage opening. At the left side of the stage is a platform where a small orchestra plays.

After the audience has assembled, a perfume, characteristic of such a show on any hot summer night when it is beginning to cool off from the heat of the day, arises. It is the odor of trodden grass, moisture, dust, and tents, made more intense by the heat of the electric lights in the canvas auditorium.

The orchestra plays a medley of popular tunes of the day. The curtain rises, and the troubles of Red Feather begin. When tempted too strongly by a white scoundrel, he takes a drink of firewater, and after a startled moment spits it out! All of the people in the audience laugh. Red Feather's troubles become the audience's until the tension is broken by the curtain ending the act.

The break between the acts is filled with vaudeville. A blond, somewhat buxom woman steps in front of the curtain, and sings, "When You Wore a Tulip, and I Wore a Big Red Rose." She projects the song in such a way that it would not soon be forgotten by the folks in Niobrara.

At the end of the second act, the manager of the show comes out in front of the curtain, and announces the next show, *Black Bess*. It is a great love story set in the horse race country of old Kentucky.

The show is in town all week. During the day children sneak onto the lot. They are shooed off and stand on the corner, watching whatever is going on. After the show's week is over and it has moved on, its vaudeville and drama acts are played over and over again by the children. The children use any vacant building they can find, but their favorite theaters were the outbuildings used for storage which were part of the Koster House establishment.[1]

This show group is what was called a tent rep show. Many others like it were playing at the same period, all over the country. The greatest concentration of reps was in the Midwest, but they were welcome and prospered in those areas which were just emerging from their days on the frontier.

The tent rep show was a frontier theater, and even after the frontier had disappeared, it still maintained its hold upon the people of the smaller middlewestern cities and towns. The companies played the same territories, year after year, and became well known and well loved. The leading lady might be a bit heavier, the leading man might be graying at the temples, the comic might be balding, and bulging in the wrong places, but they were still recognized and welcomed.

The companies always produced some of the old plays, and new plays written in the same style of the old plays. These plays echoed the prejudices and values of the audience. This was no drama to shock and make its audience think. It was drama to re-affirm what the audience already believed. It was a drama based on the myth rural audiences believed in; a ritual carried out as aesthetic purgation for the audiences.[2] The drama was played, over and over, with many variations for seventy years, always to the mirth, wonder, and delight of the audience. It was the living theater of the countryside.

It had little relationship to the theater of the metropolitan areas. When the big theaters of the cities became movie palaces, the tent reps in the country could still put the movie theater in the red while they played in the small towns.

Tent rep is little known and its glories largely unsung. The long ago issues of *The Billboard* did not feature rep on the first pages, where the big money makers of the time, vaudeville and popular music and some of the legitimate attractions were three-sheeted. The rep shows had their own department called "repertoire," where the items were understood only by those who could read between the lines.

The tent shows made money. They paid regular and better than average salaries for the time. They offered regular and secure employment, as well as opportunity for the perfecting of talent which constant performance alone can bring. The shows also made small fortunes for their owners.

In 1927, the *New York Times* said that the canvas playhouses of the hinterlands made up a more extensive business than Broadway and all the rest of the theater industry put together.[3] The *Times* estimated that four hundred companies, visiting sixteen thousand communities, played to more than 76 million customers. On December 25, 1926, an article headlined "Oldest and Largest Tent Show Title is Contested by Many" appeared in the *Billboard*. By this time the story of the beginnings of this thriving business were completely lost, or at best, hopelessly confused in the memories and minds of the oldtimers.

Some of the confusion lies in the terminology. The writer in the *Times* used the term "canvas playhouses." A more basic term in the business was "tent rep." Mrs. Neil Schaffner, a veteran of the shows in their great days of the twenties, said that there is no point in talking about "tent rep." A rep show is a rep show, whether played in a theater or a tent.

The Ginnivan Show. Probably the first show to present drama in a tent as a consistent practice. This picture is dated 1897 and is a copy of a Christmas card sent by Clarence Balleras of the Casey Concession Company.

2. A Lost Theater

What is a rep company? In the Christmas issue of the *Billboard*, dated December 16, 1916, there is a short story, by Ferdinand Graham, about one of the worst hazards of the tent show business, "The Blow-down."[4] In the opening paragraph, it succinctly stated the situation of the tent shows. The time was the beginning of tent repertoire theater's greatest development:

> There is a branch, a big branch, of the amusement business little chronicled by theatrical historians, never sung of by the writer of happenings back of the curtain-line, a life numbering in its ranks all classes of "troupers," the real actor of unlimited experience, as well as the cocksure amateur just bustin' into the business—the dramatic and vaudeville company under a tent, playing week stands. Nor is tacked to the life a mite of disrepute. Kick-a-poo, dollar-a-bottle-only-three-left, is often sold between the acts under the little top, to be sure, but ditto did the Divine Sarah offer to the admiring ·Texans, the best dramatics the world has to give.

Repertoire, as it is thought of today, and as it has always been thought of in connection with the metropolitan theater, is something different from the rep shows which reached their greatest glory playing in a tent.

The difference lies not in the form of the shows, but in their organization, their methods of operation, and in their audience appeal. The best term to use for these shows is the rural theater. This is what these rep shows, tent rep shows, one-nighters, Tom shows, minstrel shows, and medicine shows were. They provided entertainment for people far away from the big cities who seldom experienced anything to break the monotony of their hardworking and humdrum lives.

There were entertainments as soon as there were any frontier settlements. If professional entertainers did not arrive by riverboat, or horsedrawn wagon, the townspeople put on their own shows. Theatrical companies did play the towns no matter how small or remote. If they had only one show to give, they would stay one night, and then move on to the next stand. Nobody was driving them out of town because of their bad show! They would stay as long as the townsfolk had the money. The only way to get money was to give another show.

Hence it came about that companies worked up several plays, so that they could stay in one town for more than one day and night. This was a help financially, not only for refilling the company purse, but for keeping down expenses, arising from too much moving about. It was a help to the physical and mental well-being of the actors.

Traveling about the Midwest during the fast changing winter weather is difficult, even today, when the most modern means of transportation are in use. A horsedrawn vehicle multiplied the danger and discomforts many times. The railroad, when it came, was not always a comfortable experience. Being able to stay in one town and still take in enough money to make expenses gave the troupers a chance to rest and recuperate for a few days. It was for these reasons that the custom of repertory, or "repertoire," as these troupers called it, began.

After the railroads had covered the country with their transportation network, they made special rates to the troupers for personal transportation, as well as for carrying their luggage and scenery. Traveling was still difficult, but it was better than it ever had been.

In every thriving town along the main lines, small theater buildings called "Opera Houses" were built. Some of these were located on the second floor of a building, and others occupied the main floor.[5] Even on the branch line, there was some kind of hall where a play could be given. Thus, the traveling repertoire troupes came into being.

They flourished all over the country, and penetrated to the most remote frontiers.

The ever advancing technology of the modern age offered a sudden threat to their security, even to their very existence. The early movies appeared. These films could be shown in any hall that could be darkened, and they were a great novelty. The American people loved gadgets. The movies made enormous profits for their operators. To stay alive, the managers of rep shows had to meet the challenge.

They met it by moving into tents. Circuses, medicine shows, Tom shows, minstrels, vaudeville, carnivals, and even evangelistic services had been given in tents, why not dramatic shows? Who had the idea first, and put it into practice, is a question argued vehemently among tent show people. The date of the first dramatic performance under canvas can be set very early in the nineteenth century. Tent shows did not become a common sight on the landscape, until competition from the movies closed indoor theaters to them.

The small town audiences streamed in. In the good old days of unconditioned air, people did not enjoy the hot and fetid indoor theaters, where the silent movies were playing.

Eventually, the motion picture novelty wore off, and the period of greatest prosperity for the rep shows began. A tent rep manager could make enough money to lay off for the entire winter if he so wanted. Most preferred to troupe the countryside, however, playing the small town theaters which remained open to them.

Rep show audiences were rural, their tastes were different from the likes and dislikes of the big cities. The city was not only more sophisticated, but it was a place of sin.

In describing the mores of the rural population among whom he grew up, Clarence Darrow said: "There were some things they did not merely believe. These they knew." Among the things they knew, was that Protestantism was divinely inspired, no matter how many conflicting creeds there were. They believed that the Republican Party (substitute Democratic, for anyone from Missouri to the deep south) and all of its doctrines were divine revelations. Above all else, they firmly believed that the farmers and the rural population as a whole, were "the backbone of the country, and the most intelligent people in the world . . . . (and) that the cities were evil, and the country was good."[6]

A certain type of dramatic play came out of this theory. It was a play suited to the tastes of small town audiences. In the earlier days, plays had been few. Plays adapted to the tastes of the countryside were nonexistent. However, in the last years of the nineteenth century, play brokers in Chicago began to supply dramatic material, especially adapted to the tastes, and beliefs of the rural audience. Playwrights like W. C. Herman, Charles Harrison, Robert J. Sherman, and E. L. Paul turned out play after play, some of them minor masterpieces. They are masterpieces from a dramatic standpoint, for even today, they play remarkably well. One cannot help asking what the real difference between *Pillars of Society*, and *Saintly Hypocrites and Honest Sinners* is, outside of the fact that one is a foreign play and the other is native.

Obviously, this theater produced no great dramatic literature. Its stars were local, and its performances were routine. Its productions were at the best, conventional, at the worst, tawdry. It brought no great dramatic innovations into the theater.

What then is its importance? It is largely unchronicled; its history is rapidly fading away. An obvious answer is that it is of no importance in the history of the American theater, but is worth recording because of its oddity, and its antiquarian interest. It is easy to show that this is untrue.

If one looks at the theater audience today, he will find that it is limited to a small percentage of the population of the big cities. Most people have never known what a show performed by professional actors is like. In the days when rep shows flourished, thousands of people saw shows given by living actors, and saw them often. They enjoyed these shows and equated them with theater. Many of them would never see a New York company, or any other metropolitan production. Those who did get away from the small towns and farms into the big cities, would be attracted to the living theater for entertainment rather than to the movies. The rep shows were a support, and promotion for the metropolitan theater. These shows familiarized the great mass of the people with performances by living actors.

The rep shows were important because they were the grass roots theater of the country. Their's was the audience of the common people. The upper middle class, the "pillars of society," and the functionaries of the churches, looked down upon the tent theater because it was pure entertainment. The puritan tradition has always been against anything that was solely for fun. The mass of the people went to the shows and enjoyed them.

The plays are important because they represent the tastes, and prejudices of the audiences of their era. People saw on the stage, the difficulties, illusions and ambitions of their own.

They saw the young minister torn between upholding his position as the most respectable person in the town, or acting like a true Christian. They laughed at the village gossip, her daily life preoccupied with spreading the news. They admired the stalwart young hero, clad in blue shirt, and overalls, ever enduring the slanders of his envious family and friends, only to clear his good name, and win the beautiful heroine in the end. They despised the man of humble origin whose financial success in the big city had warped his values. They laughed at the crude and ugly comic, and deep inside themselves, rejoiced when he outwitted the smart and the sophisticated. The audience identified with the comic, because they felt that they were ugly, crude, and stupid themselves. They envied the abused hired girl who became a Hollywood movie star. They saw in these plays what they believed to be true. In this way, the rep plays are a social history of the times.

The one genuine folk hero of the American theater, Toby, was created out of the rep shows. Toby was not the creation of any playwright or group of writers. His beginnings had existed in the American theater for a long time. His creation was the work of audiences who were fascinated with the acting of a superb comedian, Fred Wilson. Although the Toby character was grotesquely distorted by inept comedians, one cannot help regretting that the mechanization of entertainment caused the end of Toby's development and his disappearance.

These are the reasons for recording the story of tent rep. Its history, the kind of lives the actors lived, the way the show worked, the story of Toby, and the decline and fall of the shows is the story told in the following pages.

The Choate Show about 1888. No one in the Choate family is sure whether this was a small dog and pony show or a dramatic show.

On The Prairie   9

Exterior of the Opera House, Traverse City, Michigan.

Kickapoo Indian Medicine Show at Marine, Minnesota circa 1890.

Old opera house days. The town Hall and Opera House, Vermontville, Mich.

II CHRONICLE

1. Earliest Rep Shows

E. L. Paul, veteran actor-manager, and playwright of the rep shows, said that the first repertoire performance was given in 1848, in Cincinnati, Ohio, by Ludlow's Kentucky Comedians, starring Richard Stanton. This statement was found in a small notebook presented to Wallace Bruce of Hutchinson, Kansas, shortly after the death of Mr. Paul. Where Paul got this information is unknown, for Noah Ludlow provides no record of any such performance, in his memoirs.[1]

There is an interesting connection between Ludlow and his troupes, and the later rep shows, in the person of James H. McVicker, pioneer Chicago theater manager, whose name still flashes on the marquee of a theater in Chicago. McVicker got his start in show business with one of Ludlow's troupes in the mid 1840's in New Orleans. McVicker arrived in Chicago, in May of 1848, and joined J. B. Rice's company as first low comedian. McVicker was associated with theatrical enterprise in that city from that time on. Robert L. Sherman, Chicago theater man and theatrical historian of that city, credits McVicker with taking the first pioneer repertoire company on the road out of Chicago.[2] Sherman was using the word repertoire in the sense that it was later used by the companies supplying entertainment to the rural theater. He was associated with these companies during much of his lifetime. Sherman said that, "there had been such companies playing week, and three day stands, when they were filling the time between two permanent stock dates. They were not, strictly, "repertoire companies."

J. B. Rice's theater burned on July 30, 1850, which left McVicker out of work, and with no income. He saw an opportunity in the actors who were without work. With Thomas Archer as his partner, he formed his first theatrical company. While Rice was busy laying plans for a new theater on Dearborn Street, McVicker and Archer took their newly formed company to nearby towns playing on a commonwealth basis. During that August, they played such towns as Aurora, Geneva, St. Charles, Naperville, and Galena.

Rice got the construction of his new theater building underway, gathered his troupe back together and went to Milwaukee. The company remained there until January, 1851. The repertoire idea had been started, if only for a brief time, in Chicago, a city which later became the headquarters for many companies of this type.

E. E. Meredith, reviewing Sherman's book in the *Billboard*, indicates the existence of other repertoire companies in the Midwest during this early period.[3] In their respective memoirs, Noah Ludlow, and Sol Smith have described the life in the pioneer theater.[4] Studies such as Joseph Schick's *The Early Theater in Eastern Iowa*, have supplied greater details and local interest.[5] Covering the period after the Civil War, between 1870 and 1900, there are only two books, Luke Cosgrave's *Theater Tonight*,[6] and M. F. Ketchum's *Bound to be an Actor*,[7] which give any first hand account of the rural theatrical life of the times. Each of these books was privately printed, and is not readily available. Other information must be obtained from the theatrical journals of the times, or from the reminiscences of old timers appearing in magazines such as *The Billboard*.

There was a tremendous potential audience in the smaller towns and cities, which becomes readily apparent from these sources. This audience was there in spite of the religious inhibitions of the times. The severity of this religious prejudice is described in Ernest Elmo Calkins' *They Broke the Prairie*,[8] which recounts the development of Galesburg, Illinois. The plays allowed to be shown in a small town were those such as *Uncle Tom's Cabin*, a play with not only a strong moral message, but one which reminded the audience of the nation's recent tragic history.

Three different types of shows evolved from the original tent show idea to entertain the rural audience. These were the medicine show, the one-nighter, and the rep show. The simplest in operation and organization was the medicine show. It was perhaps the first of the wagon shows to give a dramatic performance in the small towns. The success of these shows was in the fact that they could travel with a minimum of personnel and equipment.

The one-nighter was a much more elaborate outfit. It required a greater financial stake on the part of the manager. The show had to move everyday and the railroads did not provide credit. The manager often owned the living car and the baggage car which always provided quarters for himself and family, if for no one else. The railroads carried the whole production, including the laborers needed to set up the show. The one-nighters had one advantage over the third type of production in that they had to know only one play.

The one-nighter presented such things as a minstrel show, or a play like *Uncle Tom's Cabin*. Bills like *Jesse James*, and *Rip Van Winkle*, were sure draws. In later years, dramatizations of such popular novels like *The Winning of Barbara Worth* were always good. Westerns, such as *Arizona*, could be depended on to draw a house. These plays foreshadowed what was to be the staple of the rep shows, the fascination of their audiences with the believable myths.

The developing rep shows, because they had several plays learned and ready to present, could stay in a town for more than one day. This cut down on traveling expenses, and perhaps offered a life that was a bit easier and more stable.

Prior to 1890, repertoire consisted of such foreign plays as *East Lynn, Lady Audley's Secret*, and *Faust*. The latter, along with the temperance plays, showed the audience's taste for something educational, as well as moral. It was the age of melodrama, and yet, except for *Ten Nights In a Barroom*, and *The Drunkard*, no American melodrama existed.

From 1890 to 1910, the rep shows reached their greatest period. They played in the popular airdomes in the summer and in the opera houses during the winter. After 1913, the movies took over the opera houses, and forced the rep companies into the tents. The greatest development of repertoire in tents took place between 1919 and 1930. Throughout the 1930's, there were still the old halls, dusty and badly cared for, which the movie houses had passed by in scorn. The rep companies could set up their shows there in the winter.

As long as the movies remained silent, and during the late 1920's when people were growing tired of them, movies were no real competition to the living rep shows. Dramatic shows and vaudeville were booked into the movie palaces to increase attendance during that period. In 1927, the Hazel McOwen Stock Company played circle stock in movie houses, bypassing the neglected opera houses.[9]

When the movies began to present sound, they not only gained back their old popularity, but even increased it many times over. In the 1930's, the Great Depression was at its peak. A large amount of theatrical real estate became unused and profitless. Movie interests took over a major share of the theater buildings and used them for their own profit, or let them lie idle, rather than allow use by any competitive group. The rep shows, whether in house or tent, were no longer an important part of theater by 1940.

Typical small town Opera House audience in early twentieth century.

2. The Earliest Shows in Tents

There is evidence that dramatic shows had been presented in tents as early as 1825. A passage in Sol Smith's *Theatrical Management,* tells of performances under canvas in the summer of 1825:[10]

> Finding there was no hopes of an engagement in the metropolis, I applied for, and obtained a situation in a company of Mr. H. A. Williams, about to commence a circuit in the western towns of New York. My salary was to be eight dollars per week. I took leave of my New Brunswick friends, who had been very kind to me, and mine, and proceeded to Albany, where I joined my new manager. Our Company performed three nights in Schenectady, and about a fortnight in the town of Little Falls, with tolerable success; after which we took up our summer quarters at Utica, where we converted a circus into a theater.

Smith does not say what plays were given in this first tent theater, in 1825, or whether the show was organized on a stock or repertoire basis, or how long the show played. He does say that he left the production, and formed his own company in Rochester. No further mention is made of tents in his memoirs.

This may have been the first dramatic production under canvas. American show business was just beginning, and played very little part in the life of American society. The records are few, and what we do know has little connection with the great theatrical development that began after the Civil War. One item that should be noticed, however, is that Smith and his friends "converted a circus into a theater."

The significance of this statement lies in the fact that for the first time, the idea of using a tent for theater performance had entered the mind of a theater troupe manager.

The use of a tent as a performance auditorium is the only characteristic common to tent rep, circus, carnival, and medicine show, which were regarded in that order of social respectability. This common feature gave the tent shows a slightly inferior status, not only in the eyes of the general public, but in the mind of the theatrical profession.

Sherman, however, dates the first performance under canvas, as the summer of 1848.[11] Yankee (Fayette Lodavik) Robinson presented *The Drunkard*, in a tent, in Rock Island, Illinois. This play had made a great hit in Boston, and had saved the Boston Theatre from financial ruin. Other historians simply state that Robinson made his first tent there, made it with his own hands. One of his biographers said that "as each tent was worn out, its successor would be much larger."[12] According to this same source, Robinson made the tents, because the halls of the time could not accommodate his production or his audiences.

Yankee Robinson's performance in Davenport, Iowa, on September 9 and 10 of 1851, is regarded as the first performance under canvas in theatrical history. *The Davenport Gazette* lists the "officers, and cast of the company," numbering thirty ladies and gentlemen, many of whom stand at the head of their profession as performers, vocalists and musicians.[13] The tent was seventy feet by forty feet, with elevated seats for an audience of a thousand people. On April 14, 1852, Robinson returned to Davenport, and this time the dramatic presentation was *The Drunkard*.

If we accept Sherman's tale of McVicker's founding the first "repertoire" company, Robinson then should have just as much credit. According to his own account from 1848, until his show became a circus, Robinson was playing what we have called repertoire.[14] He used plays like *The Lady of Lyons*, *The Idiot Witness*, *The Drunkard*, and such farces as, *A Secret*, or, *A Hole in the Wall*. Robinson produced *Uncle Tom's Cabin*, as a feature, during the summer of 1854. He played halls during the winter, and tents during the summer, very much like the repertoire activity of the 1920's.

Robinson had given up his dramatic performances by 1866.[15] He returned to what he called the "foot of Randolph Street," with a show billed as "Yankee Robinson's Colossal Moral Exhibition, Nine Shows in one—largest show on the American continent—400 horses and men." No actors appear in the list of featured performers. The bill lists only a lion tamer, a principal clown, an equestrian director, and a band leader.

As time went on, Robinson's interests turned more toward the circus, and he added horses, training them for the circus business. In 1854, he "succeeded in using large tents, and was enabled to introduce some gymnastic feats in the afternoon." This sounds a great deal like the vaudeville specialties which were an essential part of small town shows some sixty years later.

Robinson met an itinerant organization known as the Ringling (Rüngelüng) Brothers, while trouping his circus along the Mississippi River during the 1880's. The Ringling Brothers had started their career in McGregor, Iowa. The Ringlings and Robinson launched a show billed as "Yankee Robinson's Great Show Combined with Ringling Brothers! Carnival of Novelties, and DeMar's Museum of Living Wonders." After a very satisfactory season, Robinson left the circus to visit his son, who was playing with a repertoire company at one of many theater houses throughout the Midwest. As he was changing rail cars, at Jefferson, Iowa, Robinson suffered a paralytic stroke, and died like a regular trouper, "with his boots on." The great showman was buried at Jefferson, and his grave may still be seen there.

Yankee Robinson sold his theater tent and dramatic business to a certain Jack Emerson, before going into the circus business. Emerson is supposed to have carried on the business, presumably in a tent, until he sold it to J. S. Angell, a well-known manager of the rep troupes in the late nineteenth, and early twentieth centuries. Angell was still playing his shows in a tent in the 1920's. There is no substantiation for this story; it should be considered a legend, attempting to link the tents and shows of Yankee Robinson, with the tent shows of the great period of rep theatre. In *Born to be an Actor*, M. F. Ketchum mentions Jack Emerson as a member of the first Angell troupe he worked for in 1898.[16] Ketchum played throughout Michigan and Wisconsin, during most of his acting life.

There are no dates in Ketchum's book, not even a publication date. The only way to date the actor's activities, in his book, is by his mention of the 1893 World's Fair. Ketchum was twenty years old at that time. His book was printed in Newton, Iowa, where he ran a printing business for shows. He had learned the printer's trade as a youth.

Ketchum makes one important statement. On page nine, he states that there were no tents at the time of the 1893 World's Fair. It is reasonable to conclude, that until the twentieth century, there were few tent shows of the later repertoire style, that of companies presenting a series of plays under canvas. This does not include the many Tom, and minstrel shows which often played in tents.

It is pointless to look for the first tent show. Tents were being used for all kinds of assemblies, religious as well as secular. The best conclusion to draw is that shows played wherever they could find a home.

The tent rep developed out of the rep shows playing the opera houses. One show played its whole existence in a tent, and deserves the accolade of being the first real tent rep. The show belonged to the Ginnivan Family.

Mrs. Frank Ginnivan, of the Ginnivan Dramatic Stock Company, said that during the spring of 1870, her father-in-law, John W. Ginnivan, opened a vaudeville show under canvas at Monmouth, Illinois.[17] This was Ginnivan's first venture in a tent with a program he apparently continued for ten years. In 1881, he changed the format of his show.

Ginnivan and his wife, Della, organized a dramatic repertoire show to play under canvas. He engaged H. B. Keller to act in the capacity of stage director and actor. The playbill offerings consisted of *Faust*, *The Flying Dutchman*, and *The Haunted Man*. Ghost show effects were produced by the use of mirrors, a theatrical device that had been developed in London. The show played three-day stands, and traveled by horse drawn wagons. The Ginnivan Dramatic Company operated only in the midwestern states.

During the early years, the principal members of the Ginnivan Company, aside from the father and mother, were the daughter, Norma B., and the son, Frank. In 1903, Norma Ginnivan organized a company. This new organization put two Ginnivan companies on the road.

The established territory of these two companies was Ohio, Indiana, and Michigan. In 1926, Mr. and Mrs. John Ginnivan were living in retirement at Dayton, Ohio. In *Bill Bruno's Bulletin*, of June 23, 1938, under the caption of "Still with the Show," there is this story about the elder member of the family:

> John Ginnivan, more familiarly known to everybody as 'dad,' the founder of the Ginnivan Dramatic Company, and now in his 87th year, is with the Frank Ginnivan Company again this sum-

The Footlights

mer, and in the best of health. He has not missed a season in the sixty-eight years the company has been on the road.

The notice of Frank B. Ginnivan's death in 1959 helps substantiate this show as the earliest of the modern tent rep shows.[18] Its playing history as a dramatic show under canvas, continued, without interruption, from 1881, until after the beginning of World War II in 1942.

In issues from the early 1920's until after 1950, notices keep appearing in *The Billboard* and *Bill Bruno's Bulletin*, concerning the dramatic shows which were playing tents in the 1890's. Colonel Swain's show should be mentioned as well as the Christy Obrecht show.[19] There is a notice in *The Billboard* that the Obrecht show was off the road for the first time since 1896.[20] This break in the show's record was due to a fairgrounds fire in Rochester, Minnesota, which destroyed all of the organization's equipment.

J. Doug Morgan stated that the tents during the period of 1890-1910 were gradually supplanting the houses as playing spots. He recalled that he started with the Howard-DeVoss Company in 1898.[21] The company was playing only houses at the time. The company was later known as the Flora DeVoss Company. Miss DeVoss, who headed her own company, and played the leading roles for many years, eventually found it necessary to issue this unique slogan in her advertisements: "Perhaps you knew Miss DeVoss, perhaps you knew her mother, perhaps you knew her grandmother."[22] At the end of the tent rep period, Miss DeVoss' husband, J. B. Rotnour, who had joined the show as a piano player, operated the show under his own name.

In 1900, the Jessie Colton Company, one of the most popular troupes in Illinois, bought its first tent from Murray and Company in Chicago.[23] The Chase-Lister Company, another well known show, which had been in existence as a house show since 1895, opened for the first time under canvas, on May 2, 1902.[24]

One of the many farewell tours of that great show woman, Sarah Bernhardt, in 1905, gave impetus to dramatic presentation under tents.[25] The Divine Sarah had been boycotted in the theaters of the West, because she was too popular in every theater. After her appearance, patrons had no money left for any further theater-going. The usual explanation for the boycott is that Madame Bernhardt disagreed with the theatrical syndicate of Klaw and Erlanger. Klaw and Erlanger at that time controlled most of the theaters in the country. Madame Bernhardt was under the management of Sam and Lee Schubert, and William F. Connor, who were challenging the theatrical trust.

Madame Bernhardt's solution to this problem was a simple one. She suggested to her managers that the presentation be given "sous la tente." The publicity resulting from this "extraordinaire randonée et la façon ingenieuse," made this tour one of the most profitable Bernhardt ever made. People came from far and wide, some made a two or three day journey to see her. Her fame had become so great, that many people knew of her name, without knowing exactly who she was or what she did.

The story is told that a cowboy arrived half an hour after the beginning of one of her performances, in Omaha, demanding admission to the show. When told that there were no seats available, he threatened the cashier with his revolver and shouted, "I want to see Bernhardt. I have come three hundred miles to see her. I will see her!" The cashier could only furnish a very bad place in the corner of the tent. "That's all right," said the cowboy, "If I can see her for only a minute, that's all I ask." As he was entering the tent, he suddenly turned to the cashier, and said, "By the way, this Bernhardt, what does she do? Sing, or dance?"

The crowds, thronging to see Bernhardt, filled an immense tent, which seated 4,800 people. The tent had a large stage, and was as elaborately equiped as any theater of the day. As huge as the tent was, it could be taken down, moved, and set up again, in another city, after two or three days, just like the smaller tents of the rep shows and the one-nighters.

Bernhardt's profitable tour made such an impression, that the following year, the North Brothers, out of Topeka, Kansas, an organization which became one of the largest producing companies of the Midwest, toured the southwest. Their major attraction was Genevieve Russell, in *Camille*. The tour brought the North Brothers organization into the tents, and earned them a lot of money. It also made Miss Russell (Mrs. C. Chapin North) a star.

The shows proliferated during the first years of the twentieth century. Tent shows increased; at the same time airdomes lost their attraction as places of summer entertainment. This period of rising success and popularity was temporarily interrupted during World War I. Will H. Locke, veteran actor and historian of small time show business, stated, in *The Billboard*, that male help of any kind, for show activity, was extremely hard to get during the war. As a result many shows closed down between 1917 and 1919. Those which kept running, used their men in every way they could. Locke said that all the men in the troupe he was playing with at the time, worked on the lot "puttin' up, and takin' down."[26]

In 1921, small-town theater began to flourish as it never had before. During the winter small town production companies played in the old houses if the summer in tents had not been too profitable, or if the lure of playing a show proved irresistible. Rep activities in the earlier issues of *The Billboard* are found in the section devoted to stock. In 1921, repertoire had achieved recognition as a definite segment of show business, as witnessed by a section of the magazine headed "REPERTOIRE." On either side of the caption are "house," and "tent." The section gave news of any show playing in a tent. It even gave notices from boat shows.

For the next ten years, rep shows were among the most popular and well established parts of show business. They attracted audiences jaded by the silent films. Two catastrophes at the end of the decade, the Great Depression and the talking pictures led to the rep show's downfall.

It is best to date the demise of the rep companies from Bill Bruno's death in 1940. In the twenties, Bill took over the publication of *The Opera House Reporter* from the Cox family of Estherville, Iowa. Later he sold the *Reporter*, and began *Bill Bruno's Bulletin*. *The Bulletin* came out during the most prosperous period of the rep companies, and Bill continued publishing until the end of his life.

Bill Bruno's whole life was associated with repertoire theater. His earlier career was spent trouping in the rural theater. He strongly believed in the superiority of live entertainment, and continued to ballyhoo it, and believe in its inevitable resurgence until the last moment of his life.

SARAH BERNHARDT IN FRONT OF THE GREAT TENT, CYCLE PARK, DALLAS, TEXAS

Sarah Bernhardt's Triumphant Tour in the West

Frank Winninger in *The Old Wagon;* A young man playing a G-String.

The young Winninger brothers who trouped "Houses" in Wisconsin. The famous Charles in top, left.

Gussie Andrews Johnstone, leading lady and wife of O. H. Johnstone, founder of the American Theatrical Agency, largest employer of actors in Chicago.

The famous Trousdale Brothers of Iowa. Left to right: Winn, Merle, Earle, and Boyd.

3. Circle Stock

Circle stock, another original development of the midwestern small town theater needs mentioning.[27] This development was made in response to the limited audiences of the small towns and cities, and for the comfort and well being of the troupes.

One-nighters were a strain on the troupers no matter what comforts train travel provided, or how efficiently tent set-ups and tear-downs were managed. Tents were, of course, impossible to play in the winter. Houses had to be played, and traveling from town to town everyday was very tiring, even with the elimination of the tent. During the winter season, rep troupes could stay in one town, only if they went into stock. The smaller towns could not support a stock troupe for more than six or eight weeks at a time. There was, also, always the chance that engagement might not pay out.

The Trousdale family, who are credited with inventing circle stock, exemplified all of these generalizations. Circle stock was a term applied to a company that traveled the same route of towns weekly. The earliest record of circle stock activity has the Trousdale Company playing these Iowa towns: Lake City on Monday, Ida Grove on Tuesday,

Sac City on Wednesday, Rockwell City on Thursday, Manson on Friday, and Fonda on Saturday. Sunday was always the day off.

The Trousdale brothers were identified with repertoire, and one night stand companies. Their success with *The Man On The Box*, a one nighter, with Boyd Trousdale playing the leading role, made them believe that one-nighters were the only sure kind of success. The brothers were never afterward identified with a week stand show. Boyd Trousdale was an exception, for he successfully managed stock companies in midwest cities. Late in the 1920's he was doing repertoire under canvas. The success of *The Man on the Box* had made such an impression on the other brothers that one of them put out a one-nighter, *Abie's Irish Rose*, as late as 1930. This was long after the one-nighter had gone out of style, and was no longer practical from an economic viewpoint. By 1930 circle stock was the usual winter activity of the companies which played under canvas during the summer.

Winn Trousdale, who had retired and gone into the hotel business in Ida Grove, Iowa, said in 1936:

> As far as I know, we were the first to open a circle stock, "circuit stock" as we called it at the time. I opened one the latter part of December, twenty-two years ago, on December 27, 1914. . . .
>
> The theaters in the towns played were all upstairs houses, and at this time, all are closed as such, except the theatre in Fonda, which I believe is still operated by the same man as in 1914—the Mullin Brothers, who were always good friends of show folks. All the towns were good ones, and the business all winter, in spite of the unusual cold and snow, was very good.
>
> Some weeks later, in January, Boyd and Earle saw the possibilities in this new form of repertoire, and each opened a circle stock, the former in Minnesota, and the latter in southern Iowa. . .
>
> As for who might have originated the idea: I can't recall whether it was mine, or if one of the others first thought of playing on a merry-go-round. At any rate, we were pioneers.
>
> And I have never run across any argument against one of the Trousdale brothers having the original idea. It seemed such a good idea to the other managers, that in the years before World War I, there were many of them traveling a cold and windy round of towns throughout the Midwest. Government regulations of the coal supply curtailing not only train travel, but hotel and theater heat closed them in the early part of 1917. During World War I, and for several years after the circles were entirely off the road. After the war, the managers for what reason, no one seems to know, preferred week and three night stands.

Winn Trousdale said that circle stock revived with the drop off in show business in 1929. However, during the season of 1927-28, the Hazel McOwen Stock regularly visited the Rivoli Theater in Hastings, Nebraska, two nights a week. They played standard shows, and included all the rep company trappings, such as vaudeville, between the acts. The other four days of the week were spent playing in Kearney and Grand Island, Nebraska. A small company regularly visited a small hall on a side street, south of the main street, in Hastings during the spring of 1928. This company remained true to the tent repertory. Its first production, advertised as "that great pastoral drama," was *Saintly Hypocrites and Honest Sinners*.

According to Al Pitcaithley, Elwin Strong was operating a circle stock, playing Beatrice, Nebraska, and other nearby towns. The troupe traveled by train.

1926-29 were the years in which more plays were produced on Broadway, than at any time before or since, with a resulting increase in numbers of theaters. There were more stock companies in the country and city than there had ever been before. People had money to spend, and were bored with silent pictures. Money rolled in at the theater box office.

The summer of 1929 was disastrous among show people. Financial depression hit the shows before the stock market fell. During the years from 1929 to 1935, which were more disastrous for show people than for any other group, all winter activity was in the circle stocks. They were the means of pulling a large number of actors through that lean period.

Winn Trousdale thinks that it was Charles McCollister, agent on the Jack and June Alfred show in Texas, who had the idea at this time for a circle under the sponsorship of the merchants in each town played. The Alfred show is said to be the first to try this experiment. The company played towns of every size, from cities to villages. "No manager ever made a fortune in operating them," said Winn Trousdale, "the low admission making large gains impossible, but the circles have served their purpose."

The difficulty of finding a firm date for the first time any of these related theatrical enterprises, dramatic repertoire, tent rep, and circle stock played, is illustrated by this notice in Luke Cosgrave's book: "We formed a little circuit to play each town, two nights a week for four weeks—Arbuckle, Williams, Colusa, and Woodland; then over the hill to Wheatland, Lincoln, Gridley, and Biggs."[28] This is circle stock of a sort, and it happened during the late spring of 1890, in California. Many other companies before and after this, did the same sort of thing for a short time, and their numbers can never be accurately counted.

Not until tent rep shows became profitable for managers, and offered steadier employment to actors than any other type of show, did they become conscious of tent reps importance. Written records had disappeared by that time, and the memories of the outstanding players and producers were hazy and often inaccurate.

Restored interior of Opera House, What Cheer, Iowa.

A typical opera house show. This particular show is late in time, 1932, but the setting represents the best of the house show type. The show was a Justus-Romaine production of *Peggy O'Neill*. The Grand Opera House, Kansas City, Missouri.

III THE SHAPE OF THE SHOW

1. Families and Friends

The actors and managers who gave the rep show its characteristic shape, did not dream they were creating anything new or unique, but between the Civil War and World War I, they performed several astonishing feats.

They took the traditional organization, and materials of the theater as it existed, and made them fit the demands of the audiences and economic pressure of their times. Their repertory system was a new kind of theater for the rapidly increasing and prosperous population of the countryside. Their shift to tents as housing for their entertainments met the first challenge of automation in the theater with cleverness, ingenuity, and overwhelming success. They developed a theater literature to suit their particular audience, and it had little relationship to that produced in the metropolitan theaters of their era. These unique plays were a native product of the Midwest.

The manners and behavior of the troupers almost succeeded in overcoming the inherent puritan prejudices against the theatrical entertainer. In an age of increasing commercialization they very nearly succeeded in creating a genuine folk theater.

The repertoire troupes began as families. Even in the early days of Ludlow and Smith, the family was the core of the troupe, if not the whole troupe itself. The Joseph Jefferson family, which adventured in Illinois and Iowa, was a prototype of the later rep show. Shows found this type of organization adaptable to the demands of casting and to the varied hardships of theatrical life.

One of the earliest writers on the tent shows, Earle Chapin May, said that tent reps were inclined to be domestic.[1] "Each is owned," he says, "by a family which prefers to employ other families." Not only the actors, but the musicians, ticket sellers, ushers, and canvas men were ruled according to the existing social code.

The rigidity of such a code in theatrical life may seem strange, but one must remember that in the rural mind the lives of show people were considered lurid and scandalous. This viewpoint was based on inherent puritan prejudices, and the romantic notions the presentation of the shows aroused. In some towns, such as Galesburg, Illinois, few companies were allowed to show their work.[2] In others, the presence of a foreign population German, Italian, or Bohemian, mitigated the harsh disapproval ·of theater entertainment.[3] Some of the plays popular with the rep troupes, such as *Saintly Hypocrites and Honest Sinners,* reflect the showfolks' natural disdain of the ruling puritan elite.

This disdain was based on the actor's feelings of self righteousness. They felt that they were just as good, or better, than anyone else. This pride, accordingly, modified their behavior. If the show was in the hands of a patriarch, like Colonel W. I. Swain, or a matriarch, like Miss Jessie Colton, the behaviour of the troupers was watched closely.[4] If any one of them offended publicly, he was quickly banished. The easiest group to control, of course, was the family.

One of the most famous of the families in the rep business was that of Tom and Fanny Williams. They came to this country from England, in the early 1880's. They formed a company in Rock Island, Illinois, and tourned the eastern and southern states.[5]

Harry Harvey, Sr., one of the present generation of the family, whose children, grandchildren, and great-grandchildren carried on the show business tradition, said that the company did not show in a tent until late in its career, but played "what they called in those days Concert Halls."[6] Before Tom retired from show business in 1900, to operate a hotel and saloon, in Rock Island, his family numbered six daughters, Ina, Fannie, Marie, Ona, Katie, and May Blossom, and four sons, Tom, Joe, Al, and Johnny.[7]

This family was so large, that many hotels refused to take them. Old Tom had to buy a Pullman car to transport his family and show.

When the children married, they branched out to form new companies, such as the Ina and Billy Lehr Company, the Mason-Williams Company, the Harry and Katie Keene Company, the Robert and Ona Demorest Company, the Marie DeGafferelly Company, and the Elmer and Marie Lazone's Original Williams Stock Company.[8]

The famous Payton family of Centerville, Iowa, was another very colorful family. Their activities were never connected with the tents. Their most famous member, Corse, carved out a career in the metropolitan theater as the "world's best bad actor."[9] They were a part of the rural theater tradition.

If the troupes were not the usual family of husband, wife, and children, they were often headed by a manager and his wife. The married couples gave their names to the shows they headed. Names such as the Jack and Maude Brooks show, the Clint and Bessie Robbins show of South Dakota, the Neil and Caroline Schaffner show, and the Justus-Romaine show, were well known throughout the midwest.

Often, the wife's name was used to identify the show, such as the Hazel McOwen Stock Company, which played southeastern Nebraska. Hazel McOwen was the leading lady, and the wife of the manager, and leading man, Ralph Moody. It was the husband's name only which often appeared in the advertisements. The Elwin Strong show, known in the business as the "white collar show of the road," had his name on the marquee, but had as its principal attraction, his wife, Violet Manning.

Mrs. Walter Savidge, whose husband operated one of the largest shows in the western part of the Midwest, is unique, because she is one successful manager's wife who had no desire to act.[10] Her husband did not want her to act, and she never set foot on the stage professionally in her life. She contributed to the show in other ways. Mrs. Savidge's forte was business management.

Many of the managers had been married for several years, by the time they became owners and managers. Charles Worthan married his one and only girl, Sadie, before he took to the road with his show, in 1913.[11] She was a talented piano player he had met in Humboldt, Iowa. They kept up a steady correspondence from their first meeting. They had seen each other only three times before they married. Charlie was playing with the Christy Minstrels, in Nevada, when the piano player took "French Leave." Charlie sent Sadie a telegram asking her if she wanted to come out to Nevada. Receiving an affirmative reply, he told Christy about the situation, whereupon, Christy sent her a ticket to Las Vegas, from Indianapolis. The young couple, each of them only sixteen years old, was married the night she arrived in

Las Vegas. They continued with the Christy Minstrels for a season and a half. Sadie got ptomaine poisoning in Middleton, California, during the second season, and nearly died. She recovered, and they left the Christy show, to come back to Charlie's home, in Cedar Rapids, Iowa. Charlie took out his own show, shortly afterwards. One of the feature attractions on this show during its history was the orchestra. Sadie was an expert piano player, and her contribution to the show was equal to that of her husband's, as a comedian.

Show folk couples were devoted to one another, although there were the usual separations, divorces, and remarriages common to American society. In a letter to Alex Pitcaithley, Gertrude Ramsdell, wife of Franklin Ramsdell, who headed the Londale Theatre Company, playing week stands in Iowa, South Dakota, and North Dakota, between 1901 and 1904, said:[12]

> We played *Hazel Kirke* with that company. Frank played the father. His line was character, and heavy. At that time, I was second woman, and while I had to wear a cast for a bad back for five months, I played women characters just to stay on, and be with my husband. We have been married sixty-one years, I never worked a day alone, we always took joint engagements, no matter what was offered us.

The family organization of the rep shows went much deeper than mere domesticity. Each of the women mentioned, and many more, made a real contribution to the shows as a very important member of a husband and wife team.

There were always the "talent free" leading ladies, and matronly ingenues, who happened to be the managers' wives.[13] Perhaps, earlier aspirations to theatrical fame had led them in this direction. "We can shove the Little Woman into leads," was a good standby joke in rep troupes. Managers' wives often took a part, to save a salary, as well as for vanity's sake. In many cases, "they made the overnight leap from teaching school or typing to full-blown leading ladies." Many of them became quite capable, while others were never able to live up to the position suddenly thrust upon them. Some of them capable and good-looking in their youth, refused to believe that advancing age made a difference.

One woman who dared to play leads though past her fifties has been described by a colleague as "short and chunky. Her legs reminded everyone of inverted milk bottles. She had dead-black dyed hair, and a voice which could shatter glass." Her dramatic talent was "that of a ten-year old playing the third witch in a fourth grade production of *MacBeth*." Even as the owner's wife she could not always manage

The Footlights

to take the lead. She would wait for an opportunity and when her husband, who had tried to relegate her to the position of guest star, wasn't looking she would claim the part of a "shrinking, innocent young maid. She clumped, and screeched and batted her eyelashes through three acts of pure hell for the rest of us." When the troupe was playing circle stock in the little towns where she had "been known since the Ice age," she would make her first entrance in front of "the unsuspecting audience. Their 'Oh! My God!, Again!', suppressed groans could be heard clearly, backstage." The faded leading lady never seemed to be a bit conscious of her effect on either the audience or the other actors.

A rep show wife, with no one daring to challenge her position in the company, could go on playing ingenues, long past her time, or as one correspondent said, "as long as the corset industry held out." Many managers' wives played retired or older women.

Men who later became owner-managers met their future wives in their earlier years in the business. Many a young actor and actress met on a show, and lived out their lives playing in one of the companies. Romance on the road was usually frowned on.

Wallace Bruce, of Hutchinson, Kansas, whose troupes were well known in the southwest, said that he seldom engaged single girls just to avoid trouble.[14] A young girl dating with a "towner" would give the show a bad name. Show people working under undeserved stigma felt that the young man's intentions must be "strictly dishonorable." What the townspeople thought was worse.

Bruce did not worry as much about the single men, and their associations with the local people. Nevertheless, a young man who dated a town girl could bring trouble. Early in his career, Bruce was working with the Grandi Brothers Company. He played Shamrock, Texas, and roomed with a young man who had quite a reputation as a chaser.

One evening, this fellow came rushing into the room, out of breath, and white as a sheet. He had met a pretty girl in the bakery and had gone out with her. He took her home and her father chased him off the place with a shotgun. The sequel to this story is ironic.

Several years later Bruce was managing his own company. He engaged a leading man whose reputation as a chaser went ahead of him. The young fellow joined the show for the season and brought with him his new wife. When Bruce got acquainted with her, he found that she was from Shamrock, Texas. She was the same girl who had caused the shotgun episode a few years earlier.

The show people are human. Scandals were whispered about from troupe to troupe. Stories were circulated about a manager whose lust for young girls caused one of them to follow him from town to town. She hoped to become a great actress but finally committed suicide. Another story told of a manager who fired a leading and talented player because the actor accidentally walked into the leading lady's room while the married manager was making love to her. There was the mink-coated leading lady of a prominent manager who became the lover of a local business man while her husband lay dying of cancer. Rumors floated around concerning two brothers in a business partnership, one of whom was reputed to have helped himself to an unfair share of the show's profits. While these stories were only rumors, they do make the show people sound very human.

Great success came to the shows after World War I. Many incompetent and unscrupulous men, not really showmen at all, shoved their way into an activity where they thought they could make a quick and easy dollar. These managers would start out on the road with shoe-string capital, or as was said in the business, "with thirty-five dollars, and a line of paper." Fourth-rate showboat companies took to the land.[15] Medicine show troupers suddenly went into the rep business. Rep shows became associated in the public mind with shady practices and unpopular morality.

The Tent Rep Managers Protective Association (TRMPA) was formed in Kansas City in the hope of eliminating immoral practices and illegal, dishonest business habits. Its activities were largely ineffectual because of the highly individualistic nature of the managers.[16] The standard show's most effective weapon was its own established reputation for good shows, good behaviour, and honest business practice.

During the successful years from 1919 to 1930, the honest shows flourished as never before. They successfully battled the fly-by-nights. Cheap shows did not last long and when the great decline in business came in 1930, only the well-established standard shows were able to continue.

Great old troupers, who formed the rep show companies in their prosperous years, have been described with affectionate humor by Claude Allen Lewis, a scenic artist with the reps during that period. *The Billboard* for August 28, 1948, carried his succinct description:

> The manager often had a fat wife, who insisted on being the leading lady. The managers were sometimes pretty good actors. The character woman usually had a child billed as the Child Wonder featured in children's roles during the week. The

The Footlights

Child Wonder always did specialities and always looked and dressed like Little Eva.

The leading man often wore a blonde wig in some parts. His entrance thru the center door was a studied art, surpassed only by his three-sheeting ability in front of the post office at mail time. The juvenile sometimes doubled on props. The character man had been with Booth, and expected the young upstarts to respect him. The comedian was always on the make, and kept his bald red-shell-wig in a cigar box, tied with a shoe string. The general business man made his own stickum, and kept it in an olive bottle he obtained from a boarding house. He owned all shades of crepe hair, and possessed seven wigs, and a pair of whiskers on wire. The heavy woman would own a black-spangled dress which she wore as Kate Burke, in *The Man of Mystery*, and *The Woman in Black*. The general business woman aspired to be a leading lady. She was versatile, changed specialities for a week, and always made it her business to see who had the best dressing room. The heavy man could make a realistic mustache, paint scenery, and banners, and do specialities. He often was wedded to an outsider, who married him so she could see the country, and to kill time, she would visit from one dressing room to another, and often stirred up a little hell.

These were the families and their friends, the hard working troupers, with all their skills. Their human virtues and vanities provided theater for rural America, during the seventy five years following the Civil War.

Della Pringle in her later years.

Jolly Della Pringle in 1896.

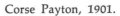
Corse Payton, 1901.

Bessie Robbins in 1900 at age 18, a popular actress.

Etta Reed, leading lady and wife of Corse Payton, 1902.

C. Chapin (Sport) North.

34   Plate I

Richard Henderson as a young actor.

Richard Henderson of Henderson Stock Company as Svengali in *Trilby*.

Al Hunt and Dick Henderson, 1930's.

Glen F. Chase, early rep manager (Chase-Lister) for both house and tent shows.

Plate II   34

Violet Manning (Mrs. Elwin Strong) popular leading lady.

Elwin Strong, popular leading man in 1905.

Worthan's first show troupe in 1913. Charles Worthan, second from top right, Sadie Worthan, bottom right.

1928-1932 The Stage Band. It was the "Best in Midwest" said Charles Worthan, seated in center with music.

2. We Do Wander Everywhere

The chief responsibility of the manager for these companies was to see that the company moved efficiently. In the earliest pioneer days shows moved by river boat, and the river was often the nearest route to the cities, as well as the settlements. It was the easiest way of moving.

The only other way to move across country was by horse and wagon, if transportation by boat was not possible. Circuses had always used this means of transportation, and continued to do so even after the coming of railroads. Circuses got the title "mud shows" from this practice.

Rep shows used the roads because they were the cheapest means of transportation. Individuals, caught in either a transportation or financial crisis, sometimes adopted the most primitive means of transportation, walking.

Luke Cosgrave, who gained his first experience with the F. W. and Grace George Company, traveled west from Kansas City in 1888.[17] He described one of his many walks in furthering his career as an actor.

After a few weeks of successful playing in El Paso, the company set out to try their fortunes in New Mexico. Luke had ridden on horseback from Pinos Altos to Kingston as advance man for the company. Mr. George decided that the ladies and one of the men would go by wagon around the mountains. Mr. George, Luke, and Phillip Snow would go across the mountains on foot, saving seventy-two miles around the mountains.

The three men got instructions about the road and set out. They expected to arrive at Kingston that night, put up their advertising, and make preparations for the arrival of the rest of the company. Around ten o'clock in the morning, they came to their first landmark, two broken-down sheds. They kept on walking until nightfall, assured that they were going in the right direction. Darkness found them back at the same sheds. They were going around in circles.

Cosgrave gave an account of the night: "We made campfire, and bedded down, this time without nourishment, except cigarettes, of which Snow had the makings. Even Mr. George smoked one—the first and only time I saw him smoke." They made beds of branches, and slept in sheer exhaustion, until morning.

They started early for there was no meal to delay them. Their only object was to keep moving. At noon, they came upon a cabin, with chickens in the yard, surrounded by a fence. No one was around. They went into the cabin, and found a large bowl of custard on the table. They caught and killed two of the chickens. "We made a fire in the fireplace, and it was wonderful how soon two of the chickens were roasted. And how good the custard was! We left a note on the table, and some tickets for the show, and were soon on our way again."

That evening, as they were preparing camp, they raised a flock of wild turkeys. They had no firearms so the turkeys got away. On the fifth day, sometime after noon, they met five men, leading three ponies, who were "looking for some show fellows, who might have missed the trail." The show had arrived in Kingston, only five miles off, two days before.

Luke said the fasting had apparently done them no harm. They felt as good as when they started, but they were very glad to be able to ride the last five miles to Kingston. When they arrived in town, the first news they heard was that Benjamin Harrison had been elected president.

Walking, as a means of getting about the country was the George troupe's response to emergency. Their usual means of transportation had been a horse-drawn wagon.

The wagons carried shows into the frontier country before there were any railroads. Wagons were used continuously for many years after the railroads had offered every inducement to show people to use their faster, and more comfortable means of transportation.

Roads were not well marked, if they were marked at all. The circus people used a time honored trick to prevent the caravan from losing its way.[18] A wagon was sent ahead of the main caravan, as a scout, to find the road. Whenever a crossroad was encountered, the driver would get out, pull down a rail from a convenient fence, and lay it on the road, pointed in the right direction. Gil Robinson, in his memoirs, described this as a technique used right after the Civil War. Ernest Jack Sharp said that it was still in use as late as 1909.[19]

Herb Walters gave a vivid description of moving his first dramatic show, by wagon, in 1915.[20] The troupe left Kansas City on June first, after a very rainy spring. They had hoped that by this date the rains would stop, but rain continued throughout the summer. "The weeds in the field were taller than the crops and it was almost impossible at times to make our moves. The roads were axle-deep in mud, most of the time, and a great many bridges were washed out." They had to begin their travels very early in the morning, while the rain was still pouring down, because "at that time of day, in the slush and water, we could move better than we could later in the day when the sun came out, and partly dried the roads so that the mud clogged up the wagon wheels." This was Missouri River gumbo mud. It "rolled," as the farmers said, making huge mud "tires" on the wheels which got so big, that even the stoutest team of horses had to stop for rest. Pools of standing water could hide holes that were dangerously deep.

The Walters Company of four men and four women moved about in "two farm wagons, old fashioned country farm wagons." Farm wagons were used for transporting grain or any other kind of produce or material, at that time. This wagon consisted of an oblong box, three feet deep, three feet wide, and ten feet long. It was set on a springless frame, between heavy wheels. It had a removable seat, resting on leaf-springs on either side, and a place for the driver's feet. Teams of mules or horses, each animal hitched to a whiffle tree and a long center tongue, supplied the power.

In a eulogy for an old-time trouper, Fred L. Cronk, a *Billboard* correspondent, summarized the spirit of show business in those days.[21] "In the '30's, I used to listen to him tell of the wagon teams getting bogged down under the load of tops, poles, scenery, props, and camping gear. He used to talk about the bravery of cast members who stuck through blowdowns, and washed out bridges when swollen streams had to be forded, and often wagons and horses were swept downstream, until they found footing on some sandbar, or rocky out-cropping."

In those old days, the trails were quagmires, and the mountain grades were not yet cut down. There were hailstorms and blizzards. None of the towns had electricity. Often the troupes ran out of provisions. One time, in the early 1900's, the whole troupe shucked corn in Nebraska, in order to move on when they went broke in the financial panic.

Cronk's troupe would enter mining towns, forts, and western villages, where no show troupe had ever set foot before. The inhabitants were so interested in these characters who had come from afar, that they would go without meals, to watch the strangers set up their tents on the lots.

Cronk and his troupers always came through. The old man ended his days on the front porch of the hotel in Moccasin, Montana, telling his tales to whoever would listen. Cronk's period was the '90's and the early 1900's. By this time, only the troupes just beginning their careers, or those who felt the urge of pioneering to inaccessible places, used horse and wagon. Those companies which had any financial status at all, quickly took advantage of the special rates offered by the railroads.

Twenty-five tickets, at a minimum charge of twenty-five dollars, were sufficient to move a company a maximum of fifty miles, and secure for the manager a free baggage car for the transportation of his equipment.[22] The troupes arrived in the town scheduled to be played, and the baggage car would be spotted on a sidetrack, convenient for both the show and the railroad. It was left there until the conclusion of the engagement.

Twenty-five fares often demanded a larger sum than the twenty-five dollar minimum, because of a longer jump. Managers had to pay the minimum, every time the show moved, whether seven miles, or fifty, so they had to figure out a route that was economically efficient.

After World War I, the railroads raised their rates. The minimum fare went to fifty dollars, even if the managers owned their own trains, as many of them did by this time. Trains carried sleepers, and added a surcharge of twenty-five cents a berth, plus a tax, making a total of one hundred and three dollars the usual minimum charge.

The Aulger Brothers Show had a seventy foot baggage car, which had an opening at the back end. The wagons carrying the tent, scenery, seats, and other equipment, to and from the lot, would be loaded at the lot. They were driven to the side track, and loaded into the car in the order in which they would be unloaded at the next stop.

The Aulger Show carried from six to seven workers who traveled in the baggage car. It was often necessary to carry an extra worker or two. If the conductor was considered "bad," that is, one who abided strictly by the rules, the extra workers could be hidden in the "possum belly." This was a rectangular receptacle, with movable covers, located in the floor of the car. The extra men stayed there until the train was moving.

The rep companies had living cars, along with baggage cars. When the Pullman Company wanted to discard a car, it was sold to a Chicago firm, Hotchkiss and Blue. They in turn, sold it to a circus, dramatic show, or some other kind of outfit which depended on the train travel. These cars were known as Pullman Palace cars. The Aulgers used these cars from 1907 until 1920, when they shifted to motorized travel.

Walter Savidge had started out using trains for his combined carnival and dramatic show, as early as 1906.[23] Reputedly, the only show of its kind in the business, he continued to use his fifteen car train, throughout the 1920's. His train cars had "mahogany berths surrounded by long, beveled glass mirrors, with silver basins, in which can be caught hot and cold running water...." In such luxury, the folks lived. Savidge did not "go gilley," or become motorized, until after 1930, when he dropped the dramatic company and toured with only the carnival show.[24] Troupes who arrived at a time when the townspeople were awake and active, could count on being greeted with wondering eyes and silent applause. Meeting trains in those days was one of the few exciting and different things to do in a small town.

J. Doug Morgan, gives a vivid description of the arrival of a troupe:[25]

> On Sundays, when the shows arrived in town, almost the entire population was down to see the actors get off the train. Every performer took a great interest in his baggage. The heavy man, and the leading man usually tried to outdo each other with their hand luggage. Each carried a fine hatbox for his silk hat, and not even the bus driver was permitted to handle this part of their luggage. The performers dressed quite a bit different from the towners, and were quite an attraction, as they walked down the street.

The transition from transportation by wagon or train to truck and auto was somewhat slower than one would expect. Early trucks and autos could not be depended upon to get over the roads in bad weather. M. F. Ketchum said that in the 1920's jumps were often made by automobiles carrying the company, and trains carrying the baggage.[26]

Complete motorization in the mid-twenties, the period of greatest expansion and prosperity for the rep shows, was quick.

Nowadays, travelling by car means efficient, easy moves with the weather presenting few problems. This kind of luxury, however, was not usual during the 1920's. Only the main roads had any kind of all-weather surfacing, and a very few of them were paved. A few more roads had blacktop and the rest of the roads were gravel. Most of the hard surfacing was found in the eastern sections of the Midwest.

There was always the problem of luggage whether travelling by train or car. The trains were the earliest and most convenient means of transportation. Train travel set the style of trunk used by the show troupes. Baggage trunks had to be easy to load on and off a baggage car. A trunk with malleable steel edges, designed by the Taylor Trunk Company, made it easy to slide in and out of baggage cars.

The Taylor Trunk Company, located at 18 East Jackson, Chicago, began business in 1859.[27] This company was the largest supplier of trunks for show business for ninety-two years. Taylor trunks were usually the ones to which theatrical children referred when they said they "were raised in a trunk."

Tracy J. Taylor, the last president of the firm, retired from business in 1951 at the age of seventy-four. He said that the company had put itself out of business because their trunks just lasted too long. The company sometimes got requests for new keys for trunks which had been made forty-five years earlier!

The saying was, "If you don't have a Taylor trunk, you aren't an actor." Among the stars on the firm's customer list were Bill Robinson, Sophie Tucker, Taylor Holmes, George M. Cohan, and most of the opera stars.

Circus people used these trunks exclusively. One time, a check was made on the brand of trunks carried by the Ringling Brothers and Barnum and Bailey Circus. Four hundred and twenty-five out of the four hundred and fifty-five trunks carried were from the Taylor factory.

By 1928, the Taylor Company had three hundred employees and three factories. When specially designed trunks for strapping to the side or back of a car were in demand, the Taylor firm became the largest manufacturer of auto trunks. In 1943 the firm quit manufacturing trunks, and confined itself to retail sales of leather goods and luggage. When Tracy Taylor, son of the founder of the firm liquidated the business in 1951, he said that he was quitting because he had no sons and did not want to leave his daughters with the job of winding up a business.

Trunks were simply highly specialized forms of boxes, adapted not only to the needs of theatrical people, but also to the requirements of their carriers. Until the end of the first quarter of the twentieth century, in the United States, the theater, big time or small time, was a traveling organization. The larger cities offered many opportunities for actors and managers to establish more permanent residence. The ambitious entrepreneur, however, would look farther afield for economic and artistic opportunity. The amusement hungry frontier would always attract him.

Dramatic End Tent.

Savidge Players audience in the 1920's. Note the crowd in the "blues."

Interior of "Skeeter" Kell's tent during 1920's. Curtain shows advertising of Paragould, Arkansas merchants.

Interior of modern Schaffner tent now owned by Jimmy Davis.

Chick Boyes' night show ready to start.

3. The Old Opera House

There were, at first, no theaters in the rapidly growing frontier community. In thriving frontier towns, such as St. Louis, Mo., no building was built for theatrical presentation until 1836.[28] Regular show presentations had been given in the Old Salt House beginning in 1826. Before this date, shows had been staged in available halls. Joseph Schick said that in Davenport, Iowa, from 1836 to 1853, all public entertainments were given in hotel dining rooms, church assembly halls, school rooms, outdoor pavilions, or in the court house.[29]

Joseph Jefferson III, of *Rip Van Winkle* fame, noted that the family company, trouping the Midwest in the early days, was often forced to offer its entertainment in the most unsuitable structures.[30] The personnel of the small company were experienced actors who could give a satisfactory performance in any kind of structure that could be adapted to theatrical presentation.

As soon as any town became established enough to realize itself as a community, some kind of public hall was built. It was not necessarily thought of as a theater. Often, it was located on the second floor of a main street commercial building. The first floor was occupied by a grocery or dry goods store.

These impromptu theaters of course usually had level floors, with stages or low platforms at one end. Built in the pioneer days, many of the early show buildings did not survive the growth of communities. A number of theaters built in the 1870's and 1880's, the great days of house trouping by the rep shows, still exist in the small midwestern towns, empty, unused, and ghostly with layered dust.

Claude Allen Lewis, a well known scenic artist in rep and stock, gives us a vivid general description of one of these old halls:[31]

> Then there was the old town opera house. The stage door was always up the darkest and dirtiest alley in town. It had its roll curtain and a green baize, which when turned over, was red. Then there were the bunch lights made from an old dishpan, which acted as a reflector. Nails were driven into the wall which acted as a rack for stage-braces which invariably fell during a quiet scene . . . canvas doors that never stayed shut after locking them, and which would slowly swing open during an important scene.

Backstage old lithographs were pasted on the walls. They depicted such things as the sawmill scene from *Blue Jeans*, or one of the more sensational scenes from such a melodrama as Lincoln J. Carter's *The Fast Mail*. In the dressing rooms, there were peek-holes in the walls, showing the raw bricks and lath of the building's construction. Names were written there with red grease paint, and faded stickers of such plays as *The Warning Bell* and *The Royal Slave*, reminded the viewer of past glories. Advertisements for Professor J. Warnesson's grease paint almost always boasted its superiority in placards glued to the wall. There was often only one dressing room on either side of the small stage.[32]

The stages of these old theaters were not more than twenty feet deep, and twenty-five feet wide, with a proscenium, thirteen to fifteen feet in height. Stage lofts for rigging were almost unheard of. Curtains were used, but they were roll-up curtains, rather than drops.

The construction of these curtains was unique and efficient. The bottom of the backcloth was rolled once, and glued to a drainpipe which extended a few inches at either end. A length of sash cord was attached to each end of the drainpipe, and then to an eyebolt in the ceiling. These cords acted as stoppers, necessary if the drainpipe was to roll the curtain. Another length of sash cord was rolled once around each end of the drainpipe, and passed through a single pulley at one end and a double pulley at the other. The two lengths of sash cord

The Footlights

were tied together beyond the double pulley, and attached to a single rope which extended down to a tie board. The curtain could be rolled up to the ceiling, out of the way, or let down in full view of the audience by means of this apparatus. The diagram shows how this worked.

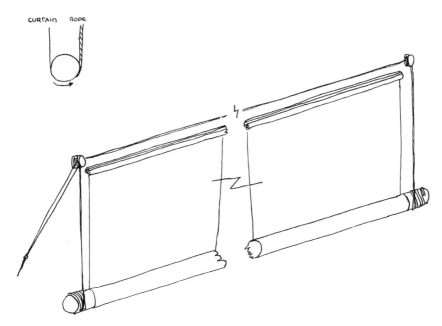

CURTAIN   ROPE

The front curtain also rolled up and down in this fashion. It was decorated with some masterpiece of the sign-painter's art set in the middle, surrounded by baroque scrolls. Around the sides, and the top and bottom, the advertisements of local merchants were usually painted.

This practice originated in the Le Claire hall at Davenport, Iowa, where, during the engagement of Hough's Lyceum, the drop curtain was placarded with advertisements of local business enterprises.[33]

The play house furnished the scenery for use by the visiting troupes before the invention of diamond dye scenery. It was physically impossible to carry anything except the props and costumes needed by the troupe for the productions. Whatever the bill, the same four sets were always used: front and back, timber and town. Stock flats, legs, and wings were furnished in some of the better houses.

Jesse Cox invented diamond dye scenery in Estherville, Iowa, around the turn of the 20th century.[34] The diamond dye scenery meant that travelling troupes no longer needed to depend on the stock scenery provided by the houses. This new kind of scenery material, which was hung from battens, could be folded after the show closed and packed into trunks. Jesse Cox's invention obviated the use of flats, awkward to handle, and always needing to be crated for shipment. Diamond dye scenery enabled the troupes to advertise "Carloads of Spectacular Scenic, and Dramatic Effects." Carloads, however, usually consisted of four or five trunks of diamond dye scenery.

Jesse Cox got into show business by playing in the band, taking small parts, and acting as property boy for the old Long Dramatic Show. His interest in shows came to him naturally, since his father was the original publisher of the *Opera House Reporter*.

The Long troupe needed scenery and Jesse decided to try his skill at painting it. The scenery worked. He went home to Estherville to start the Cox Scenic Studios.

One day, a one-night-stand producer came to Cox and said, "Can't you build me some scenery that doesn't require a whole baggage car for transportation?"

Cox started experimenting. He bought packages of dyes, the kind women used for touching up an old dress or scarf. He had special soft bristle brushes made, with short hairs, and he learned a trick that required other scenery men years to discover. In watercolor art the highlights are painted. In dye scenery, the highest highlight is provided by the cloth. The painter works down from the highlight, instead of adding the highlights.

At the height of his scene painting industry, Cox had a standing order for two thousand yards of cloth a week. The business became a big international one. The scenery was easy to pack and load. Most important of all, it would not crack or flake, because the dyes, as the color medium, became a part of the scenery fabric.

The Cox Studio, built with a high, off center gable construction designed to accommodate the great scenery paint frame, is still standing today, ready to produce a large scenery job. The scenery frame can also be used for highway sign sections. The principal activity of the Cox Studio today is the design and construction of advertising signs.

The business is now carried on by Robert Cox, who was in partnership with his father before Jesse's death in 1957. Jesse, even at the age of seventy-eight, was still active in the business and could, in a few minutes, turn out a rough sketch for a neon job or highway bulletin.

Lighting, as an effective theatrical device, was not developed in this country until 1925. Its use throughout the first quarter century was largely confined to a crude, general illumination. A night scene effect, where it was required, was achieved by turning on a circuit of blue bulbs. Many of the towns played by the rep shows did not have electricity as late as the second decade of this century.

Small town theaters provided kerosene footlights and some kind of overhead lighting device, both using the same fuel. The invention of the Coleman gasoline lantern provided a brighter, safer lighting medium. Air was pumped into a receptacle, filled with gasoline, causing gas to form, which escaped through lighted wicks, providing a more effective illumination. These lamps were used as late as 1929 in towns that didn't have electricity.

The early nineteen hundred's tent shows, such as Karl Simpson's first outfit, used crude and dangerous gasoline torches for illumination both of the theater and of the stage.

The rep shows played anywhere and everywhere, adapting themselves to all local conditions, no matter how crude. The Wight Theater Company would play such isolated towns as Aberdeen, South Dakota.[35] These towns, although large for their area, were far enough distant from the centers of technical improvements so as to lack electricity in the local theater.

The overhead stage lighting in the Aberdeen theater consisted of a Rochester lamp, fueled with kerosene, hanging in the center of the stage. During one show the lamp fell, spilling kerosene all over the stage carpet. The carpet didn't catch fire because the excessive amount of kerosene smothered the flames. But for this lucky chance, the actors and audience would have burned with the building.

Many of the old playhouses often lacked adequate facilities for the presentation of a play. They seldom provided facilities for the most obvious and necessary creature comforts. Modern plumbing was unknown. Hot and cold running water or any kind of water faucet arrangement was a great rarity. The actors would often have to put on their makeup, dress in cold discomfort, and undress and wash in the same way. A bowl and pitcher for washing, a slop pail for wash-water and comfort station, might be the best available facilities. Dressing room space was often completely lacking. Central heating was unknown. Managers who wanted to keep their troupes going during the winter, decided to "Go South."

Those shows which could not or would not "Go South" invariably ran into the old-fashioned and inefficient heating arrangements. The first thing one sees when entering the old opera house at Shelbina, Missouri, is the old-fashioned heating stove, placed on a high platform, in front of the stage right proscenium wall, above the heads of the occupants of the first row seats. This opera house, the finest of its day, has been locked up for some forty years. It is opened occasionally to allow the curious visitor to disturb its ancient dust.

Why did the shows play such theaters? Actors love to give shows, and managers love to present them. There was a huge profit to be made, even at low prices, if there was an overflowing house. In the larger and more show-minded towns, mining towns, and towns with a large foreign population, some very fine and well-equipped playhouses were built.

Miss Lucille Spooner said that the Italian population of Centerville, Iowa, largely employed in the soft coal mines nearby, gave great support to the Drake Avenue Opera House.[36] In Niobrara, Nebraska, the Bohemian element of the community was responsible for the very fine Z. C. B. J. Hall, still standing today.

The German population of Davenport, Iowa, loved their beer gardens, shows, and jolly times. A strong association of German theater lovers, the *Liebhabertheaterverein* (the love-to-have-theater club) built the first real theater in the city, equipped not only for shows, but for balls, dances, and card games.[37]

All fun, sinful in the view of the average pioneer as taught him by the Protestant churches, was for foreigners and riff-raff, not for the pillars of society.

The use of the terms "opera house" and "house" to describe the centers for small town entertainment in the preceding description of non-metropolitan theater activity, and the infrequent use of the term "theater" has been noticeable. This usage has been purposeful. The native born American, obsessed with the religious prejudices of his ancestors, looked upon any kind of theatrical activity as something less than respectable. In his mind, any kind of show was associated with aristocratic sexual immorality, drunkenness, and any other kind of social misconduct that could arise from the apparent instability of the life of the theater. Actors wandered from place to place and had no settled home. They did no work in the generally accepted meaning of the term. They "played."

Music had for centuries been a respectable art as it had always been associated with the worship of God. Opera is music. Strange and unintelligible as it is to most people, the term opera house came to be applied to any place devoted to shows.

Americans are great believers in names. They are great name callers and name acceptors. If the name given to anyone or anything conjures up the right image, it will be immediately accepted. The respectable members of society in the small town could attend an entertainment in an opera house without blushing in embarrassment.

Even so, actors or any person connected with any kind of show were always looked upon as outside the bounds of respectable society.

Terms other than opera house were used to blunt this general prejudice. In the smaller towns, town hall was as common as opera house. The words, town hall, brought to mind a general meeting place of the people for any purpose whatsoever, even a church service.

When the rep shows took to tents and became very popular, no such euphemism seemed necessary. The reps advertised themselves as dramatic companies, providing continuous entertainment, with their specialty numbers between the acts. Perhaps the innumerable Bijou, Crystal, and Empress theaters throughout the country devoted to the silent films helped break down the prejudice against the word "theater."

Justus-Romaine Company, 1923, at Verdigre, Nebraska.

Charles Worthan troupe 1926-27. Owner Charles, wife, Sadie and daughter, Bonnie in box office.

On The Prairie

Baird & Wilson Company: 1) Ed Armstrong, 2) Joseph Baird (Wilson's partner), 3) Fred Wilson, 4) Bill Stolman, 5) Jack Carrington, 6) Ruby Rumley, 7) Mrs. Rumley, 8) Pearle Wilson, 9) McDonald, 10) Whitecomb.

Horace Murphy Company, 1911. Fred Wilson (Toby) tenth from left.

Baird & Wilson Company, Eugene, Oregon, 1922.

4. The Shows Move Outdoors

The use of a tent as a place for presentation of a dramatic show goes far back in American theater history. Most of these presentations were intermittent, and made on the principle of using any available place a show could be presented. There had always been a demand for summer entertainment by audiences and by actors wanting work. As soon as the railroads could provide dependable transportation, and the towns provide opera houses, small town trouping became an extensive and profitable business.

In the mid nineties the airdome, another unique American contribution to theater housing appeared.[38] These outdoor theaters flourished in large cities and small towns, until World War I. Wallace Bruce operated one in the city park in Hutchinson, Kansas, as late as the early nineteen twenties. The airdomes were so profitable that two large circuits were organized to provide programs for them.

The Bell and Ollendorf, and the Crawford circuits operating out of Kansas City on a guarantee and percentage basis, were the best known. They presented stock, vaudeville, and rep in the earlier days, and when the movies achieved popularity, silent pictures.

51

The simplest type of airdome was a canvas wall, with a box office at the front, and a canvas covered stage with the dressing rooms at the back. The middle area was filled with rows of benches.

Another type of airdome was built in Peru, Nebraska, in 1915 to show pictures and vaudeville.[39] The wall was made of corrugated iron sheets both high and slippery enough to prevent anyone from climbing over it. It had a covered stage at the rear, and was fronted with a box office.

During the nineties, every town of any consequence in Texas, Oklahoma, Kansas, Iowa, Nebraska, and Missouri had an airdome theater. It was usually located on a choice lot in the heart of town. The airdome at Omaha was located on the site of the future Brandeis Theater. The airdome stage at this theater was permanently roofed.

Some airdomes had an adjustable canvas roof to stretch over the audience for protection in case of rain. The facilities for play productions were well equipped with a stock of permanent scenery. Airdome seating capacity ranged from five hundred to one thousand five hundred seats, depending on the size of the town.

One of the most famous airdomes was located in Cycle Park, Dallas, at the end of the streetcar line at the old fairgrounds. Today, this spot is the home of the Texas State Fair. The main feature of the park was the twenty foot wide, mile long, oval-shaped race track, built of white painted wooden planks, for bicycle races.

On one side of this oval was the grandstand, with a seating capacity of two thousand. In front of the grandstand was a large stage, with an apron extending twenty feet out toward the grandstand. The orchestra sat at one side of this apron. There was a distance of sixty feet between the stage and the audience as the width of the racetrack and additional space of forty feet intervened.

One of the actors who played there with the Ruble-Kreyer Theater Company in August, 1897, the first rep company to play the airdome, said that the actors had a real problem in making themselves heard.[40] They all had good voices and succeeded in making themselves understood.

Airdome theaters, according to E. L. Paul, reached their greatest period of expansion about 1908, and proved a godsend in at least two ways for the repertoire companies and their actors. Because of their location in the far Midwest, they changed the center of the rep business from Chicago to Kansas City. Kansas City was a more convenient home base for the companies than the conventional midwestern Chicago. Winter engagements became easier to book and cheaper to produce. Up to this time rep actors were still placing their ads for employment in the *New York Clipper*.

Several reasons are given for the sudden decline and disappearance of these open air theaters. E. L. Paul said that the coming of the musical tab show, tremendously popular in the houses, never caught on in the airdomes. The airdome managers, after seeing their popularity, had booked them in place of dramatic shows, to their own undoing. The unforeseen effect of continous dramatic fare through winter and summer apparently gave patrons a surfeit of plays. The novelty soon wore off turning audiences to other kinds of outdoor entertainment. The companies of this period were still starving for new plays, and audiences refused to pay a higher price for the same old plays that they had seen during the winter at the ten-twenty-thirty-cent price schedule.

The airdomes were a blessing for the rep companies. They provided opportunity for the expansion of these companies. The decline and eventual disappearance of airdomes was one of the forces turning the rep shows toward the use of the tent as a summer theater.

Use of tents for religious revival meetings, ironically enough, has a strong connection with their use as theaters. Famed revivalist Dwight L. Moody used tents all the time. His friendship for Walter Driver, later one of the founders of the United States Tent and Awning Company, started that young man on a brilliant career in tent manufacturing business.[41]

Driver, whose family had moved from Canada to Chicago when he was thirteen, was a newspaper boy at the corner of Madison and Halsted streets. He attracted the attention of one of the neighborhood clothing store owners who presented him with a Little Lord Fauntleroy suit.

A youngster, dressed in this kind of suit and selling newspapers, caused quite a stir. Moody happened by one day, and noticed the boy. The two became great friends and one day, Moody asked him, "Are you going to sell newspapers all your life?" Walter had no answer for that question. "You come with me," Moody told him, and he took Walter to the Murray and Baker Company where at that time Moody bought all the tents for his evangelistic performances. He often placed many of his Bible students in jobs with the tent manufacturing firm.

Walter Driver started his career there as errand boy, and stayed for ten years, working his way up to plant superintendent. He foresaw a future for himself in the outdoor show business. Driver turned his attention away from the making of evangelistic tents, which up to that time had been one of the principal activities of this company.

In 1885, with two friends, Edward P. Newmann and William Leeper, and ten thousand dollars which the three of them managed to scrape together, he founded the United States Tent and Awning Company. The company began operations in a rented building in Chicago.

At this time the Murray and Baker Company partnership had broken up, Mr. Murray staying with the Chicago plant, and Baker moving on to Kansas City, where he started the Baker and Lockwood Tent Company. Driver went on to a career as head of one of the largest and most successful tent manufacturing companies in the country. The basis of his success was his personal contact with the managers and owners of show business in tents. At the time of his retirement in 1938, he said that he had sold canvas to every circus and tent show in the country.

After the invention of the dramatic end tent, most tents were made according to its specifications. One of the finest of these was that made by the Rogers Tent and Awning Company of Fremont, Nebraska, for the Aulger Brothers Stock Company which was first used in the season of 1930.[42]

The canvas auditorium swelled from the stage end to an eighty-four foot width, with a length of one hundred and thirty feet, allowing a total seating capacity of one thousand, four hundred. The seats, all numbered and reserved, were covered with green canvas, and provided with fairly comfortable cushions. Reservations were put on sale in advance of the engagement at the local stores, and the opening night was often sold out.

This fine Aulger Brother's tent was the first of its kind made by the Rogers Company. It was considered an innovation, since it could withstand the wind better than any tent previously manufactured.

The first tents used for dramatic shows were the simple roundtop tents. To make a place for the stage, the back wall of the tent was not hung, leaving an opening where the stage could be set. The stage end of the tent roof sloped very little. A floor which served as a stage was placed on jacks and stringers in this opening. There was a canvas roof, and canvas side walls to close off the stage and dressing room areas.

The roundtop tent's main disadvantage was the big centerpole. It stood flush against the stage center blocking a clear sight line. There is no record available of who invented the first dramatic end tent. This invention eliminated the center pole, and allowed for clearer sight lines. Mr. H. C. Somerville, grandson of C. J. Baker, said that this type of tent was used a number of years before the turn of the century.[43]

A man by the name of Knabenshue, a carnival operator in the East, brought a damage suit against the Baker-Lockwood Company in 1905. His suit claimed that he had invented the idea of eliminating the center pole in front of the stage.

His patent covered the idea of using masts for each of the front stage poles, with a cable stretched between the masts. In the center of this cable, a block and tackle was used which lifted the canvas at a point midway between the two masts. This device eliminated the necessity of inside support at this place in the canvas roof. This tackle allowed for a higher stage opening, without having much "bag" in the canvas, and with no poles to block a clear view of the stage. The idea of using masts at the two front stage poles with tackle in between, was used before 1905, proving this. A 1905 photographic illustration of a tent made for Tom Franklin Nye, who ran one of the earlier tent shows in Texas, showed this setup being used.

The catalogue showed photographs of the inside and outside of the dramatic end tent. The inside photograph showed a "tack card" pinned to the front of the stage proscenium, with a date on it. Mr. Somerville gives Monday, June 12, 1905, as an "illustration date," saying that he does not remember the exact date. He also said that the United State Government has a bound volume of Baker-Lockwood catalogues, from 1900 to 1910. The government would not release the volume after the suit, although the company tried very hard to have the volume returned. Since proof had been established that dramatic end tents were made before 1905 Knabenshue's patent was declared invalid.

Mr. Somerville said that most dramatic tents have been made with push-poles for the two proscenium poles. The other type of tent used for dramatic shows is known as the bail-ring tent. Since the idea of the rigging of the dramatic end tent was proved to have been invented before 1900, the invalidity of the patent was declared for both types of tents.

The general principle in raising and lowering, or packing a push pole tent is that there is no raising, lowering, or packing, until the tent is on the ground.[44] The opposite is true of the bail-ring tent. With this type, all poles and rigging are set where they are to be used before the tent is raised.

In the early days of the tent shows the tents were not water-proofed. Bob LaThey Johnson quotes one early manager who said, "If it rains, they won't come; if it rains after they come, it doesn't matter." The managers soon discovered that following this dictum was unsatisfactory, because the mildest threat of rain would keep people away. A method of waterproofing had been invented. It was dangerous because it used highly flammable materials—a combination of gasoline and paraffin. During World War I, Colonel W. I. Swain invented a safer formula, but this formula was taken over by the government for use in the war, and was never released for general use until after the tragic Ringling Brothers Circus fire in 1944.

The old form of waterproofing consisted of mixing paraffin wax, diluted with about four parts of gasoline or benzine.[45] When large areas like the top of a big tent were waterproofed it was a thinner mixture since the goods treated would lose flexibility if spread with too heavy a mixture.

The tent canvas would be spread on the ground and the waterproofing preparation sprayed on. Watering cans were thought well adapted for this purpose, if the nozzle was covered with a fine wire gauze. This way of spreading the preparation required less effort, and could be done with a minimum of waste. A strict no smoking rule, of course, was always in force when tents were being waterproofed.

Canvas could not be treated before the tent was sewn, because the preparation stiffened the material. Stiffened canvas would not only make the sewing by hand or machine more difficult, but would cause the needles to leave perforations too large for the thread to fill. These small holes would cause leaks in the finished tent.

When tents had been treated with this type of waterproofing they could burn with lightning speed, and to complete destruction. On July 30, 1928, the new tent of the L. Verne Slout Players, set up for engagement at St. Charles, Illinois, burned to the ground in less than ten minutes.[46] Those few minutes destroyed the tent, as well as company and personal equipment. Someone had dropped a lighted cigarette into a pile of dry leaves.

A fire like this was the worst kind of disaster. Fire was considered even more dangerous than a blow-down. The Slout Company had to call off the remainder of that season's engagements. Encouraged by the esteem of their friends in the towns of the company's established circuit, they worked and planned all winter, and were back on the road again with a show in the spring of 1929.

Murphy's Comedian's baseball team.

Plate IV   56

Billboard paper from Walter Savidge Shows.

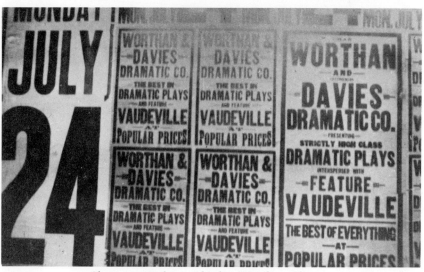

Show paper from Charles Worthan Show.

Flyer from Jack King's Comedians, Jack King is "Freckles."

56   Plate V

Flyer from Baird & Wilson's Comedians.

Letterhead of the Worthan Dramatic Company.

Plate VI   56

The Baird and Wilson Orchestra, 1913. Joe Baird with the cornet.

The Justus-Romaine band, Verdigre, Nebraska, 1923.

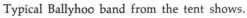

Typical Ballyhoo band from the tent shows.

5. Bands, Baseball, and Ballyhoo

When the show arrived in town it had been anticipated by the people for some time. One-sheets, paper posters twenty-eight by forty-two inches, had proclaimed its arrival for at least a week before the show hit town. These posters hung in the windows of empty store buildings, as well as in those of thriving businesses. For the large shows, twenty-four sheets flashed their messages from the sides of blacksmith shops and barns, as well as from billboards.

Most shows hired an advance man, who went ahead of the show, a week or two, and saw to it that a lot was located, a license for showing obtained, and that a proper amount of billing was put up around the town. Sometimes, in later days, when attendance had begun to decrease, this man would arrange for sponsorship by some local organization.

Billing consisted of paper "sheets" of various sizes, based on the conventional one-sheet, prepared for the shows by printing houses which specialized in turning them out.[47] Some of these posters were specially designed for the plays produced. Many of them were made

57

up ahead of time, in conventional form, leaving only the dates and places to be added.

Many of these theater print shops were located in such cities as Kansas City. These were cities which shows considered headquarters, and the shows provided a profitable supply business. Some of the printers were located in small towns. M. F. Ketchum, of Newton, Iowa, operated Ketchie Show Print after his retirement from show business.

The most used sizes, other than the one-sheet, and the three-sheet, were the eight, sixteen, and twenty-four sheets. All of these were multiples of the twenty-eight by forty-two inch one-sheet. They were printed in strong clashing colors, usually red, blue, and green on white. They may have been crudely designed, but they got their message across.

The shows also developed a special flyer, announcing the plays, vaudeville acts, and picturing the cast, as well as describing any special features. This kind of flyer is used by the one or two show companies that remain active today. It was usually seven to eight inches wide, and twenty-one to twenty-four inches long, printed on colored news-print. The advance man would distribute these to stores and mail them to all rural boxholders.

Some shows developed a special publication of their own for similar use. Charles Worthan's show mailed a special four-page maga-zine called the *Red Wig*. The Slout Players mailed a similar publica-tion called *Toby's News*. At the beginning of each season, the Vermont-ville, Michigan, *Echo*, the newspaper serving the show's headquarter town, devoted a special supplement to the show.

Nothing was too sacred to use for ballyhoo. Lodema Corey's marriage to Ralph Clem, on the Ed. C. Nutt show, in Alabama, in 1916, was done for two effects.[48] The audience, as guests at the wedding, would spread a great deal of comment, and the towners would feel more rapport than ever with the show. The prevailing puritan prejudice against the theater would be dealt a blow by having one of the local ministers perform the ceremony. If the minister felt that it was proper for him to unite these two young people in matri-mony right there on the stage then why would anyone in town feel that it was not respectable to attend the show?

The gods or fates that presided over these shows did not always bless the publicity stunts that had been dreamed up. Wallace Bruce playing in the airdome at Hutchinson, Kansas, in 1932, had booked a mentalist for a "special added attraction."[49] On Monday night, the mentalist put a young woman to sleep in a downtown store window. She was to stay there sleeping until the coming Saturday, when he would awaken her on stage. All week, throngs of people watched her as she lay sleeping in the window. The proprietor of the store told Bruce that the equivalent of the entire population around the small city had stopped to gaze into the store window.

The stunt had also caused lots of talk about the town. Mr. Bruce was looking forward to the biggest house of his career on Saturday night. The advertised time for the awakening was the evening show at eight. When the house opened at seven thirty, the rain began to pour down "in buckets full," and continued until ten o'clock.

The potential audience never arrived. The dozen or so people who defied the elements to see the show were asked up on the covered stage to see the mentalist awaken the girl. Bruce added sadly, "My mother told me that there would be times like this!"

After a show arrived in a town, the manager and actors set out to establish a suitable image in the minds of the towners. These images ranged from folksy and friendly, to glamorous and distant. This effect varied according to the personalities of the managers and the kind of show they were putting on. Harry Hugo, whose show was not a polished one, visited with all the farmers and townspeople, as if he were really one of them. Fred Wilson was well-known for his delight in talking to the local people. Elwin Strong worked for a different effect.

H. L. Carlstrom, who lived next door to Strong in Fremont, Nebraska, and knew his show very well, said that he used to parade around town in a tall silk hat and Prince Albert coat.[50] Carlstrom said that Strong gave the word to the actors not to speak to him if they met him on the street.

When the actors on a show adopted this same kind of attitude, it was known in show lingo as "three-sheeting." The leading man and leading lady would get dressed up in their flashing best and visit the post office, or merely walk up and down the streets of the town. In the days before skirts were shortened, and when hats were still hats, the leading lady could dazzle the eyes of towners accustomed to their own drab everyday clothes. The leading man, in checked gray and white suit, with a diamond stickpin, (and it could often really be a diamond) in his carefully knotted four-in-hand, and a derby hat on his head, invited the secret envy, but open scorn of all the men, and appeared in the women's dreams as their ideal.

Frank North, one of the famous North Brothers, told Carlstrom that in the old days all the actors on the show dressed in their best when making an appearance on the street. The managers tried to see to it that they themselves, and their principal actors were invited to dinner at the better homes, usually the homes of the town bankers.

The principle behind this was that the rest of the people of the town would follow if you could get the rich and well-known to attend the show.

Managers aimed their efforts at establishing as great a rapport with the towners as possible when the shows were really flourishing in the mid-twenties. Most of them went out of their way to be "just folks." The great Harley Sadler was not only a fine actor and expert show manager, but sincerely liked. He took an interest in the members of his audiences as individuals.

After the last performance of an engagement in Lubbock, Texas, while the tent was being taken down, and all its equipment was being loaded on the railway car, Sadler saw a small roadster nearby that was obviously in trouble.[51]

A woman and two children were sitting in the roadster. The father of the family was cranking furiously in front of the car. Sadler recognized the group as old patrons, who lived thirty miles south of town. It was midnight, rain was threatening, and all of the complications of the teardown demanded Sadler's attention. Nevertheless, he went up to the struggling farmer, asking him concerning the trouble. The farmer answered him by saying that he supposed the car would eventually start, but the ignition was apparently not what it used to be.

Sadler returned to his railroad cars to watch the loading of all the paraphernalia an up-to-date tent theater carried. After a while, he turned around, and noticed that the farmer's roadster still hadn't started. He had some of his canvas men pull the stalled car into the street. Sadler then got into his own car and pushed the balky roadster. It finally started, and buzzed away homeward through the night.

Incidents which made the audiences feel as if they were truly important to the shows could be multiplied many times. The established show's rapport with their audiences was so great, that the towners often thought of them as established local institutions, even though their visits came once a year, and were never any longer than a week.

Therein lay the rep shows great strength. Fred Wilson's salute to his audiences, "And when you see me, say 'Hi! Tobe! Have a cigar!'" made him loved and famous, all over the midwestern and southern territories which he played.[52]

The bands and baseball teams carried by the shows were the greatest and most ordinary means of attracting attention to the shows. Brass bands are the oldest, and to this day, the most popular kind of instrumental musical groups in the Midwest. In the past, every

The Footlights

town had a municipal band. They played on summer evenings in a specially erected bandstand usually in the town square. Rep show bands, small or large, playing in the town square at noon, parading the downtown streets, or playing in front of the tent before the performance, were a great attraction and a delight for the towners.

The band was always dressed attractively, often in conventional, semi-military uniforms, other times, as can be seen in the accompanying pictures from the shows, in linen dusters and caps. The groups varied in size, according to what the manager of the show could afford to hire. The bands ranged in size, from five or six people, to as many as fifteen. Many a youngster got his start toward being an actor or manager, through his ability to play a band instrument. On most of the shows, the actors had to "double in brass," or the musicians had to play parts. Few shows could afford to hire musicians for band work only, or actors only for acting.

The Seven Cairns Brothers, who began their careers in show business in their home town of Decatur, Illinois, were musicians. The family had originally come from the neighborhood of Jerseyville, Illinois, where they were born. They spent their childhood on a farm, about twelve miles from town. Their father was a man with a great deal of musical talent which he never had a chance to develop fully. He did, however, have a fine reputation as a country fiddler.

In a letter to Al Pitcaithley, Roy Cairns described how they began in show business.[53] After the father died, the family moved to Decatur, Illinois. George, the oldest and the first to take up a musical instrument, learned to play the horn to perfection. When he found out that there was no place for a horn except in big bands and symphony orchestras, he took up the trombone. He mastered the trombone so well that he got a job with the Primrose Minstrel Show, afterwards the Primrose and Dockstader Minstrel Show, and worked in that show for many years.

As each of the other six brothers, Herbert, Walter, Roy, Harry, Warren, and Rolland (Cotton), in order of age grew old enough to play, George would pick out an instrument for him, and see to it that he got instructions.

Before they started their own show, the brothers had a number of years experience in dramatic shows and vaudeville. Roy said he cannot remember just when each of his brothers made his debut in show business. He does say that he and his brother Walter started out by joining the Bradshaw Players in Tuscola, Illinois, in 1906.

"I loved the tent game," Roy continued, but he was not very crazy about permanent stock, which the company played, beginning in 1928. It was "hard work keeping up in new bills, and pleasing the public."

Shows always presented some kind of music, if only a piano and drums, if a band was too costly or impractical. This was necessary, because of the requirements of the vaudeville, presented between the acts. Often, a calliope was used for pre-show ballyhoo. The advertisements in the *Billboard, circa* 1910-1919, feature many improved varieties of this old circus and carnival instrument.

The Slout Players advertised a "New Tone Calliope," manufactured by the National Calliope Company, of Kansas City, for their 1929 season.[54] Its appearance on the street took the place of the old band parade in the pre-show afternoon. The Slout Krazy Collegian Orchestra furnished a special musical program every evening before the performance. J. Doug Morgan, advertising in *Bill Bruno's Bulletin* for the summer season of 1930, announced a calliope for street advertising, as well as Joey La Palmer, and his Eight Morganians. Today, a calliope is only obtainable as an antique.

Baseball teams were another way of attracting attention to the show. "If you could play ball, and double band," said H. L. Carlstrom, "You were in!"[55] The show ball teams would schedule a game with the local club in the afternoon. The townspeople would come to the ball game in the afternoon, then go to the show at night. If they came from the country, as a great many of them did, they would pack an evening lunch for the family, and make a great day of it.

The Seven Cairn Brothers were famous for their baseball team, as well as their band. All seven of the brothers were members of the team. They played all positions outside of the battery. "Brother Warren," said Roy, "was a fine pitcher, and of course, pitched a lot of games. When he pitched, it hurt our infield, because he was a fine shortstop. I played third base, the hot corner, and loved it."

Horace Murphy's Comedians carried a team of eleven men, in 1911-1912.[56] Les "Skeeter" Kell's show was famous, as late as 1930, for its skilled baseball players. Baseball teams would always prove to the hardworking villager, or farmer, that the actors were real men, not sissies. This established another kind of rapport with the public.

6. Inside the Tent

Describing the raising of the show tent, Mrs. McKennon remarked on the difficulty of the final job: putting up the sidewall.[57] "...even in the bright glaring sunlight, your dark canvas shuts out the light, and you must work in a difficult gloom." Inside the tent during the day it is very dark, and often hot, unless the sidewalls have been raised.

A story comes from several sources, about an old, hill-billy type towner. He wandered into the tent during the day and inquired what was going to take place. He was told that there would be a show that night. He replied, "Tain't no use, nobody'll come. It's too dark in here."

Brightly lighted in the evening, the marquee, and the auditorium did draw big audiences. They had eagerly awaited the night's entertainment. The feature of the evening was, of course, the play.

It should be said that the tent was never an ideal place for a dramatic presentation. Hilliard Wight and Wallace Bruce, maintain that they would rather play in a house. The tent theater was only an expedient.

The acoustics were bad, until the invention of sound systems. The poles, even though they were strategically placed for sight lines, forced all who did not sit in front, to stretch and peer around their neighbors for a good view of the stage. This was because the audience floor was on level ground.

The tent theater was modeled on the conventional proscenium type developed during the Renaissance and eighteenth century and finally reaching its perfected form around 1900.

A proscenium was always used, as elaborate as the resources of the company could afford. Every opera house and tent theater had some of the characteristics of a royal opera house. Christy Obrecht who took over the show from his father, carried a beautiful velour proscenium complex, grand drapes, teaser, and front curtain, the only one of its kind.[58] On a show like this, or the Aulger Brothers, or the Elwin Strong Show, the proscenium would be of sufficient height to give a proper lift to the scene behind it. Other shows, with a lower proscenium, could not get this effect. Often, the top proscenium curtain sagged, making it a poor frame for the play action.

Some shows used specially painted banners for advertisements of local businesses, to guarantee the weekly "nut." This was traditional in all kinds of theaters. The early silent movie houses threw advertising slides on the screen, while the operator was changing the reel. The tent shows, after the invention of sound systems, underlined this "pitch" for local merchants. They used an announcer, placed backstage, to read ads for each sponsoring business, while the audience gathered.

The front curtain could be raised in the usual way of metropolitan theaters. It often parted in the middle revealing the setting, or the olio curtain, which provided the background for presentations between acts.

The stage was always a temporary structure. It was sometimes wide and deep enough to include dressing rooms for the actors. The Elwin Strong show was noted for providing this additional comfort. The actors in most shows dressed at either side of the stage with the ground for a floor.

There was no device invented for the metropolitan theater that the tent managers did not try. Sets were conventional flats and drops, or legs and drops, dressed as well as possible with stage props. The props were carried by the show, or borrowed from local stores. As time went on set changes were eliminated by the use of one-set plays. Thirteen scene changes needed in the four basic sets for *Ten Nights in a Barroom* can be a stagehands' nightmare.

The first-class shows kept their sets freshly painted and newly designed. The small shows, the "fly-by-nights," and the "hardly ables," were shoddy and careless in their sets, as well as in their acting. The sets were unattractive because they were badly soiled, or they were badly painted by unskilled artists. Even the best of shows carried sets which were unattractive because they were poor imitations of the conventional settings of the period. The play was the important thing with the shows, not the stage set.

Clint Robbins said in the early days of both house and tent that rep plays were few and hard to get.[59] The English influence dominant in the early nineteenth century continued with presentations of plays such as *Lady Audley's Secret, East Lynne,* and *The Lady of Lyons.* These plays were common productions into the early years of the twentieth century.

Plays like those and other metropolitan successes such as *Dr. Jekyll and Mr. Hyde,* and *Trilby,* were always presented in the rep shows by actors such as Elwin Strong and Richard Henderson. Small town audiences, however, developed a yearning to see plays representing life as they knew it, or life as they felt it ought to be. When Clint Robbins said that plays were hard to get, he probably meant that plays appealing to the audiences he played to were hard to get.

In these early twentieth century years of explosive social and industrial development, rural America ceased to be the dominant element in the population. Cities were growing enormously in wealth and population, drawing ambitious young men away from the farms with dreams of wealth and success.[60] In self-defense the rural population developed certain myths, believing them as actual facts. The myths consisted of premises such as the belief that the city was a wicked place which could corrupt the best of men, the country was the home of all virtue and honor, and that the poor and meek, even the stupid, would eventually triumph over the rich and clever.

Plays patterned on these myths became a ritual, enacted nightly before hundreds of audiences. They became so popular that a flourishing dramatic literature developed, aimed at midwestern rural audiences. In 1898 Alex Byers began his career as a play broker.[61] He named his business the Chicago Manuscript Play Company. Among his writers, were people such as W. C. Herman, Nelson Compston, George Leffinwell, and Lem Parker. Byers directed his company from a cubby hole office in the old Palace Hotel in Chicago. W. C. Herman could turn out a play for Byers for twenty-five dollars and feel well paid, even after turning over the copyright to his employer.

Plays such as *Clouds and Sunshine, The Call of the Woods,* and *Sheriff Jim's Daughter,* became semi-classics, both for the audience and actors. The two latter plays presented the popular literary genre of the time, the Canadian Northwest and the American Far West. The first one mentioned, *Clouds and Sunshine*, represented a special class of play invented to advance the cause of rep shows as a moral and educational influence. Shows such as this were called preacher plays.

Charles Harrison, actor, manager, playwright, and play broker, whose career runs from the days when tent shows were just beginning through their greatest period of success in the twenties, is credited with creating this type of play.

The hero of the play is a small town minister, a strong and virtuous man about to be corrupted by the influence of the village hypocrites, usually the banker and the old maid gossip. He finally sees through their pretence and selfishness. The minister begins to appreciate the true virtues of humility, honesty, and generosity.

The two plays most widely known are, *The Only Road* and *Saintly Hypocrites and Honest Sinners*. The latter play is probably the greatest of these "lost" plays of the American small-time theater. It has often been said that it has been played more times, and has been seen by more people than any other play produced in this country, except for one or two of the English classics. When read, the play seems to be written in diction too stilted, flowery and old-fashioned to be spoken in any kind of conversational style. When played, one sits back in honest wonder at how well the play works its effect on the audience. It is not a play that can be "hoked" or "hammed" in spite of the writing. It cries out to be given straight, with complete honestly and sincerity, with no modernization or improvements.

The characters seem to be types: the greedy and dishonest banker, and his sycophant, the old maid gossip of the town; the minister, and his wife, too much possessed by her importance as the minister's wife; his brother who has seen something of the world, and the two young people, the sister-in-law and her sweetheart. All of them have the elements of real characterization. They seem so convincing that even sophisticated audience members leave the theater saying, "you know, I know somebody just exactly like that!"

Harrison's other well-known play, *The Awakening of John Slater*, follows the ritual pattern set by such plays as *Won By Waiting*, or *Out of the Fold*. *Out of the Fold*, although a New York play of minor success, achieved considerable fame among the reps. George Crawley's *Sputters* (sometimes known as *The Girl of the Flying U Ranch*) presented a combination Western and Toby comedy. *Sputters* did this even though Toby had not yet been established with his name and reputation, as later known.

This was only one branch of the stream from which the flourishing rep literature of the first quarter of this century flowed. Plays from the metropolitan theater, serious plays with a strong moral implication, were given another version, more acceptable to rep audiences. Plays such as Nelson Compston's version of *Dr. Jekyll*, *Strongheart*, and *The Squawman*, based on romantic myths about the Indian, were examples. They were given different names in order to avoid royalty payments. *The Heart of Wetona* and *Red Feather and His Squaw* are examples. E. L. Paul's *Tropical Love*, very well known throughout the rep shows is a re-written version of the popular hit of the twenties, *White Cargo*. When mystery terrifiers like *The Cat and the Canary*, and *The Bat* were nationally popular, one rep company was presenting a play entitled *The Spider and the Fly*.

All of these plays, original or re-written, were copyrighted and offered to the rep companies at extremely low royalties not only by Byers, but also by other play brokers such as Robert J. Sherman and A. Milo Bennett in Chicago, E. L. Paul, Herschel Weiss, Karl Simpson, and the Murdoch Play Bureau of Kansas City.

Charles Harrison, with his partner, J. D. Colgrove, operated the Harrison-Colgrove Play Bureau in Denver. Robert J. Sherman was probably the most prolific of all the playwrights supplying drama to the reps.[62] Some of his plays survive not only in presentation, such as *Tildy Ann*, but are still offered in the catalogues of two nationally known play publishers. *Melvina's Courtship* appears in Baker's Plays catalogue, published in Boston, and *Spooks*, is offered by Samuel French, at twenty-five dollar royalties.

The managers often wrote their own plays. They wrote to avoid the expense of royalty, as well as to satisfy a creative urge. Hilliard Wight, for example, has two plays, *The Squarest Man in the World*, and *The Best Laid Plans*, written for his own use but fully copyrighted.[63] The manager-playwright was many times quicker to notice a trend of the times and use it as the theme for his play. In 1930, Neil Schaffner advertised a play called *Chain Stores*, which became a big rep success because it hit at a sore place in small town economy.

The rep play above all other things must be clean. It generally pointed to a moral. A well-known play like *Camille* was seldom given by the reps. No presentation of it is reported except for the North Brothers tour in the year following the great Sarah Bernhardt's tent production. *Camille* was popular in cities and mining camps, but not in small towns and rural areas, for obvious reasons.

Suggestive titles and advertising were sometimes used. Puritanism encourages the prurient mind. The show itself, however, must be really clean. Neil Schaffner's two plays, *Three in a Bed*, and *Natalie Needs a Nightie*, have purposefully suggestive titles, yet the action of the plays is good, clean, uproarious farce.

In the later years of the reps, when they were trying to attract any kind of audience, "blue comedy" was used, especially by Toby comedians. This was not typical of the shows in their prime. The general rule about gags was, "If you are doubtful, it's dirty, and must not be used." Another statement was, "If you can't tell the story Sunday morning in church, you can't tell it Monday night on the stage," except maybe in the Saturday night concert. Most of the shows also avoided suggestive advertising in those days.

The tent shows thought of themselves simply as part of the show business world. They never dreamt of creating anything unique or original. Their object was to present a program which would draw an audience. The unique and original are seldom created self-consciously. Few people today realize that the reps created a flourishing literature of their own. They also developed two original folk characters: The G-string, a garrulous, chin-whiskered old man, and more especially Toby, the crude yet clever country boy.

Tent rep attitude was always that of pleasing their particular public. The programs they presented were a mixture of the two types of plays previously noted. The plays were written to the tastes of the midwestern rural public, and were usually re-written versions of metropolitan hits which had elements of strong moral appeal. Many of these plays did not need to be re-written for the midwestern audience. Plays like *Turn to the Right*, and *The Family Upstairs*, were stock pieces with companies who could pay the higher royalty. These plays needed no re-writing.

Managers of the better tent outfits were always alert to trends and changes in the metropolitan theater. They were accustomed to making annual pilgrimages to New York and Chicago to keep up-to-date on plays, settings, lighting, and other techniques. Clint Robbins always spent part of the winter season in New York watching shows and picking his repertoire for the following summer.

Fred Wilson's wife, Pearle, who worked in rep and stock for over thirty years, once made a trip to New York for the first time in several seasons and saw most of the hit plays.[64] She was amazed.

> I went to *Harvey*, and *Oklahoma*, among others. The way some of the minor roles were played was a disgrace to the profession. A good tent show never would have permitted lighting like they had in *Oklahoma* where the actors threw shadows on the backdrop which represented a field of grain. I felt so let down!

The Footlights

The rep companies, both house and tent, played everything from *Hamlet* to *Sis Hopkins*. Between 1907 and 1910, Hilliard Wight trouped the county seats and larger towns of the Midwest, playing *Hamlet, Don Ceasar de Bazan,* and *Monte Cristo*. Other ambitious managers, such as Elwin Strong, and the Aulger Brothers played current Broadway plays like *Outward Bound,* and *East is West*. The average rep bill, however, was chosen from old, established plays, or plays coming from the play brokers and so-called "hack" playwrights in Chicago and Kansas City.

Elwin Strong Players flyer.

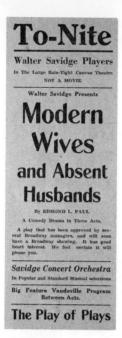

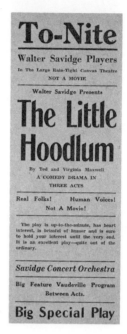

Flyer from Walter Savidge Players.

Handbill, Brainard's Comedians.

Theater Program from Walter
Savidge Amusement Company.

70

7. Doubling in Brass

Vaudeville became a standardized part of the rep shows for two reasons. It was a way to entertain the audience between set changes, and was an attempt by the rep shows to capitalize on the most popular entertainment form of the period. After the change from the variety of the honky-tonks to the vaudeville bills appearing in respectable theaters, vaudeville's popularity became comparable to the tremendous vogue in TV, and television performers today.

A casual glance at the two outstanding magazines devoted to show business, *Variety* and *The Billboard*, proves this. Vaudeville brought some of the glitter, glamour, self-confidence, and specious cleverness of the cities to the rural audiences.[65] During the hey-day of the rep shows, the twenties, vaudeville had become an extremely necessary part of the program. When rep shows began their decline in the thirties, it became almost as important as the play itself.

An advertisement of the J. Doug Morgan show, in 1930, bannered as "America's Biggest Tent Theatre," and the "World's Greatest Tented Amusement Enterprise," failed to mention a single play offered that season.[66] The show presented "A Grand Triple Alliance of Musical Comedy, Drama, and Vaudeville. Traveling in Our Own Special Train of Fifteen Big Modern Mammoth Circus Wagon Trucks. A Collosal Aggregation of the Best Talent in the Repertoire Field." The names of all performers are given, their status as lead, heavy, etc., and the variety acts they do. The plays are not mentioned, and have apparently become less important as a drawing card.

The acts could be anything. There were the singers, dancers, and instrumentalists. There were even puppet shows and recitations. Emile Conley has a copy of a poem he often used as a reading done to musical accompaniment, "Whispering Bill." A male quartette was one of the most popular acts, especially during the early years of the century. Every school, college, and church organization in the country, as well as phonograph recording companies featured such groups. A music publishing house, the J. A. Parks Company, of York, Nebraska, devoted itself to publication of quartette music. Bert Dexter, still active as character man on the Jimmy Davis show, got his start in show business singing high tenor in a quartette. Wallace Bruce's second job in show business required him to play small parts, and do all sorts of odd jobs, and sing in the quartette.

On a small show, specialties added a considerable burden to the actor's job. They would have to have a different act every night, if the show played week stands. On the first show Wallace Bruce owned, everybody was versatile. The company consisted of six members, all, except one woman, doubling in the orchestra. Each actor had a variety of specialties, for the show presented four acts of vaudeville every night, along with a three-act play. There were instrumental and vocal specialties, a trio (male), comedy singles, and doubles.

Hilliard Wight said that in the early days of rep shows it was difficult to break into show business if the aspirant did not play a musical instrument, sing, or dance. Jim Parsons, son of Jack Parsons owner-manager of the Manhattan Stock Company, playing Arkansas in the 1900's, relates a different picture.[67] He said there was a time when the managers hired the best actors they could get. They hired musicians for the band or orchestra and some specialty people if they were necessary. As times got harder, or managers became more greedy, they learned to save a salary here and there by looking for people who could double. Jim Parsons said that "Good specialties, and the ability to blow a saxophone, could keep a lousy actor working, while clever people had a hard time finding work. And I'm not speaking from bitterness. I did specialties and doubled on the saxophone, and could usually get work if anyone could."

72 *The Footlights*

Parsons worked for Harley Sadler in 1933. It was not one of Sadler's most prosperous years because of the economic depression. The show carried fifty people, including a fifteen piece orchestra, and everybody doubled. A show cast of twenty-two was possible, and six specialty acts were offered each night. This situation, although impressive enough in itself, is representative of the beginning of the period of decline for the shows.

The story of Art Holbrook, beginning his career on the World Players, illustrates what could happen to a versatile and talented young man.[68]

> They have a young fellow on the World Players named Art Holbrook, who originally joined to drum in the orchestra and was soon afterward forced into small parts, continuing his drumming, however. He made so good in the parts that he was given longer ones. Then he started singing with equal success. Last week the Players offered a musical comedy, "Peggy from Paris," Holbrook played one of the juveniles, and on last Monday night at Fremont all went well until he started to dance, upon which one of the ladies in the audience was heard to remark: "My Gawd! That boy has done everything but knit."

Al Pitcaithley's specialty was unique. His ambition at the beginning of his career was to be a circus performer. He had practiced his contortionist act during his high school days. He discovered in his physical education class that he had a great deal of physical flexibility.

Al said that his act was unique, because as far as he knows, he was the only talking contortionist in the business. He explains:[69]

> I talk all through my act, doing gags that fit various tricks and gags used for a stall while I get my breath. My stage training in stock and rep was valuable for this because it taught me timing and how to talk. You have only to think of the announcements made by the average acrobatic act not used to talking to get my meaning. In clubs and burlesque I could spice up my material with gags that would hardly pass in polite vaudeville. I once did my act in a tuxedo. I would come in, sing a song, then while talking hang up my derby, cane, and coat on a halltree, and go into my contortion act. This was always a surprise to the audience since from my opening and entrance a "bender" was the last thing expected. When stage hands had got careless, and forgot the halltree at one time or two, I got temperamental and switched to sports attire. Later on I switched to tux trousers and a satin blouse with full sleeves which is the easiest dress to work in I have ever found. I still use it.

An act original enough to gain fame for the actors lingered in the memory of audiences. The Lead, South Dakota, *Register*, reviewing the performance of the Clint and Bessie Robbins Company in *At the Risk of His Life* by Mark Swan, mentioned the Robbins as the couple "who put on the 'rag-doll' specialty here some years ago, the finest thing of its kind ever put on the stage in the Hills.[70] During the engagement of the Company in Lead next week, they will do this stunt at least one evening." The newspaper gives no description of the act, but since it was a dance, one can get a vague image of what it was like.

The write-up mentions another type of popular variety act of the time, songs illustrated with slide pictures. These songs and pictures were impossible to present in Lead, since at the time, there were no electrical outlets for the projectors in the play house.

A canvas dressing room, 1930's.

8. Grease-Paint and Gladrags

Every actor had to furnish a full and complete wardrobe unless he was called on to appear in a costume play like *Rip Van Winkle*. These clothes ranged from the rough costumes of the G-string comedian, the fantastic Toby get-up, and the hired-girl clothes of such a character as Tildy Ann, to full dress wear for both afternoon and evening for the men, and beautiful up-to-the-minute fashion dresses for the ladies. W. C. Herman's *The Italian's Revenge* required costuming of high fashion. Actor's salaries were adequate for the times, sometimes even high, and work was always steady for the most of them. Nevertheless, the acquisition of a full wardrobe, bought new, would be a considerable financial strain. Actors acquired their wardrobes in bits and pieces according to the roles they were playing. Many times the costumes were second-hand.

Advertisements in *Bill Bruno's Bulletin* for Mrs. Perrin's Re-Sale Shop, and other shops in Kansas City, show how this problem was solved. Society women often wore a new dress once or twice. The dress was still in almost perfect condition but could no longer be used.

The woman would offer it to a re-sale shop rather than have it clutter up her wardrobe. An actress could acquire an astonishing array of gowns for a reasonable price from these shops.

Anna Crayne's Shop in Kansas City, advertised "High class Used Street and Evening Wear for Ladies and Gentlemen," and the Patton-Lund Wardrobe Shop offered "All kinds of Good Used Stage and Street Clothing. The Place of Real Bargains for Ladies and Gentlemen, Open until 9:30, evenings. 4221 Walnut."

Charles Worthan had one leading lady on his show who dressed unfashionably, much to the disgust of the troupe. By the end of her engagement the company had snooped enough to find out that she had plenty of fashionable and beautiful clothes. She had felt it beneath her dignity to use them on a tent show.

Jolly Della Pringle was famous for her evening gowns.[71] She advertised her wardrobe as being very expensive. She featured one dress made of looking-glass beads, tiny squares of glass sewed so close together that they covered her entire figure. The costume was so effective because the glass glistened under the stage lights.

This was the day of the hour-glass figure. Unfortunately some of the women were not physically built to assume such a shape, and the padding in use nowadays was unknown at that time. Della had to wear two rubber breasts inflated like balloons to make her hour-glass figure work.

One night during the performance some of the mirrored beads cut through her dress and punctured the falsie; the air leaked out leaving Della decidedly one-sided. The audience noticed the puncture and roared in laughter. When Della had an exit she went off stage for repairs. Her re-entrance with complete bosom made the audience roar again in delight. She went right on with the show as if deflated and re-inflated bosoms were a natural thing.

Make-up, as well as clothes, added glamour to the actors' personalities. It smoothed out wrinkles, refreshed faded complexions, and aided in the creation of character parts. Shops supplying make-up were plentiful in Chicago, Kansas City, and other metropolitan centers. Percy Ewing's establishment at Cerro Gordo and Church streets in Decatur, Illinois, was the best known make-up shop among the rep show actors.[72]

Mr. Ewing carried a full line of make-up, wigs, and accessories, and was known all over the Midwest as the actors' friend in need. His business was ostensibly a newsstand. However, from the shop's beginning, around 1904 until the 1930's, it was famous as a show business establishment. This reflected Mr. Ewing's primary interest in the theater.

Rail express packages, in the days before World War I, could be sent "subject to examination." Many companies would start out on the road with very little capital. This way of sending express packages was a real boon to the cash-poor actors.

When an actor got a little money together after a few weeks of playing he would send an order to the Ewing Newsstand in Decatur. He would not have to enclose any cash with the order. Mr. Ewing would send the materials requested via railway express, "subject to examination." He tagged the packages with the full price of the contents or with an itemized price list. He often sent some extras along to tempt his customer.

When the package arrived at the train depot in the town where the actor was playing, the express agent would open the package for the actor's inspection. The agent permitted the actor to pick out what he wanted. The actor would leave the money for the goods with the agent who would make out a money order to Ewing's, enclose it with the remainder of the goods and ship it back to Ewing's.

Ewing, aside from stocking standard wigs and accessories, would order special wigs to be made up by firms like the Zauder Brothers in New York. An advertisement in *Bill Bruno's Bulletin*, gives some idea of the extent of Ewing's business:[73]

Wig Specials

Only one of each, Ladies Grand Dame Wig, purple hair, and one red, white, and blue hair, $8.00 each. Shell top, Buch made, for Jeff or Andy Gump, bald except for fringe of hair in back, $10.00, size for 7 or $7^{1/8}$ head. 240 pieces of stage money, $1.00
PERCY EWING SUPPLY HOUSE, DECATUR, ILLINOIS

Mr. Ewing generally had a regular stock advertisement in the *Billboard*, running at the same time. In 1905, he moved his shop to the six hundred block on North Water Street. The shop, now located at 761 North Water, is operated by Percy Ewing's son, Eddie. He carries a full line of theatrical make-up, and still has a few wigs in stock.

Several years ago when Wallace Bruce was searching for a new red wig for his appearances as Toby, he remembered Percy Ewing's speciality, and sent a letter to Decatur.[74] The letter was never delivered. He wrote another letter to the Association of Commerce, but got no information in reply. Finally, in desperation, Bruce wrote to one of the local newspapers. Eddie Ewing chanced to see the letter when it was published and promptly sent Mr. Bruce a new red Toby wig.

Candy sales display.

Selling candy in the "blues."

The candy man on the
main floor, reserved.

9. The Candy Pitch

The intermission between the last two acts of the play was devoted to the candy pitch. This device, giving prizes in return for the purchase of a box of candy, is usually associated with circuses, carnivals, and other non-dramatic shows. Its use in connection with the tent reps was unique among dramatic shows. Candy pitches were not characteristic of the tent shows until about 1920. Once the pitch was introduced it often made the difference between financial success and failure. It had been used in shows playing houses, but rep managers hated to introduce it into a show because they felt it detracted from the performance.

The prizes to be given away during the candy sale were displayed throughout the show, usually on a platform opposite the orchestra at stage left. Prizes ranged from carnival type kewpie dolls to electric or gas cooking stoves. Blankets, radio sets, silverware, carving sets, lamps, smoking stands, fancy sweaters, and so on, aroused the deep-seated desire of the people to gamble on getting something for nothing. Aside from the big display prizes, every candy package contained a prize if nothing more than a cheap trinket. The manager somehow saw to it that the big prizes, if they were given at all, were saved for a Saturday or feature night.

During the intermission of the play the manager, or his appointed deputy, would give the audience a sales pitch, designed to make them want to buy the candy. After the pitch the actors, or workers on the show, passed among the audience with a canvas sack full of candy on one shoulder, and a bag of change on the other. The candy was the cheapest kind, usually what was called "candy kisses." The audience would buy it, pressured by their gambling instinct, or by their children. The children were not fussy about the type of candy as long as it was sweet.

Wallace Bruce described an original candy pitch, one with a comedy touch:[75]

> Ladies and Gentlemen! We know it is customary for all tent organizations to offer some kind of a prize candy sale between acts. Well, we are no exception to the rule, only we don't come out here and make you a lot of false promises. Most shows come out and tell you that this candy is a fine, chewy confection, made in a snow-white factory, and never touched by human hands. This candy here is a regular twenty-five cent seller, but for advertising purposes, we are going to let you have it tonight for only a dime — ten cents! Now, ladies and gentlemen, I don't do this. I sell it to you for a dime, because that's all it's worth, in fact it isn't worth that much. We make our own candy by picking up used chewing gum from the bottom of the seats, mixing it with a little glue, and adding a little coloring to make it look tasty! We have many prizes in these boxes, for instance, solid gold watches from Woolworth's, baseball hose—you know the kind, full of runs, ladies' wrist watches with no works in them.
>
> No! We make no wild claims. The only guarantee I make to you is that the candy is in the box, all five pieces of it. One thing, you can buy this for the children. We guarantee this candy will not hurt the children — there's not enough in there *to* hurt them.
>
> Now the agents will pass among you. The cost is ten cents each. There is a prize in each and every box. When you open your box, please hold up your prize so everybody can see it.

Harley Sadler's pitch was also original. He is credited with saying:[76]

> You never can tell what you will get out of this candy. Two years ago, a boy and a girl found prize coupons in their candy. The boy's called for a pair of lady's hose, and the girl's for a safety razor. I suggested they exchange prizes, and they did.

And that was how they met. They got married, and last night, they came to the show. With them was a bouncing baby boy. As I said, you never can tell what you will get out of this candy.

H. R. Brandt, president of the Gordon-Howard Company, was the pioneer in the candy business.[77] Mr. Brandt was a young attorney, and had represented several persons in the amusement business.

In the fall of 1920, he and his wife were attending a vaudeville show at Pantages Theater in Minneapolis. During intermission, when the lights were up, a sharp young concessionaire appeared in the front of the center row, and made an announcement similar to this: "Ladies and gentlemen! We are introducing tonight, an unusual confection package, a package which contains a combination of Candy Delight with an article of value in every purchase. Included are such wonderful items as silk hosiery for the ladies, men's neckties, pipes, billfolds, cigarette cases, safety razors, handkerchiefs, and articles of value from many countries. Remember, in addition to the delightful confection, there is an article of value for everyone. The price is a dime, ten cents! Please, have your change ready as sales time is limited. Thank you!"

Young Brandt immediately recognized that here was an idea with a future. He learned that the concessionaire was Sidney Anschell, who was just starting his business under the operating name of Universal Theatres Concession Company with small quarters in the Pantages Theater building.

Mr. Brandt rented a third floor loft in a large commercial building in Minneapolis. He ordered cartons, shipping cases, a supply of merchandise suitable for prizes, and candy for filling the boxes. During the latter part of the first year of the business, Brandt ordered candy manufacturing equipment. After the machinery arrived, the company manufactured all of its own candy.

Mr. Brandt soon found that Minneapolis was not a strategic location. It was not a central location for the shows, especially those playing in the southern Midwest, South, and the Southwest. He observed the growing importance of Kansas City as the center for the rep shows. Brandt hired a salesman well-known to hundreds of show managers. The salesman had headquarters in Kansas City. When Brandt saw the results of his actions he moved his entire operation to Kansas City.

He began his business in Kansas City in a three story building. This soon proved too small, and a building three times the size was leased on Wyandotte Street. The move was made in March, 1923. The new building was soon outgrown. The company increased its business so much that in 1929, the peak year for the candy business, the building at Wyandotte Street proved to be too small. Then Brandt bought a large, seven story building, the Massachussetts Building, at the corner of Eighth and Baltimore Streets. The building had fifty thousand square feet of working space which Brandt remodeled. His firm occupied the whole area.

The candy business added revenue to the gross income of the tent managers. They bought new cars, diamonds and furs for their wives. When the front door business was bad the candy sales produced the money that moved the show on to the next town. Wallace Bruce said that he customarily gave his wife Ruby the profits on the candy sales. When the show was rained out, or when business was just plain bad, Ruby's candy money moved the show. Managers had the feeling there would be no end to this additional, and often, show saving income.

The blow fell as it did so many times during the later years of the tents, not only unexpectedly, but at the time the shows were struggling for their lives. In July, 1934, a complaint was served by the Federal Trade Commission on the three companies who were the chief operators in the candy business, the Gordon-Howard Company of Kansas City, Anschell's Universal Theatres Concession Company, and the Union Concession Company of Chicago. The Commission charged that this form of merchandising contained the elements of a lottery which was not permissible in interstate shipping. The Commission also charged that it was unfair competition.

A hearing was held in Washington that August. After months of efforts by the companies to answer these charges, the Federal Trade Commission issued a final Cease and Desist Order in June, 1935. An agreement in the decree stated that if the companies ceased and desisted from the practices complained of in the charge, several months extension would be granted.

The companies made plans to prepare a suitable package that would meet the Federal requirements. The new method was to sell the managers packages containing candy only as one sale, and to sell them the merchandise units as they ordered them. The candy companies would give the managers no use instructions. The show managers found no difficulty in combining the candy and the merchandise and continued business as usual. The only difference in practice was that now the show companies were the ones who inserted the coupons.

Shows displayed the ballys as they always had. They were bound only to abide by state laws. The concession companies were the ones operating in interstate commerce and had solved their problem by billing the shipments separately.

At the peak of its business, the Gordon-Howard Company had over three thousand customers. The depression, competition with the new talkies, and radio, reduced the customer list drastically. The business failed to yield its former fabulous profits. All three companies mentioned are now out of business. The Gordon-Howard Company, in 1943, changed to commercial lines, and in 1955, sold its building and liquidated all assets. H. R. Brandt resumed full time law practice.

☆　　☆　　☆　　☆　　☆

All of the topics in this section which have been treated in detail, worked together to make the show a characteristic unit. From the moment the advertising sheets appeared, to the time when the equipment was loaded for transportation to the next town, the show was the central attraction in the community. Its offerings responded to the community's tastes and prejudices. Its productions came at the time the smallest town was a real community. As a result, the shows developed into a unique theater, quite unlike anything that exists today.

A typical bail-ring tent rigging set up.

Charles Worthan's Dramatic End Tent, 1920-22. Tent was 115 by 50 feet.

"Skeeter" Kell's tent, 1920.

Chick Boyes Players tent.

IV LIFE ON THE SHOW

1. Everything was Great in Kansas City

Every spring, when the snow began to melt away, and an occasional balmy day promised more like it, the shows began their preparations for the summer season. In the veins of managers, actors, and tent men, all blest or afflicted with perennial wanderlust, blood began to pound like the waters in every little spring ripened river. Managers looked over their equipment, and decided whether the old outfit would do for another season. Actors, tired of playing halls and theaters, or bored with lounging around mediocre hotels, longed for the warm days and open air playing. Laborers with no particular residence or skill thought it a fine idea to join up with a show. Remembered only as a possibility were last year's blow-down, rain out, struggles through the mud, and poor audiences. Every year new shows were organized hopeful of making the small fortunes usually gathered by the established shows. Kansas City was the hub for most of this activity. Actors were hired there, and managers bought their tents and supplies there.

Kansas City! From the days of the Dizzy Saloon during the late eighties, and early nineties, until the waning years of the shows just before World War II, this midwestern metropolis provided vacation, and refreshment, opportunity for employment, professional contacts, and supplies for the 2500 tent show people who called Kansas City their town. It was more than a business center to them; it was their home.

Show people would head for Kansas City in their off seasons. The actors looked for engagements. The managers looked for actors, supplies, rest and recreation, especially if the old home base, such as Wayne, Nebraska, or Fostoria, Ohio, seemed a little slow to them. Home to the actors, if engagements were not immediately forthcoming, were the theatrical hotels like the Gladstone, the Mercer, and the Centropolis. One could always hear show news and gossip about what was happening, going to happen, or had happened.

The tent rep headquarters were in the Hall building. W. Frank Delmaine, and his wife Ruth, representing Actors' Equity Association, had their offices there. Most of the actors belonged to Equity during the heyday of the shows. In the earliest days of the organization, Frank Gilmore had come out to Kansas City to organize the repsters. The idea of unionization was welcome to actors in the small time. They usually had more than their share of the financial difficulties inherent in the acting profession. Charles Worthan said that one character woman on his show worked so hard for Equity that the show became a one hundred percent union shop.

The managers found Kansas City a convenient headquarters. According to one report from 1930, showmen were accustomed to spending over a million dollars annually there.[1] By the early twenties, it cost from 10,000 to 20,000 dollars to equip a good show. This is a lot more than Charles Worthan paid for a completely new outfit as late as 1918.[2]

Worthan promoted a loan of 2,000 dollars from a Blue Mound, Illinois, banker for a new tent and outfit. He sold the old one, including the scenery, for two hundred and fifty dollars. As prices increased during the twenties, expenses for the shows operations increased. This brought still more money into Kansas City and increased its prestige in show business. During this period, Kansas City ranked third behind Chicago, and New York, as a booking and general theatrical center.

Why did Kansas City become the center for the rep shows? Chicago is entitled to a certain place as a center for the shows. Chicago did business providing actors for city stock, and for the road shows produced there. These shows played cities large and small, all over the country. The old Revere House, at Clark and Hubbard, is still remembered as one of the haunts of the rep actors.[3] There were many who called Chicago their metropolitan home, especially if they had any aspirations to progress professionally. Tent reps found their greatest popularity and prosperity in the Midwest, although they played in all sections of the country, from New England to California. In the South, a region based on a rural economy, the shows also flourished. In Arkansas, Louisiana, Kentucky, Tennessee, Mississippi, and Alabama, some of the biggest shows, such as Colonel Swain's, found the South their most profitable territory. Since the shows were really a kind of pioneer theater they found great welcome in the developing states of the Southwest, Oklahoma and Texas.

Fifty thousand miles of railroad radiated from Kansas City, stretching from Missouri to Nevada, Montana and Texas.[4] The Kansas City Southern Railroad, built by a Kansas City entrepreneur, linked the city to the South. A railroad network covering 1,483,030 square miles gave convenient transportation to shows working the western part of the great midwestern heartland.

Kansas City was a great center for farm marketing. It was the largest city in the Midwest where farmers brought their cattle to market. It was a city which had not grown so great as to be utterly frightening to the less sophisticated rural folks. William Allen White, looking back over half a century, describes Kansas City as "an overgrown country town of a hundred thousand people."[5]

It was not until 1920-25 that Kansas City began to take on a real metropolitan aspect. Actors in the small-time shows, tired of the trouping from small town to small town, and longing for a bright light, although imbued with small town feelings and mores, could come here and feel at home. Whatever the validity of this reasoning, Kansas City became the hub of the universe for the rep actor.

Actors passed to and from Kansas City until 1914 through the old Union Station. In 1914 the present Union Station was dedicated. The old station, a big sprawling building, had been the center of KC traffic. The town had pointed to it with pride, as the second Union Depot in the country. As the town moved away from the West Bottoms the station became inaccessible and cramped as a railroad center. It was far away from the main movement of life in the city. Unprotected against engine smoke, it became a blackened monstrosity.

The children of the rep actors learned to travel at a very early age. Self-reliance was one of the very first things they were taught. Evelyn Barrick used to travel alone to and from her home to the Ursuline Academy in St. Louis.[6] On one journey, traveling on the train from St. Louis, she missed connections. She went at once to the

Traveler's Aid. The woman in charge took her home, gave her dinner, and put her on the next train, after wiring her parents. It was through this old Union Station, crowded with people, that she had made her own way, an amazing feat for an eight year old child.

The Blossom House, a hotel on Union Avenue, was the scene of many a story and political intrigue but it was Charley Pervis's saloon, the Dizzy, opposite the old Ninth Street Theater (later the Orpheum), which was the actor's rendezvous.[7] Charley was their friend, in calm or storm. The walls of his place were covered with many pictures of theatrical folks, all bearing affectionate autographs. Here actors met one another, when the season closed and they came off the road. There was a cafe connected to the saloon, and in Will Locke's words, "dear old Mother Fessler's rooming house . . . upstairs."

Although there were no regular theatrical agencies in Kansas City in this early period, the Dizzy saloon served as one. Managers who wanted people sent a letter or wire to Charley Pervis. He easily got in touch with actors who were out of work, or loafing around town. Managers could also wire the Ackerman-Quigley Printing Company. This company would post notices on their "call board." Many an actor or actress of the early days got an engagement in this way.

Will Locke said that Ted Sparks of the vaudeville team known as the Ragtime Boys (Ted Sparks and Leon Hahn), opened the first theatrical agency in Kansas City. During 1903 they split the team, and Leon joined Locke's troupe in repertoire when they opened in Mound City, Missouri. Ted moved to Kansas City, and opened his agency in the old Century building, opposite the post office on Grand. The back end of the hallway had a fence across it, with a gate in the middle. Ted put a desk behind the fence, and called it his office. This was the first theatrical agency in Kansas City.

Leon immediately sent Sparks ten dollars as deposit, in case he should have to wire him for an actor. Many years later, Ted told Leon that at the time, he was flat broke, and that the "sawbuck" was the first money he ever received as an agent. Perhaps it was the first ever paid to an agent in Kansas City.

Sparks had pretty tough going for a while but eventually built up a good business. He went into partnership with Frank Caldwell and formed a thriving agency and booking office. In the *Billboard*, December 15, 1915, The Sparks Amusement Company, Indiana Building, is listed.[8] The agent had become an established part of Kansas City show business.

In 1934, Karl Simpson advertised that he had been in the agency business since 1922. Mr. Simpson's name is always the first one mentioned whenever old-timers talk about Kansas City agents.[9] His agency was the biggest in Kansas City booking anything and everything connected with show business. His office door in the Gayety Theater building was lettered with the names of the various shows for whom he was the sole agent.

To get an idea of what agency promotion was like his ad in the *Billboard* for October 13, 1934, should be read. He is calling for show people for the Ted North, Chick Boyes, Harley Sadler, Wallace Bruce, Harry Dunbar, Tol Teeters, Boyd Trousdale Shows, and many more. Mr. Simpson said that he carried a quarter page ad in the *Billboard* every week.[10]

Simpson was an agent to the biggest and best of the shows. The shows were clean, and the people loved to see them come to town. Even the ministers who would inveigh against the sinfulness of showgoing were on their side. The farm women loved them. When the better shows came to town everybody from the mayor to the most insignificant citizen talked about them. The movie houses were usually deserted a week before and a week after their coming.

Simpson began his show career at eighteen. His father did not want him to go into show business. He thought that Karl should do something respectable. Nevertheless, Karl went into show business eventually opening his own touring company, Simpson's Comedians. His father was happy at his son's success since in the later years Karl was often able to help him out financially.

Mr. Simpson encouraged theatrical aspirants. If he saw any promise in a youngster at all he would take the trouble to train him until he knew enough to do his bit on a show. Then he would find a job for him on one of the established shows. The shows, during the twenties, paid a normal salary of twenty-five to thirty-five dollars a week. One half of a week's salary was the agency fee. Actors could get by on five dollars for room and board making their salary rather handsome for the period.

Other prominent Kansas City agents were Kathryn Swan Hammond, Don Melrose, Kenneth Wayne, and Schnitz Seymoure who had the longest running theatrical agency.

Harley Sadler as a cowboy "Toby."

2. Breaking Into the Business

Before the days of Charlie Pervis' saloon, actors were getting jobs in Kansas City. Luke Cosgrave's career as an actor comes close to spanning the period between the Civil War, and the great days of the rep shows. At the end of his theatrical activities he made his last and greatest success in the great silent film *The Covered Wagon*. Cosgrave's autobiography, *Theater Tonight,* describes in picturesque and significant detail the life on the early shows, and his own experiences with them. He is the first actor on record to get a job in the theater out of Kansas City.

Breaking into show business was not easy. Jim Parsons, whose father, Jack, operated the Manhattan Stock Company, said:[11]

> . . . a question I never have found the answer to is how people got *into* the business . . . amateurs were strictly personae non grata (gratas? Personas non gratis? Huh-uh) Graduates of dramatic schools were no more welcome. To this day, I automatically sneer at the mention of a dramatic school. Any dramatic school! When ambitious, even though misguided towners would ask me how to get into show business, I haven't the faintest idea what to tell them.

Jim knows that the only way to break into show business was to be born into it, "me, Madge Kinsey, Bud Rowley, Jack Sexton," or to marry into it. Marriage was not an easy way, and a way open almost only to women. If a town girl married an actor she usually spent two or three years selling tickets, playing maids and minor roles. After three or four years she would graduate to playing ingenues. If she had any influence with her husband or the management she finally got to play leads.

Professional show women disliked non-professional females on the show. "That is why," Jim said, "I took my new wife to the Happy Bill Radio-Dance Troupe, where the first two or three years could be skipped." Many a young woman bitten with the theatrical bug married a potentially successful manager and assumed all the leading parts, no matter how lacking she was in talent or how matronly in figure.

"Most managers' wives I have encountered," said Jim, "had been playing dewy ingenues for thirty years, and if the corset industry didn't go bankrupt, would be playing them for thirty years longer . . . Well, twenty-five years. In my early twenties, I lecherously pursued many a motherly young thing of fifty, all over the stage."

Clara Mae Parsons, "Findlay's (Ohio) leading musical light," married into the business. Jack's Manhattan Stock Company was playing the town in 1910 and needed a piano player. Mrs. Clara Mae Barker, an expert piano player applied for, and got the job. "Also the manager!" said Jim. Ability to play a musical instrument became in later years the easiest entree into the business. When the specialty acts, and musical part of the show developed into an essential element, ability to "double in brass" became a necessity. The tenderfoot actor-musician would be drafted into playing small parts. If he was any good, or had any looks and personality he could go on from there.

J. B. Rotnour, one of the most prominent managers of the later years, began his career playing piano on the Flora DeVoss show. He married the owner of the show, and after her death, trouped the show under his own name.

For Hilliard Wight, the way into the show world without musical ability, or a talent for vaudeville performances was a long and weary one. He ran away from home, a cotton farm in the foothills of the Ozarks near Fort Smith, to seek his fortune. When he died at the age of 97 in May, 1968, he was the oldest veteran of small-town rep and tent shows. He told an interviewer that it took him ten years, from 1885 to 1895, to break into theater.

When Wight arrived in Phoenix, Arizona the performance at the theater attracted him. Maude Granger was playing in *Slave Girl*. Her highly charged, emotional performance caught his imagination. He was smitten with the lure of the grease paint and painted canvas. He travelled to San Francisco determined to become a good actor. The difficulties, his lack of speech training, no vaudeville act and the inability to play a musical instrument seemed insurmountable. Finally he got a job as props man, and doing bit parts at the old Morosco Theater in San Francisco.

The manager of the house heard Wight's nasal twang, and offered to teach him how to speak properly for five dollars. Wight paid the fellow the amount asked. His instruction consisted of the proper pronunciation of English vowels. This gave the young man confidence, and he was more determined than ever to advance his theater career. After four years in San Francisco he beat his way back to the Midwest. In the year of Coxey's Army he took off from Strawberry Point, Iowa, for New York City.

He found work there with a repertoire company. Within six days the show folded. He went to work as a "pearl diver" (dishwasher). In his off-duty hours he visited every legitimate theater in the city. He increased his command of the English language by frequent visits to the Public Library.

Whenever a show needed an extra, or bit player, Hilliard was always available. Gradually he became expert at reading lines, lost his stage fright, and learned "stage presence."

During his early years in New York, Wight met a young soubrette from Rhode Island whose versatility so charmed him that he married her. Their courtship took place between the acts of plays they both were in, plays that seemed predestined to fold after a few performances. The Wights were determined people, and Hilliard was consumed with a great desire to play the great parts of Hamlet, Don Caesar, and Monte Cristo.

One day, he happened into a saloon where he encountered the great Maurice Barrymore. Barrymore told him that he was too small a man (his height was five feet, five inches) to make it big in New York, and didn't have the physique to stand the toughness of the struggle. Hilliard had at that time landed a juvenile part in a hit. He and his wife Amber talked the matter over for a long time; their final decision was to leave New York for the Midwest. There Hilliard might find the opportunity to play the parts he longed to do.

He traveled about the country with repertoire troupes until he and his wife saved enough money to start their own company. Finally, in South Dakota, they were lucky enough to land parts which enabled them to save four hundred dollars. In 1907 the Wight Theater Company was born. At first the company played the usual repertoire bills. In 1910 Wight and his wife began playing the classical repertoire they had waited for so long to do.

He became famous for his portrayal of Hamlet. At Yankton, South Dakota, a doubtful college official asked who Hilliard Wight was. He had come into the theater backstage where Mr. Wight was sitting crosslegged atop his trunk, with his shirt off, mending a costume. The professor said that he hoped the show would be good, and Wight replied that they would do their best. Wight added that if the professor should come that night with his students and the group found the performance less than satisfying, none of them would have to pay for the show.

After the performance the professor led a group of enthusiastic students backstage. He threw his arms around Wight in delight at the performance. The crowd boosted the actor to their shoulders, and carried him around the theater shouting his praises as they went. Such things happened in all the towns where his father played Hamlet, said Leverett Wight.[12] The people had never seen anything like Wight's show before. It was a spanking new production, with new costumes and diamond dye scenery created by the Cox Studio. Wight played Shakespearean and classical roles from 1910 to World War I. After the war he played the usual repertoire bills until 1935, when the Depression made trouping unprofitable.

Youngsters from middle class families whose parents had aspirations for them were polite about leaving home. They liked their parents, and their home ties were strong but the footlights still dazzled their eyes.

Harley Sadler's father dreamed of his son becoming a lawyer but son Harley had other·ideas.[13] Every time a rep show came within miles of his home in Sweetwater, Texas, he followed it as far as he could. Then he went home to work gathering money to repeat the adventure.

In 1909 he trailed a company so long the manager gave him a job. Harley worked at this job for two years. This was his initiation into show business.

He organized a company of his own, on the trouper's proverbial shoestring. He specialized in old-fashioned melodrama. All of West Texas liked his show for he always played Toby, or some other comedy character.

Alex Pitcaithley's parents were staunch members of the Methodist Church.[14] His mother was very distressed when he showed his strong desire to become a performer, but came to accept his profession later. During the difficult days of the Depression, she opened her home to

Al and his troupe, in Beatrice, Nebraska. She let them use the front room for rehearsals, and often boarded the whole troupe.

Some children born into the business had no use for it, and left the show world as soon as possible. Others, such as the Wight children, L. H. (Pete), Billy, and Amber, had long stage careers. Madge Kinsey, a show family child, was billed as Baby Madge in earliest childhood. She starred as Little Eva, in the Toby version of *Uncle Tom's Cabin*. She was billed as the "Phenominal Child Artiste."

Trixie Maskew's mother was an actress, and Trixie danced in house shows throughout Ohio, and Pennsylvania, at the age of three and a half years.[15] Some of these shows were very elaborately outfitted according to Trixie Maskew.

A rep company was playing a "Tom Show," in Texas, in 1905. In Texas, the whipping scene often upset the audiences for they felt that it was not typical of the way they treated Negroes. Their easily aroused emotions often caused a riot or "Hey! Rube!". There were so many of these riots that the canvasmen slept armed with brass knuckles. The "blues," or general admission seats were all put on one side so that they could be pulled down easily in case of a riot. They would be pulled at the slightest threat of a riot, even at the risk of hurting someone. During these riots the actors customarily hid under the stage until the disturbance was over.

Why did the show people ever go into such a business? Why did they suffer all the fatigue, discomfort, danger and general hardship? Those born into the show world, naturally carried on their parent's business. "For God's Sake!" exclaimed Jim Parsons, "Why would anyone want to? I loved it, and so did most other actors I suppose, but I wouldn't have recommended it to my worst enemy!"

Youngsters looking at the posters printed in blazing colors plastered outside the opera house were looking into a different world, one more colorful than the humdrum world of the small town surrounding them. Perhaps they wanted, not only to enter into this world themselves, but create it for other people. Here was a chance for an otherwise ordinary human being to become a god. Here was a chance to build a world of his own, a world that was made to his own liking, where answers are sure and satisfactory. It is a dream world, a world where the dreams are controlled to the needs and desires of the dreamer, and no dream ever becomes monstrous and fantastic.

Said Hilliard Wight in his poem: "Thespic":

> Who am I?
> Listen to the whistling wind go by!
> I am the heart,

The parcel and part,
The song and the story,
The mad-cap glory
Of all the actors from the start;
I am the slave that was, the free man,
Freed by the spoken word—
That made him seem an angel, a god,
And placed his feet where none had trod—
The silver tongued (saving manna)
Roscius, Hosanna,
I am the acting art.

Who am I?
I am creative art,
The birthing sigh
The earth gave up
To the April sky;
I am the first that was,
The last to be,
As old as young
Eternity;
I am the whole,
The acting soul.

Bill Bruno's Bulletin. Page from Volume III, Number 29; August 14, 1930.

3. The Billboard

The New York Clipper served as the business and advertising medium for show business, large and small. It was published in New York, but the West was a long way off. Early in the 1900's, a new magazine, called *The Billboard*, began publication in Cincinnati, Ohio. It soon became the established representative of all show business for pitchmen, medicine shows, carnivals, rep shows, the Broadway hits, and big-time vaudeville. It became the bible of the small-time theater. News from the shows was published, and the people from rep shows were always welcome in its offices. Because it was published in the Midwest all the show people of this great area felt that it was especially close to them.

The magazine made its first appearance as a billposter's magazine on November 1, 1894.[16] It's title was, *Billboard Advertising A Monthly Resume of All that Is New, Bright, and Interesting on the Boards Devoted to the Interests of Advertisers, Posters Printers, Bill Posters, Advertising Agents, and Secretaries of Fairs.* It was the brain child of W. H. Donaldson who had started out in an art store and picture framing business. He went into the poster printing field with his father, where he acted as a salesman. During his travels he built friendships with bill posters, show printers, outdoor advertising men and showmen. There were publications in those days which catered to certain branches of the amusement business, but none covering the men engaged in these activities.

Mr. Donaldson conceived the idea of a publication for the interests of these men. The first issue of eight pages came out on November 1, 1894. It produced barely enough money to mail the edition small as it was. The third issue aroused the interest of some people, but it was not until after the fourth issue had been sent out that subscriptions began to come in. There was no trouble about money for mailing, postage, and petty cash after the fourth issue.

The first issues were mailed from the offices of the Hennegan Printing Company, at 11 West Eight Street, in Cincinnati. Three years later the title was changed to *The Billboard*. The partnership with Hennegan lasted only a short time.

In the early years, Donaldson and his wife held down every desk. When the paper began to show a profit in the seventh year, he engaged an editor. The publication now appears weekly, but *The Billboard* began as a monthly.

The agricultural fair department, and a circus department were started in 1896-1900. These were logical developments since these amusement enterprises used a great deal of show paper. The first big special, a feature of later years, appeared March 31, 1901, devoted to street fairs. Theatrical notes appear as early as 1900. There are very few notes until October 15, 1901, when headings such as Stock and Repertoire, Music and Opera, Minstrels, Burlesque, and Vaudeville were used. All kinds of amusement departments were added when the demand arose. In 1904, offices were opened in Chicago and New York. Correspondents existed in every city, large or small, where there was news of show business nature.

The classified advertisements from the pages of this magazine indicate not only something of the life of the show, but how the magazine was used by large and small companies in show business. The advertising policy of the publication was liberal. The following quotation from classified advertising shows how *Billboard* endeared itself to the average showpeople, making them feel it was a friend as well as a source of information and news about the business. The first page of the classified advertisements in the December 9, 1914, (Christmas Issue) issue is devoted to an explanation of their free advertising policy.[17] The complete copy of the advertisement is interesting:

The Footlights

Classified Advertisements

At Liberty   FREE   Wanted Situations

Advertisements of an acceptable nature and not to exceed twenty-five words will be inserted without charge in the classified columns. Open to Actors, Actresses, Performers, Musicians, Advance Agents, Press Agents, Billposters, M. P. Operators, Rink Skaters, Stage Hands, Carpenters, Managers, or any person connected or identified with the show business.

If answers are not satisfactory the first time, we invite as many insertions as are necessary to secure what you want. We do not want you to feel that you are imposing on us by using our columns, but copy of advertisement MUST BE FURNISHED EACH WEEK. NO FREE STANDING ADS MUST BE ACCEPTED, AND YOU MUST BE READY TO JOIN AT ONCE. FORMS CLOSE THURSDAY, 6 P.M. FOR INSERTIONS IN THE FOLLOWING WEEK'S ISSUE.

Notice — Letters directed to initials only are delivered through the Post Office. If initials are used, the letter should be addressed in care of person, firm, or post office box.

What a real favor to the actor out of work! Here are some typical ads:

LADY WITH CHILD would like engagement with stock or medicine company. For full particulars, address Musical Trio, Box 211, Stanley, Wisconsin.

VERSATILE YOUNG MAN — with two years experience, but very little wardrobe; modern romantic and character leads; Shakespearean second business; 5 ft. 11 in., 160 lbs.; repertoire and stock people take notice. Ticket? Yes. Edward Dewitt, 6 Fountain Place, Kansas City, Mo.

Under the heading "Stage Aspirants" people wanting to break into the business could insert an ad, at the same free rates.

YOUNG MAN — 19; 5 ft., 10 in., 150 lbs.; wants position with burlesque or stock company; neat appearance. GEORGE APPELL, 1616 Erato Street, New Orleans, La.

AMATEUR — 18 yrs. old; 135 lbs., 5 ft., 6½ in., for stock or vaudeville dramatic sketches; some experience in dramatics, H. F. ORCUTT, 226 S. Main St., New Britain, Conn.

Sometimes the appeal was almost desperate:

TWO YOUNG MEN — Wish connection with theatrical company; will take anything. TOM HEBER, Gen. Del. Albany, New York.

Paid At Liberty ads with simple display printing, i.e., the first line and name in black letters, could be inserted for as little as one cent

On The Prairie   99

per word. Most of these are strictly informational. Some of them could take a humorous turn:

THAT DERNED OLD FRAWD, OLD RUBIN HAYSEDE, the kuntry show-man. Care Mrs. Jefferson, 313 M. St. N.W., Washington, D.C., givin' Suthern, Yanky and misserlanus reedins and ressertations. Price, one hundred and fifty dollars, and car fare both ways! Cash in advance: Heantwuthit.

There were paid ads running up to three cents per word. There were no limitations on insertions or number of words. There was no discount for time. Cash had to accompany copy and all copy had to reach Cincinnati by Thursday, 6 p.m. The magazine reserved the right to edit all copy.

In a box on page 106 of the Christmas issue of 1916, the magazine boasts its efficacy as an advertising medium under the heading "The Outburst of Figures." The article states that this particular number contains eight hundred and twenty-seven classified advertisements. This proved that the "show goods dealers, professional people, moving picture houses, and novelty dealers, have selected a popular method of advertising. We feel safe in saying that the number of CLASSIFIED ADS printed here, is larger than will appear in all amusement journals combined, during the holidays."

The Billboard ran professional advertising of all kinds outside the classified section. Artists' individual photographs were displayed, small ads inviting managers to seek the actor for work, and ads from managers wanting attractions.

The Billboard was the top national magazine of all branches of show business. One other publication designed for the rep shows and other small-time organizations was published in Kansas City. It is identified as the organ representing Kansas City show business. Hollywood was still the "illegitimate" offspring of show business.

That publication was called Bill Bruno's Bulletin, after its founder, editor, and publisher. The earliest issue available is dated 1928, and the last issue was published in 1940, a few weeks before Bill Bruno's death, in Lawrence, Kansas. Bill had a tiny office in the Gibralter building, at 818 Wyandotte Street.[18] His show business career was associated with Kansas City, but the reputation of his paper and his own name were known from coast to coast.

The facts of Bill Bruno's life and career in show business are obscure, like a great deal of the material on the rep shows, and can only be guessed at from statements made by show people.

Bill Bruno was an actor, and a good one. He retitled a tab version of a popular play Hello Bill! naming it after himself. He played it season after season, all over the north central states. Everyone in the little towns waited for *Hello Bill!* to make its annual visit. Some of the lines were old, some new, some were added on the spur of the moment. When the lines were spoken by Bill they were surefire.

Hello Bill! was what was known as a "sock opera." It was successful as long as Bill took it out. It gave the home folks plenty for their money and always packed them in. The kids ate it up because Bill kept his show clean.

M. H. Tilton, in a letter dated February 12, 1965, told of the formation of his own company, the Tilton-Guthrie Players. He said in the letter that Bill left the Bruno-Guthrie Players in the fall of 1922. He "went to Kansas City and started a publication known as *Bill Bruno's Bulletin.*" Mid and Tillie Tilton had joined the Bruno-Guthrie Players in the spring of 1922. Bill sold his share of the show to them. Known as the Tilton-Guthrie Players, the company had a show life of twenty years.

The date given by Tilton is correct for the formation of the Tilton-Guthrie Players. The date is erroneous in regard to *Bill Bruno's Bulletin*. The issues of 1929 are dated Volume II, and those of 1930 are dated Volume III. They represent consecutive years of publication. Furthermore, in the issue of September 25, 1930, in which he announces that he is discontinuing publication of the sheet indefinitely, Bill stated that his publication was started in 1928 as a joke.[19] The issue of September 25, 1930 is given as Volume III, Number 35. Since it usually came out as a weekly, this would mark the date of *Bill Bruno's Bulletin* beginning as January, 1928.

Bill's association with the *Opera House Reporter* must have begun with his leaving the Guthrie show, in 1922. When the shows took to the tents in the twenties, and the need for the little magazine no longer existed, he turned to other fields. The unimpressive little sheet that in it's heyday could, in Bill's own words, "put any show out of business, with a bad report from a house manager," disappeared.[20]

In the issue of the *Bill Bruno's Bulletin*, for July 10, 1930, in the "Do You Remember When?" column, Bill asked, "Do you remember when E. K. Pitman bought the *Opera House Reporter*, and moved it to Northwood, Iowa, renaming it the *Amusement Reporter?*" At any rate, one can conclude that Bill bought the *Opera House Reporter* sometime in 1923, and sold it before 1928, when he started *Bill Bruno's Bulletin*.

When Bruno fulfilled his threat and ceased publication of *Bill Bruno's Bulletin*, cannot be accurately ascertained. One researcher stating that the little magazine was suspended in 1932 for four years does not say where he got his information.[21] This writer has seen no copies of the *Bill Bruno's Bulletin* between 1930 and 1935. From 1935 until 1940, just before his death, Bill put out *Bill Bruno's Bulletin* regularly. *Bill Bruno's Bulletin*, throughout those troubled days, was the carrier of hope, encouragement, and cheer to the dwindling tent rep companies. After his death, the publication in its original format became history, although for several years it was published by Bob Feagin and his wife in a mimeographed form.

Bill's real name was William H. Brunnhofer.[22] He left behind no great amount of money, but he won the love and respect of all in the Kansas City show world. Bill stood for fair play and live dramatic shows. In his editorials he castigates the stage hands' union for their exorbitant demands during the period following 1929. Business for the shows had sharply declined, and in view of the weakness of the actors' union, Actors' Equity Association, he stood for the straight dramatic show as the rep shows' principal objective opposing their desperate attempts to increase business by musical tabs and presentations.

Bill Bruno was a friend to the actors who were out of work. If a heavy or an ingenue, or anybody else was out of work, Bill would insert an At Liberty ad in his paper and say to the actor, "Pay me when you become a Wallace Beery or a Priscilla Lane."

Juveniles who showed up looking as if they hadn't been eating regularly, could always count on Bill for help. He would produce two dimes and order the youngster to run down to the restaurant and bring back two bowls of soup for their lunch. He always admonished the kids to bring back plenty of free crackers.

No. 4R3098
4 rose diamonds
ruby center
Each......$1.50

No. 4R3101
12 rose diamonds
very pretty
Each......$3.75

No. 4R3104
12 rose diamonds
turquoise center
Each......$5.25

No. 4R3107
15 rose diamonds
very fine
Each......$6.75

No. 4R3110
12 rose diamonds
ruby center
Each......$6.50

1902 catalogue cut for diamond stick pins.

4. Grouchbags and Diamonds

Sixty to ninety years ago when the rep shows were beginning money was not as plentiful as it is today. The old joke about starting a show with thirty-five dollars and a line of show paper was not so much of a joke. Actors and crewmen were always available. There were many people who had no particular training for any specialized kind of work looking for jobs. Always there were those who were willing to take a chance of making a few dollars. They often demanded nothing at all if travel and adventure were part of the prospect. People were not as security conscious, as they are today. Some were simply dazzled by the idea of working on a show.

The shows began with small personnel groups. They were simple shows, with minimum scenery requirements. Admission prices were low but would yield a profit, if the money was carefully managed. The standard ten-twenty-thirty cent ticket price scale was followed. By the thirties a reserved seat, plus admission to the tent totaled sixty cents. All shows carried "blues" or bleachers, for general admission, while the "orchestra" seats were sold at a higher price as reserved seats.

103

Addison Aulger said that the price for the show was gauged by knowing the price of a dinner in the town. If a dinner could be bought in a local restaurant for thirty-five cents then the admission to the show would be the same.

As the show's manager prospered so did the actors. The actors flourished financially if the audience came in crowds. One commentator said:[23]

> Tent rep salaries are small though reasonably sure. From early spring until late November it is pleasant for those who like gypsying to sleep on the lot in 'living' cars and motor each Sunday morning fifty or sixty miles to another green pasture, where, barring Monday afternoon street parades and an occasional rehearsal, there is little to do but act each evening. A life like that beats "walking the weary" on hard New York streets between casting agencies.

This was not an age of the great show business salaries. Actor's wages did rise from ten dollars a week to the Equity minimum of forty-five dollars a week during the twenties. Most of the standard shows employed Equity actors. Small shows might avoid the union, and pay as low as thirty-five dollars for a team, and fifteen to twenty dollars for a single. Prestigious outfits like the Elwin Strong show, paid as high as one hundred and ten dollars per week for a leading man. This salary was an exception.

Bill Bruno's Bulletin quips in a "Do You Remember When" column, about the time when thirty-five dollars a week was a high salary for a leading man. Shows in the great days of the reps paid fifty to seventy-five dollars a week for the principal actors.

Beginning actors started out at pretty good salaries. Lee Reinhardt joined the Harry Hugo Players at the age of eighteen as a musician.[24] He was paid thirty dollars a week which he said was a big improvement on what grocery clerks in small towns were paid.

The troupe played small Kansas farm towns. Many of these towns had no cafes, or cafes that were worse than none. In such towns the company sought out the local boarding house. These were often excellent accommodations serving good food and plenty of it. In one of the towns there was no market supplying fresh meat. The troupe was fed home grown fried chicken twice a day for a week. "Not so good, for someone who doesn't like chicken," Reinhardt said.

Financial misfortune seemed to happen more often in show business than in any other. The actors realized this, as did the managers. They became mistrustful of one another, and of such sound institutions as banks.

The Footlights

No wonder!—in those days of the greatest financial prosperity the country had ever known banks all over the midwest were failing. As a means of protecting their own financial interests actors and managers invented a very personal sort of bank called the grouchbag. Al Pitcaithley said it got its name from actors who saved their money, and were not free spenders; hence were called grouches.

The grouchbag was the actor's bank. It was the answer to his need for financial security. Lee Reinhardt said:

> You would come in to K. C. from a good season with a few hundred dollars saved (it would buy something then). You would keep this in a little crocheted, envelope-like bag, called a grouch bag, pinned to your undershirt.

The grouchbag contained current savings, money put by for an emergency, or the total worldly possessions of its owner. This "safe" was pursed up by a string and never left its owner's undershirt.

The grouchbag describes its emergency use. That money was not there for everyday spending. It was there to help out in case of non-payment of salary; as a defense against an unfair and unpleasant manager, for use in case of sudden sickness, and accident, or for any other "act of God." If the actor had to use the contents even justifiably, it would make him grouchy, hence its name.

The women of the troupe wore their grouchbags around their necks. If the show was unusually daring, and the women wore low-necked dresses, they tied the precious little packages about their thighs. They wore long skirts in those days. Sometimes, Mrs. Barrick said, they pinned the grouchbags on their brassieres (or camisoles, as they were called then), or tucked in the corset.[25] Mrs. Barrick tells about Etta Patten, who lost her grouch bag shortly before the birth of her daughter. All her savings, the money she had saved for the doctor and the hospital were in the bag. Her husband Bert was not angry with her. Everyone on the show felt tremendously sorry for the couple, but Mrs. Barrick cannot recall what was done in the emergency.

A manager also carried a grouchbag. Often he struggled against wet weather and the crowds who refused to come to the show. The string was loosened to pay the actors' salaries. It would be loosened when he was banking a surplus, paying a bill, or yielding to the request of improvident actors for an advance on unearned salary. Whenever he did have to loosen the string, he too became grouchy.

Diamonds in the older days were thought of as real security. They were about the only security a performer had. In some instances diamonds were better than money. Ward (Pop) Hatcher said that the underlying principle was that no matter where the actor went broke, he could pawn a diamond.[26]

Diamonds were good financial references. Often actors had good bank credit in their home towns, but if the show closed suddenly and the manager disappeared into the middle of the Mojave desert, banking references did them little good.

Performer's diamonds were fairly standard but good quality. Women had diamond earrings and a diamond ring. Men wore the biggest diamond they could finance, usually in a ring setting. Lodema Corey was famous as the leading lady with the diamond in her tooth. In 1965, she said that she still had the diamond though it was no longer part of her dental work.[27]

The theory was that the actor could get quick money any day in any town with a diamond. It generally happened that the worse he needed the money the less he got for pawning his diamond. The first time any performer in the old rep show business got a "yard" ahead (a "yard" was the term for one hundred dollars), he would buy diamonds with the money.

Diamonds also gave the performer prestige and class in addition to a feeling of security. They were flashy things to wear. Towners had no idea of the actual value of the stones, and if the actors wore a lot of jewelry towners figured they must be good, and would come to see the show.

There were diamond hoarders on the shows. It is said that older performers having nothing else to do used to sit in their boarding houses fingering their precious stones.

Oscar V. Howland,[28] one of the great comedians in the business bought a number of beautiful pear-shaped diamonds. He sewed these in little pouches next to the button holes in his long underwear. At one time during the thirties diamonds dropped in value. Oscar became careless and left his diamonds in a small chamois bag on his dressing table. A little comedian in the show who was a dope addict stole Oscar's diamonds. At the same time he broke into the local drugstore and removed a number of drugs. He was never caught and Oscar never recovered his diamonds.

Stories of the grouchbag and diamonds seem quaint to us today. Financial disaster stories are often told, and make interesting reading. Their appeal lies in their sensational aspects. The lurid robbery-murder has more reader appeal than a wedding anniversary. Most of the standard show companies were run in a businesslike manner, and made excellent profits for their owners with little crime or misconduct on the part of the members of the troupes.

Mrs. Walter Savidge said that every time her husband came home from his summer tours he bought another farm.[29] Chick Boyes owned a number of farms around Hebron, Nebraska. Lodema Corey said that she invested in stocks and bonds. It is impossible to make an accurate run down of the success or failure of the rep managers and actors. One gets the impression from visiting with those who are still alive that the majority of them were successful in their business, and invested their money wisely. One famous exception was Colonel Swain.[30] He owned what was probably the biggest show in the business, but died in a shanty near his home town of Dwight, Kansas.

How much banking business the rep people did remains a question. Charles Worthan said that he borrowed money to replace his tent from a local bank in Blue Mound, Illinois. Fred and Pearle Wilson banked in Noel, Missouri. This was the home of Grandpa and Grandma Pickering, Pearle's parents. The Wilsons would send money to the bank for deposit by post office money order. They used Grandma Pickering's address as their permanent mailing residence, and she would forward their mail.

An advertisement in *Bill Bruno's Bulletin*, from 1930, shows that regular banking practices were very common among the repsters. The ad read:

BANK BY MAIL

We will be glad to give you full information so that you will be able to deposit your earnings of the summer where they will at all times be safe, and at your easy access when you return to Kansas City.

Let us take care of your banking needs. Do not take unnecessary risks in carrying funds. Your business can be handled by mail.

WEST SIDE BANK OF COMMERCE
Twelfth and Broadway
Kansas City, Missouri

The tent shows prospered on the old Woolworth principle that if you can sell something for a nickel or a dime and sell a lot of it you can make money. The managers made a great deal of money from admission prices from as low as ten cents to a high of sixty cents.

Show paper for the Millikin University Town and Gown Players.

108

5. Showmen vs. Appleknockers

Non-professionals especially those making up the audience were towners to the troupers. This term was used if they were friendly and came to the show in great numbers. If they were perverse, actively hostile either individually or as a group, and stayed away from the show they were called appleknockers. Sometimes, they were just plain cash customers. Upon the customer's attitude depended the success or failure of the show.

This attitude was a strange mixture of admiration, wonder, and extreme disapproval. These viewpoints represented two different philosophies of life, two different ways of life. The theories overlapped in actual practice, but the thoughts were completely separated.

Two small town institutions, the church and the livery stable, symbolized these extremes. Most of the people belonged somewhere in between these two, and crossed over to one or the other, as fancy lured or necessity dictated. Very few people belonged completely to either extreme. Those intimately connected with the church exercised a powerful influence. On the other hand the great majority of the population could not resist the glamour of the shows.

To the small towner life in the large cities as described in the Sunday supplements seemed exciting. To them the shows brought a safe, though vicarious experience of metropolitan life. Outwardly they might scorn it, but inwardly they were titillated.

Life on the farm was isolated. The automobile was uncommon. Surfaced roads did not exist. Farm work was hard and the hours long. A weekly trip to the nearest village was an event. The coming of a show became a major event, a welcome break in the monotony of seeing the same place, the same people, and doing the same tasks every day.

Bess Robbins, one of the owners of the Clint and Bessie Robbins Show, famous in the prairie towns of the northern Midwest, learned of the importance of the shows to the people of these regions early in her career.[31]

She had spoken sharply to a newspaper friend after the night show, of how she had been annoyed by babies crying during the performance. Her friend rebuked her by saying "Bess Robbins, the mothers of those babies have saved egg money for months, to get to see you tonight. Some of them came forty miles by horse and buggy, because you are the brightest spot in a very dreary existence. Any time your audience boasts a baby, it means the mother is a devoted fan — and you be grateful." Bess said she never forgot the rebuke. It taught her not to seek applause but to give happiness.

The visits of the established shows to each town became an annual event. Relationships with the towners developed to a very familiar level. H. L. Carlstrom relates that the towners in Harry Hugo's territory would say, "Harry Hugo! Doesn't have much of a show or outfit! But he is a down-to-earth person. He can set down with a farmer and talk shop with 'em; and they like that." This attitude brought them to the show. It also made money for Harry Hugo.

When a show arrived in town the actors soon caught up with what had happened during the past year. They often knew more about the scandals in town than the towners did. Mondays were spent making the rounds and being seen in the right stores. They greeted local people who wanted their friends to think that they were well acquainted with the actors.

Visiting was a good time to find out what names were unwise to mention in turning show gags into local jibes. Joe shouldn't be mentioned this year; he ran away with the minister's wife. Bob ought to be skipped; it has been discovered that he took samples home from the bank where he worked. The townspeople didn't mention these derelictions. They just pretended Joe and Bob didn't exist. The showmen had best do likewise.

Often new towner babies were named for favorites on the shows. Ward "Pop" Hatcher provided entertainment for a Des Moines editor when a buxom girl shoved a wriggling baby into Pop's arms and said, "You never met little Ward, have you, Pop?"[32] Pop said he was very happy to see the girl's husband come up to explain.

A flyer from Arch Marshall of Perry, Oklahoma, recounts in a showman's own words what the shows thought the town people thought of them; what the show as a group thought of the towners in the up-coming engagement, and what both groups expected from one another. The flyer is a handbill from Brainard's Comedians, a vaudeville show, dated November 20, 1898. It was circulated in Avoca, Wisconsin, when the show advertising an up-coming engagement was leaving the summer tent for performances in houses during the winter.

WHAT YOU EXPECT,

"A bum show outfit" no Musicians, no Singers, no Performers, no Knowledge of Entertaining an Audience, a Non-legitimate Combination of Straggling Gentry, Without Clothes enough to Flag a Hand Car, or Money enough to Stop a Bread Wagon. Yes, you expect us to be Drunk when we reach Town, and Our Trunks to be in Soak for a Board Bill Before we get to your City. You will be Disappointed if we do not come in afoot, in Fact, you expect us to be "ALL BUT HUMAN."

WHAT WE EXPECT,

A Poor Town with Poor People a Poor House with a Bum Manager, Poor Hotel with Poor Accommodations, a Cranky Landlord, who will Saddle Every Tough Show Outfit that ever stopped with him onto Our Shoulders, and Treat us as he now wished he had Treated the Other "Gang." He will put us in the Poorest Rooms in the House, Place us at a Side Table, and call it a "Cut Rate" as if We would not know that we Simply got 5 cent meals for 25 cents Rates, Like the Shoe Dealer who Shows a Pair of $5 shoes, but in order to Sell them to his Good Customers at a reduced Rate, Wraps up a $2 pair Instead.

WE EXPECT,

Everybody to Know our Business Better than We do, and All to Tell us, Before we leave Town, Exactly How to Run it. Business Men Must not Allow a Bill in Their Windows, People Might Know we Were Coming, and Again, we Might, by Accident Receive an Accommodation.

Now we have Both told what we expect. Come to the Show, and then Pass Judgement on what we can do and what we know.

On The Prairie

We Claim to have a Neat, Clean and Strictly Up-To-Date Vaudeville Company, Each One of the Said Company to be First Class Artists, and Ladies and Gentlemen. Come and See for Yourself.

WATCH FOR DATE AND PRICE

A story from Ward Hatcher shows how dangerous a towner could be.[33] A youngster by the name of Vivien used to play the town of New Madrid, Missouri, year after year. He was a scrawny little fellow, just not very impressive physically. One Monday he was in a bar with a towner friend when the local bully entered. Every small town had its "tough guy" in those days, and probably still does for that matter. "Drinks for all," the bully ordered. Vivien reached for his, started to drink it, still talking, then stopped suddenly and set it back on the bar. "That's not what I'm drinking," he said, "and I don't want it." "Drink it!" the lout yelled, "or I'll fill you so full of lead you won't fall." "I'm talking to my friend," Viv declaimed in the voice he used to denounce the villain every night from eight to ten-thirty, "Go away! Don't bother me!" The town tough reached into his pocket, and came out with a weapon which looked like a cannon to Viv. The men along the bar scrambled for cover using tables and the bar. Vivien suddenly realized that this might be the final curtain. Unlike the guns he was used to night after night on the stage there were no blanks in the one pointed at him. There was real lead.

He looked up, his brain seemingly on strike, as in a bad case of stage-fright. His mouth automatically opened and out came the last line from the second act of Saturday night's bill. "Shoot! you Coward!" he shouted, turning toward his tormentor and baring his breast to the expected slug. "You haven't got the guts!"

The pride of the Missouri toughs lowered his head, pocketed his gun, and slunk out the door overwhelmed by the realism of Viv's acting.

Vivien fainted on the floor. He awoke surprised to find he was still alive. "Probably," Pop said, "there are some people in New Madrid who still remember Viv Varney as the only man to cross the town tough guy and live."

The towners had a feeling of sin mixed with their desire for glamor. The sin made the experience all the more delightful. They also had an ingrained and self-conscious feeling of inferiority toward the apparently more affluent and sophisticated city dweller. City denizens were, in many plays, haughty and unscrupulous dowagers, effeminate fops, conceited and utterly selfish types who were usually bested by the simple virtues of the country folks. The playwright put his characters in situations where they made fools of themselves by their inability to perform the simplest kind of farm tasks, tasks even the most witless bumpkin in the audience could perform with ease.

The good city folks, as described by Jim Parsons, "included both male and female rough diamonds from the slums, and the sons and daughters of the haughty dowagers and greedy stockbrokers... who took an immediate liking to country life and farm folks and nearly always married one of them. They always demonstrated very quickly that at heart they were just as common as an old shoe, and freely admitted how laughable was their inability to milk a cow."[34] In these preferences for the humble and meek, the outcast, the forlorn, the poor, the audience was expressing its feelings of fear and self-consciousness toward the rich, the powerful, and the successful. Audiences accepted the popular moral theological legend of the diamond in the rough, the ever present story of rags to riches for the good of heart.

A copy of *Mr. Jim Bailey*, another Charles Harrison play, is not available, but Jim Parsons has written a lively summary of it. Its plot is typical of that of the rep plays. It well represents the tastes and prejudices of the rural audiences, and is worth giving in full:

> *Mr. Jim Bailey* concerned an ignorant farm boy, and his ignorant old farm dad, versus the haughty, villainous stuck-up city folks. When oil was found on the Bailey farm, Jim and his dad became fabulously wealthy so haughty, impoverished Mrs. Belmont snares him as a husband for her haughty, beautiful daughter, Gladys. Then both Mrs. B. and Gladys make life miserable for Jim, by sneering at his ignorance although Gladys occasionally has twinges of conscience between feeling sorry for herself, because she has to endure such an uncouth millionaire. Mrs. Belmont begins to encourage a divorce with a fabulous settlement, of course, in order to marry Gladys off to a nasty society type, when Jim's diamond-in-the-rough old dad comes for a visit and this is more than Mama and Gladys can bear. So they kick Jim out, and he resolves to get eddicated at the end of the second act. The third act is a couple of years later, in Paris, Jim is the glass of fashion, and the mould of form, flinging ten-syllable words around like they was nothing. Dad didn't change, of course. And they run into Gladys just in the nick of time, as she is about to give in and marry the society fellow; and she realizes that she always loved Jim and she tells Mama to get the hell out and take her high-toned gigolo with her; and everybody lives happily ever after.

The opposition from the local churches ranged from mild disapproval to fervent opposition. Church bodies passed the shows by as not being worthwhile, or characterizing them as the gateway to hell. Perhaps the violent reaction of the clergy to the reps was a reflection of anger and annoyance at the competition. Even today the evangelistic minister often operates in a tent. The emotion-packed sermon along with the simple singable music usually presented by professionals makes up quite a show of its own. These services take the place of theatrical entertainment for many thousands of people and can be designated as a kind of paratheater.

One of the featured acts of the Ruble-Kreyer Company was a fire dance by the soubrette performed on a plate of glass set in the stage floor.[35] Red and blue lights and smoke shot up from underneath the stage. Brilliant colored designs were projected from a stereopticon onto the waving, white serpentine dress.

One Sunday in a Texas town, Locke and the leading lady, a woman of culture and education, went to a local church. After the minister had finished his sermon he picked up a clipping from the local paper and read, "See Corinne LaVaunt in her fire dance at the Opera House, Monday night." Then, assuming a sombre and tragic tone, he exclaimed, "Oh! Some day that will be a fire dance," dramatically pointing downward. He followed with a bitter, scathing peroration of the evils of the theater.

As he finished, the leading lady arose from her seat, asking to say a few words. Thoroughly startled the preacher gave her permission.

> Your words are unchristian like, and not in keeping with your calling and the doctrines of your church. They are perverse to the lesson we learn from the seventh chapter of Matthew and the teachings of our beloved Savior who turned not his back on any creature no matter how lowly. Your pulpit is a holy place, consecrated to God, Love, and Truth. It is not a place to be defiled by narrow-minded censure and stigma. I am an actress, a member of an honorable profession which you defame and denounce without knowing wherof you speak.

The preacher was thoroughly taken aback. Fortunately for his composure the organist picked up the cue and started playing the doxology as the congregation arose and hurried out.

Some troupers invaded the ranks of the ministry. Jack Collier, who managed a show touring Nebraska in the thirties, was an ordained minister of the Methodist church. He was the son of a minister and his wife's father was of the cloth. Al Pitcaithley said that during many of his between-the-act announcements he would weave much theological discourse into the praises of the local merchants for bringing the sunshine of his troupe into their lives.

Bill Bruno's Bulletin, May 15, 1930, carried this item:

The Billie Angelo Comedians, management of Hal Stone, opened last week in Murray, Iowa, playing to good business in spite of much rain and storms. The entire cast of the show was entertained on Thursday night at the home of the Reverend and Mrs. Leslie Ross. Mrs. Ross will be remembered as Ruth Angell, a member of the famous Angell family who operated in Iowa for many years.

J. S. Angell received much publicity in 1929, for his latest play. An Associated Press dispatch from Iowa was being featured in Eastern newspapers as well as in others throughout the country. The story carried the caption: "Famous Church will be Feted in Drama:"

Nashua, Iowa, March 12—Having been lauded for many years in story and song, the famous little wayside shrine will be given new publicity in a play "The Little Brown Church in the Vale" written by J. S. Angell, of Murray.

Mr. Angell, who spent his youth in Charles City, was a leader in the Nashua band about forty-two years ago. He was a friend of Dr. William S. Pitts, author of the song, "The Little Brown Church," as Dr. Pitts was the leader of the band at Fredericksburg at the same time.

Mr. Angell will also be remember by old timers through his connection with Angell's Comedians, who used to visit Nashua every season for a week's stand at the opera house.

We are constantly reminded that our old rural culture dominated by a farm economy, has changed to an urban culture dominated by industry. The small towns are still here. Many of these towns have attracted industry which provides employment more profitable than that of working as a farm hand. The rural economy still thrives in the business blocks located around many courthouse squares. The rural attitudes still exist.

Where are the shows of yesterday? The old opera house is probably still in the upstairs of a downtown building, with dust heavy on the floor, and its remaining equipment hanging on rusty nails. A warm night breeze comes through a broken window in the old hall, and the tattered curtain flaps emptily in the wind. The movie theater, once the proud rival of the tent shows, does poor business and in some places, has closed down completely. Where is the eager appetite for theater, the excitement and glamour of the living show, built to the tastes, needs, and beliefs of these people?

The typical small town audience inside the tent during the play, 1930's.

6. Drunks and Dynamiters

Managers feared two kinds of anti-social behavior more than anything else. Drunkenness and dynamiting could ruin a show quicker
than a blow down. The term dynamiting needs definition because of
its unusual, yet effective name. Gossip and backbiting are common
characteristics of human behavior in any social situation. The intense
egoism, and the resulting professional jealousy especially common
among theatrical people can become dangerous to the morale of the
close knit company. Carried to an extreme by a viciously inclined
actor these traits can destroy the show. Actors come on a show and
begin criticizing the manager and his ways. They talk one way to one
person and another way to the next. They run down the show and
everything about it, and in a very short time have the whole group
thoroughly angry and upset.

A person of this type can soon be spotted. Actors would often
join a troupe and deliberately set out to cause trouble usually for
reasons of personal ambition. Dissatisfaction among the actors leading
to disloyalty to the company, and filling it with tension and division
are always threatening diseases. If not checked at the very beginning

it can become an epidemic resulting in complete destruction of the troupe.

An editorial in *Bill Bruno's Bulletin*, December 17, 1936, described such a situation. Bill said that he had received a letter in the mail describing loyalty, a virtue which had become almost obsolete. A young actor playing circle stock with a company in the south had written to him. In fact, he had written two letters. The first letter described the company as a "nice lot of folks," and told how much the young man was enjoying himself. Four weeks later a second letter arrived, describing a great change.

During the second week of playing the "dynamiter" made his appearance in the person of an actor who wanted his own show. He had evidently joined the show to disorganize it, get the present manager off the job and take over the show.

In his letter to *Bill Bruno's Bulletin* the young actor said:

"When I first wrote you, I didn't realize that the reptile you refered to as a dynamiter was at work. This particular one has one-half of the company fighting the other half, and is trying to get rid of the manager so he can take the show over himself. I, however, have refused to have any part in the doings and have told the dynamiter that the moment Mr. _____ stepped out of the management, I was leaving also. Not liking my stand, the troublemakers are making life very unpleasant for me. But I am staying with the show in spite of them. Until Mr. _____ steps out at least.

I have been taught and believe that if a manager was honest and above-board, as this one has certainly been in the face of bad luck and dissention on the show, one owed him at least a little loyalty. So I am not leaving here so long as Mr. _____ needs me and wants me, and the dynamiters can't drive me off. Whether I get salary or not, I'm staying on because this manager has been square, worked hard to put the show over, and is not to blame entirely.

Bill Bruno in his editorial comment, "But One Way to Handle Them," said:

There is only the one remedy for dynamiting; the moment dissatisfaction starts among your people, find the dynamite and get it off the show. And do it QUICK! Such a course may put a hardship on you for a week or two, but you will be rid of continual and never-ending trouble when you get the dis-organizer off the show. The sooner the better. Because other actors will listen and also become dissatisfied. Then you have trouble on your hands which you will have to get off the show sooner or

The Footlights

later. So why not get it over with at the start? . . . There is nothing which helps organization and performance so much as a general good feeling among the company. The audience is quick to note it. Don't fool yourself that they miss the undercurrent of dissatisfaction. They do. They at times feel the dynamiting long before the manager does . . . There is nothing so harmful as the disorganizer —the 'dynamiter' if you like—and there ought to be no place for him in the business. Whether he be actor or manager. In the later case, he won't be a manager long.

Al Pitcaithley describes the dressing room arrangement on the Christy Obrecht Show, as a very elaborate outfit, which had canvas booths housing two people to a dressing room.[36] He said that this was Obrecht's way of preventing dressing room gossip and the resulting dissension.

On another show the scenery and property trucks were pulled up with their back ends opening on the tent, and used as segregated dressing rooms. The manager who always acted in the show dressed with the men, and his wife with the women. Generally, dressing room gossip is a sneaking sort of thing, and the presence of the manager and his wife in the dressing rooms prevented any kind of gossip.

The general attitudes of the troupers toward their shows usually were ones of great loyalty and devotion. They loved show business. It was a way of life to them, and they enjoyed every minute of it.

In the great days of the shows drinkers were usually individuals and easily disposed of. Equity had a firm rule against drinking. An actor who acquired a reputation as a drunk could just as well get out of the business.

Drunken actors can sneak up on managers. A talented and otherwise acceptable person appearing on the lot intoxicated ruins the show's current performance. He also gives the company a bad name which may follow them for years. Drunken actors were tragic occurrences for the repsters to whom the show was life.

One exception to the no drunks rule was Bush Burrichter, one of the greatest, and most popular comedians. He was a very small man, slight of build. He was admired by actors and audiences for his abilities. "A clever and likeable fellow, but a spasmodic drunk," said Al Pitcaithley.[37] "He could go for weeks without touching liquor, and then suddenly let him so much as smell a cork, and he would be drunk for days."

Bush had been married very early to a girl whom he fell madly in love with at first sight. He and his young wife were playing on a well established midwestern show, one of the first in the business.

One night the manager called him in and gave him his notice, along with two weeks salary.

Bush was thunderstruck. He wanted to know the reason why, since everything had been going along smoothly. The manager calmly told him that the notice was for him alone. Bush would leave his wife behind. The manager intended to marry her. This may be the reason for Bush's infirmity. Some people who worked with him think it was.

Al Pitcaithley, in his autobiography said, "Lest the reader get the wrong impression, I consider Burrichter a good friend . . . a valuable man on a show and a most likeable personality, but a domestic tragedy gave him a thirst for drink that was a great hindrance to his career."

Al met Bush on the Trousdale show playing stock in Cedar Rapids, Iowa, in 1932. When Al joined the company, Bush had been drinking during the show, with a new bill to open the following day's matinee. Bush didn't know a line of the thirty-four side part in that play. After the show Al thought the only thing to do was to get him to bed, so he took him to his room.

It was a real struggle. Bush did not know Al, and his usual acumen was dulled by drink. Al propped him up against the foot of the bed, and tried to get his clothes off. Bush struggled against him crying, "No! No! Don't!". Bush had a horror of homosexuals, and he didn't know who Al was. He thought a male deviate was trying to take advantage of him. The struggle became vicious when Al tried to take his trousers off. Al finally got him to bed and stayed in the room with Bush while the show's manager called a friend of Bush's in Des Moines.

The girl friend was an Amazonian redhead. The manager had often paid her to keep Bush sober. Al was awakened by her arrival at six in the morning. She saw Bush dead drunk in Al's bed and immediately jerked him to a sitting position. Bush in his daze didn't know whether he was seeing a ghost or a real person. Alice slapped him, first to the right, and then to the left. She stood him up, and banged his head against the wall several times. Al felt sorry for him but the girl was such a big, strapping creature that he dared not interfere. All through this punishment Bush would whimper, "Been bad boy, Alice! Been bad boy!." Her only response was, "You sure have!" coupled with another slap.

After she had punished him she sent for black coffee. Alice set him down at a table and taught him his lines. The lesson took the rest of the morning, but by matinee time Bush was ready to go on stage in a fair degree of sobriety.

Three years later Al arrived at Pauls Valley, Oklahoma. He found Bush acting as both comic and director. Bush was again in the same sad state. Al felt panicked. There were the last rehearsals, the setting of specialties, and many other last minute details to be done before the show could open. The manager was so disgusted that he was ready to close the show. Al had no wish to be stuck in Pauls Valley so he told the manager that he would be responsible and would have Bush sober by show time.

It was a little after noon at this time. Al took Bush to his room and locked him in, after putting him to bed. He left orders to the clerks and bellboys to see that Bush stayed in his room until Al called for him at 6:30 p.m. By that time Bush had slept off the effects and Al had poured black coffee into him. Bush was ready for the show and he finished the day by giving a fine performance. Al added that there never was a harder worker for the interest of a show than Bush, when he was sober.

Bush died on November 30, 1947.[38] He had lain down on his hotel bed holding a burning cigarette. The resulting fire burned him so badly that, after five days in the hospital, he died. In spite of his failing, Bush was respected and admired. There are humorous over-tones in these experiences but his life over-all was tragic.

The objections to drinking on the show are explicitly stated by Jim Parsons.[39] Show people were not puritanical but a show is really a twenty-four hour a day job. The performer can never forget the evening deadline at any time. When he is not working, and if he wants to have a riotous time, there is no one to object. Everybody needs to let go once in a while, and show people, naturally tolerant, recognize this. Charlie Worthan even brags with a grin about the time he got a little bit under the weather at a T. R. M. P. A. (Tent Rep Managers Protective Association) party in Kansas City, and danced with Sport North's wife.

On the show having to nurse a drunk "was bad enough, because of the embarrassment and constant vigilance required and having our own work spoiled. There was a serious financial element too. We could all be thrown out of a job if the drunk couldn't make it—or at least have to lay off without salary until he could be replaced," said Jim Parsons.

Jim told of two drunken experiences in his professional career, one of them accidental and one purposeful.[40] These incidents show what drinking can do to a show, and to the attitude of the company.

One time when Jim was on the Jack Brooks show he went to a nearby town during the afternoon to visit one of the Cairns girls,

Eileen. "This sounds a bit racy, but at this time she was happily and prosperously married, and nothing could have been more platonic," Jim said. She had a bottle of saki, a new and exotic drink to Jim, and they killed it. "Mostly me, I'm afraid," added Jim. That night he knew he was still high but felt sure that no one else would suspect it if he watched himself, and was very careful. "No stumbling or mushy enunciation from Parsons."

"I walked firmly and steadily and spoke-every-word-with-the-greatest-precision-and-clarity, congratulating myself that no fault could possibly be found with my performance—until after the first act, Tom Brooks drew me aside and whispered, 'Mother said it's all right this time, but don't do it again, and *for Heaven's sake, don't talk so loud!*' "

The second incident happened on the Happy Bill Radio Troupe. The experience was not a happy one for Jim. The director who starred in the main show, and in the dance afterward, was a drunk. "A very nasty person to boot, as comics in every branch of show business are inclined to be." This director was half-drunk every night, and often was well over the half way mark. This was no fun for the troupe or audience. Jim resented the manager's letting him get away with it night after night with no reproof. Jim finally said to himself, "To hell with it! Let's see how Bill likes having two drunks on the cast." He deliberately poured down as much liquor as he could before the show. He took a bottle backstage to nip on between the scenes. He has no memory of the performance. Apparently it must have gone all right but the dance after the show was a nightmare. He began to get very sick, close to the vomiting point. Whenever he would put his saxophone to his lips and start to blow he would come dangerously near the edge. "Not that I gave a damn, this was what I had started out to accomplish, but my wife was only in the business a few months, and this was her first job." She was frantic as she sat beside him all through the dance begging him to play whenever he took the sax out of his mouth. "I'd stop, and she'd plead, 'Jimmy! Please play! Please! Try, Jimmy!' And so I'd try, and start to get sick, I'd stop and she'd beg, and I'd start to get sick, and so on and so on, and so on."

122

7. Children on the Show

Show folks are not supposed to have children, but children inevitably happened. The children were not allowed to become little vagabonds but were brought up as well, or better than children from families of more stable professions. Their parents were concerned about their education. Children learned the quality of self-reliance from the very nature of their parent's profession. They found out very early the ways of the world, and how to cope with them.

Fred and Pearle Wilson's children, Evelyn and Neil, were very properly brought up under these difficult conditions. They were sent to school at an early age away from the show.[41] Evelyn went to St. Louis, and Neil spent several years at a military school in Cleburne, Texas, operated by an Episcopalian priest, Dr. Johnson.

The Wilsons stayed in private homes rather than boarding houses and hotels while the children were too young to go to school. On one occasion a woman didn't want to rent to them simply because they had children. Fred exploded, "Dammit, lady! I'll shoot the children." The lady relented, and every year after that when they played the town the family stayed there. The landlady had the best rooms in town; the beds were equipped with the best mattresses, a comfort to tired showfolks.

The landlady finally decided that show folks had better behaved and more informed children that any she had ever seen. Children are children and cannot always behave no matter how well they are trained. Evelyn Barrick added ironically, that she and her brother were being especially good at the time.

Jack Parsons and his wife, knowing well the dislike landladies usually have for children, dressed four-year-old Jim up to look like an angel and went out searching for rooms.[42] They were trying to convince a more than skeptical landlady that she would simply love having little Jimmy in the house. "Oh! Jimmy is so very well behaved, that he's no trouble at all. Say hello to the nice lady, Jimmy," said Clara Parsons. With a furious shriek, Jimmy answered, "NO!" Drily, his father said, "Come on, Clara!"

The Parsons family when staying in hotels, sneaked a little in-room cooking on the side, even though it was often strictly against the rules. One afternoon, when young Jim was left to his own devices he did a little cooking of his own. He stirred up a lovely little mess of mentholatum and sugar, in the chamberpot which he had just used. He set it boiling atop the little coal oil stove the family had brought in for cooking. There was a honeymoon couple in another room on the same floor. Jim went to the room and borrowed the bride's ostrich plume picture hat. Jim then served the mess in the new hat to the horrified couple.

The Wallace Bruce Company first broke down the barriers against children at the De Soto Hotel in Dalhart, Texas.[43] At noon on the first day they were staying there Mrs. Bruce set her baby girl in a high chair dressed all in white. The child ate her noon meal quietly, without any fuss or muss. She showed the same behavior during the supper meal.

The hotel manager's wife was having lunch and supper with her grandchildren. She had quite a time feeding them. They kept getting all smeared with food. Finally she came over to the Bruce table introduced herself, and asked Ruby, "How do you keep your baby so quiet? How do you get her to eat without spilling food all over herself?" Ruby answered, "I have taught her from the start to be neat and not to act up in public." The Bruce child's behavior helped to re-enforce the good impression the troupe made during its initial stay at the De Soto Hotel.

Mrs. Barrick and her brother were never allowed to go barefoot as children.[44] They had to dress at all times as if they were going to make a public appearance. Amber Wight Rebein tells the same story of her childhood. Mrs. Rebein was not sent away to boarding school. She had to attend school in whatever town the show happened to be playing. She was often taunted by other children because she belonged to show folks. One girl whose dress and attitude were particularly superior so aggravated Amber that she pushed the girl into a convenient mud puddle. Jim Parsons in his earlier years went to school in whatever town the company happened to be playing. He attended a different school each week during spring and fall when the troupe was on the road. Jim's school residence was a more permanent one when the troupe went into stock in the winter.

One time after school was out Neil and Evelyn arrived at the tent after the performance had started.[45] They made so much noise playing that their father stopped the show, went to the footlights and said, ("Will I *ever* forget it," exclaims Mrs. Barrick) "Evelyn and Neil, be quiet! These people paid their money to see a show and see it they will! *Behave!*" He returned to the stage and began the show over again. The children were so quiet that they were completely forgotten. After the show the parents were in the restaurant eating. They suddenly remembered the children and hurried back to the tent. The children were asleep on two benches. "It was punishment enough," says Mrs. Barrick, "to be scolded in front of all those townspeople." Their actions were in sharp contrast to the behavior and attitude of another tent show child. This child would interrupt performance after performance and receive no reproof. How popular he must have been not only with the audience but with the actors as well!

Mrs. Barrick recalled her proudest moments were when she walked down the street with her father and the people told him how well behaved his children were.[46] "Perhaps," she says, "other parents were not as strict as ours but we knew we were loved. Our parents were always fair and a whole lot of fun."

Evelyn once arrived on the show during a matinee at Christmas time. The show was in Tulsa. She was hugging her father when his cue came. He took her right on the stage, introduced her to the audience and told them she had just arrived, and that he hadn't had the time to welcome her properly. The audience roared and applauded its approval. Fred hugged and kissed her and then took her to the wings where her mother was waiting for her.

Evelyn was about ten or eleven years old when the Wilsons were playing Oiltown, Oklahoma. She arrived in the town and found no one to meet her. She went straight to the theater. The troupe hadn't arrived for the show that night and the manager was so angry that he didn't give her the wire from her parents saying that the train had been wrecked and that they wouldn't be there until the next day! The wire also mentioned they had made arrangements for her to stay at the hotel. Knowing nothing of this but being very self reliant, she went to the boarding house where the company usually ate. The people there cared for her, refused payment and took her to the train the next day to meet her parents.

Those were the oil boom days in Oklahoma.[47] They were wild frontier days. Life was not sacred nor safe for there were daily killings. Because there is supposed to be safety in numbers the whole company often slept in the tent; the actors slept in the men's dressing room; actresses slept in the women's and the canvasmen slept on the stage. The canvasmen usually slept there throughout the season. One young couple was newly married and could not stand to be separated so they made their bedroom under the stage!

The natural drinking water of this area is brackish, alkaline, and apt to make people ill. In many places bottled drinking water was shipped in. Mrs. Barrick said that the water made her ill quite often. When the company was playing at Jennings, Drumright, and Oiltown, the two children were sent to visit relatives in Topeka, Kansas. Evelyn's mother could eat anything any place after trouping the oil boom towns. Evelyn, much to her mother's disgust, had a weak stomach. It was always a pleasure to be invited to someone's house. She and Neil could play with the children and the parents could talk. She described all these experiences as a happy time for her.

There were many natural hazards in Oklahoma, especially high winds and tornadoes. Oklahoma is a notoriously dangerous section of tornado alley. When the company which included Fred and Pearle Wilson was playing in Purcell, a tornado tied a knot in the steel center pole of the tent. The Wilson children heard their father say that the company would probably not make enough money to get out of town. They decided to help out. Evelyn and Neil went to the local merchants and told them that their parents were broke and couldn't get out of town. They asked the storekeepers for tin foil to sell. Fortunately for their parents' pride, one of their father's friends sent word to him; the children no longer "helped." They were not punished as Fred Wilson realized he had not properly explained the situation to them.

Mrs. Barrick said that in many ways her father was an odd man, especially in his attitude toward his family and toward the show. He liked to talk to everybody and had an easy manner with the general public, but he wanted his family kept away from the public.

Fred's mother had taught him that when a woman married, she should stay home and take care of the kids. That theory didn't work with a wife like Pearle Wilson and it later led to domestic difficulties. Fred and Pearle's marriage ended in a divorce. Fred's second wife Hazel conformed to Fred's domestic views, although it was really not in her nature to do so.

Mrs. Barrick attended her first dance when the show orchestra played for a dance sponsored by a local American Legion club. Evelyn was never permitted to talk to the town boys as a usual thing, but as her mother was chaperoning her she was allowed to dance this time, but only with the boys from the show. However, Pearle did not dance. Mrs. Barrick said that if she had danced with the local boys or if her mother had danced her father never would have forgiven them. Even so, he was so angry and upset for fear that people of the town would talk about them, that he didn't speak to his family for a week.

Actors often trouped pets on the show even though this gave them more than the usual trouble in getting rooms. Jim Parsons said that he has heard rumors of an eccentric character woman who trouped a cow but he doesn't believe it is so.[48] There was an actor on the Parsons show, "name long since forgotten," said Jim, who trouped a wolf. He didn't keep the wolf in hotel rooms but tied it up on the lot, to the vast disapproval of Jack Parsons, who refused to believe that the wolf was as tame as its owner said. He lived in a constant state of fear that young Jim would wander within reach of the wolf and be chewed up.

One day while the grownups were rehearsing young Jim was left to himself in the dressing room. He began to play with the makeup kit. He took off all of his clothes and striped himself with greasepaint from head to foot. He said that the effect was too spectacular not to be admired. Jim decided to give a show and wandered down the street looking for an audience before whom he could perform. Without difficulty he found one and put on a few dances for the people in front of the bank. This was in Mena, Arkansas. He was a great success for the audience kept growing.

One of the canvasmen saw the crowd and wondered what it was all about. He joined the group only to find the boss' son dancing stark naked, covered with grease paint, mostly red. He took the boy into the nearest store, bought him a pair of pants, and headed back for the tent. The crowd followed behind.

The actors had by that time discovered Jim's absence. Everybody had been delegated to search for him before something dreadful happened. Jack looked up the street and the red-painted body of the boy in the canvasman's arms confirmed his worst fears. Jack didn't wait to check on anything. He grabbed an axe and headed for the wolf, bent on revenge. The tale ends happily, even for the wolf, because somebody stopped Jack in time. Jim doesn't say whether he suffered any consequences.

Show parents fully realized the difficulties of life for children on the show. The bad food and water, the constant moving from place to place, the danger from insects, disease, and the hazards of continental weather all took their toll on the children.

Pearle Wilson.

Fred Wilson as a young actor.

8. On the Way to the Center Door Fancy

Any live show no matter how well rehearsed is threatened with the physical and mental lapses of the actors, slips of the tongue, wrong turn or wrong cross, sudden loss of memory, the uncontrollable interferences from the dumb forces, a falling flat, the prop which twists out of the hand, the failure of lights, and even the wind and rain. Each living performance is a different performance in spite of thorough direction, hours of study and rehearsal and thorough penetration into characterization and meaning. This is because the show is alive.

The Loranger show was one of the first to play the wide plains of the Dakotas. When in its later days, Jim Parsons was playing in the troupe, Bess Loranger was in her late sixties, had dyed red hair, swore like a truck driver and was rumored to smoke cigars.[49] In Jim's opinion, "she was one of the sweetest old girls I have ever known in my life although her language embarrassed me at times." The troupe was playing *The Family Upstairs,* a Broadway comedy. It was as much a staple play of the rep shows as *Saintly Hyps* because of the old-fashioned family story it told. Jim was playing the teen-age son, Willie, and Bess was playing Mama. Poor Mama, at one point completely upset because she had lost an argument with someone else, whirls on Willie with the line, "Willie! You go upstairs and wash your neck and behind your ears!" Bess got her tongue twisted. "Willie" she yelled as she turned to Jim, "you go right upstairs and wash your behind!" Suddenly realizing what she had said, she stopped cold for only a moment and then burst out with a stentorian guffaw. When something struck Bess funny it was impossible to cover. Naturally the audience caught the line and the show was stopped for five minutes. "It was the best laugh I ever got," added Jim, "and, damn it, I didn't get it—Bess did!"

Outside interference was always a hazard not only from the elements but from human activities. Trains, automobiles, and airplanes often interfered with a performance.

Wallace Bruce once used the train noise in Hutchinson, Kansas to the advantage of the show.[50] During the Depression, the Bruce Company was using a burned out store building as a theater. The troupe cleaned the place up, painted it, and put in a new front. They set the stage end in the back. There was no roof over the audience. At that time in Hutchinson the street cars were still running. There was a car switch right in front of the theater and the switching of the cars from one track to another made lots of noise.

The Santa Fe railroad was only a few blocks from the theater. This was in the days when steam engines were still using shrieking whistles and loud bells. During the performance of a very sad scene in one play where a woman was dying and the other characters had gathered around speaking very softly, a Santa Fe train came bolting through town, its whistle blasting away, and its bells ringing madly. Bruce thought he had better save the situation in any way he could. He stepped down to the footlights and started singing, "Hear Dem Bells." He got an appreciative laugh from the audience.

One time Wallace's company arrived in a South Dakota town too late to attend to every detail. The company had to open with *Turn to the Right*, a Broadway show which the reps often fell back on.

In the same show, Lois Darr, a very pretty little ingenue, was playing the lead. As she left the stage, she turned just outside the center door and waved to her mother. On this occasion in a hurry to get the tent set up the crew had stretched the tent so that the back drop was a little off the line and leaning in at the top. The cast had to cross behind the drop, but at each edge was a set of steps. The actors came down off the stage on these steps, placed well out of sight of the audience. When Lois turned to wave she took one step too many and fell between the drop and the back edge of the stage. When her

The Footlights

mother turned to wave at her all she could see was a beautiful silk-clad leg sticking in the air.

Most of the companies tried to present the best kind of stage production possible. Scenery and properties were standard in terms of the current practice of the day. The J. B. Rotnour show, one of the established outfits, was noted for using worn-out, faded scenery simply because the owner refused to replace it with new scenery. Jim Parsons said that J. B. was a pinchpenny—a pinchpenny only in regard to the tent outfit and equipment for he never owed salaries. The tent was a real antique. It had been patched and repatched until it looked like a crazy quilt. J. B. had no intention of replacing it. When the final blowdown came it wasn't the canvas that gave way but the stitching to the ropes which had rotted away year after year, needing only a vigorous pull to make the tent fall out completely. The canvas tore loose under the force of the wind and sailed away, leaving every pole and rope standing, a skeleton with no skin or flesh.

J. B. followed a similar thrift policy with the scenery. All drops had been painted by some artist back in the Old Stone Age of the theater, and were so worn and faded by years of use that it was really difficult to tell what they really represented.

The worst of the set lot was used for the Saturday night western bill. No matter that the script said that the fare was a western, the kitchen set was used. One season the company was using *Jealousy* as the Saturday night western.

The script called for a palatial ranch house. The fabulously wealthy cattleman was bringing his bride from the East. Up went the kitchen set. On one Saturday night it rained. The tired and patched old tent leaked copiously. The Saturday night furniture consisted of a couple of wooden kitchen chairs, and a battered old kitchen table. Three or four streams of water were pouring down on the stage floor. The chairs and table were shifted to the dry spots on the stage. Buckets and dishpans were placed under the leaks. When the curtain went up on the first act and the leading team entered, Jewel Parsons was playing the bride. "She looked around at this poor old gray rag of a set, streaked with trickles of water, the tired old wooden chairs and table, held together with wire, and placed helter-skelter around the stage, the rain splashing away busily in the dishpans and buckets, and read her first line, "Oh! John, it's beautiful!"[51]

Call of the Woods by W. C. Herman was the rep show's answer to the immense popularity of novels, films, and plays about the Canadian Northwest. First presented in the days of the house reps in DeKalb, Illinois, by Robert L. Sherman's Company it was a standard repertory piece throughout the twenties.[52] It was shown up through the final days of the tents because it contained a character, Eben Quackenbush, who could easily be turned into a Toby. Sherman played the leading role of Dave in the first production.

During the performance on the Harley Sadler show in 1933, Willis, the heavy, burned the all-important letter tossing it into the fire place. Moments later a member of the cast noticed that the fireplace was burning. Desperately, every member of the company on and offstage, was trying to decide the best thing to do. Ring down the curtain? Stop the show, and put the fire out, or what? Sadler playing Eben, solved the problem at once and without fuss. He walked on stage, nodded to the heavy, picked up the fireplace and took it offstage.

Call of the Woods is a play Jim Parsons remembers that caused another almost lethal onstage accident. Before the accident can be understood, we need a resumé of the plot. It seems melodramatic and silly now, and Jim's resumé which follows, makes it all the more so. We must remember that its story and characters are written in terms of the popular novels and films of the period. It certainly held its place as a play for many years. Jim's resumé is worth quoting in full:[53]

> . . . younger brother Willis, a mealy-mouthed hypocrite, has for years been stealing money from blind mama's strongbox, and putting the blame on his blue-shirt-lead older brother, Dave, a noble, stalwart type who had been forbidden to darken mama's door again and lives in a cabin in the woods where he makes a living, hunting and fishing, and smooching the wealthy Judge's daughter, Grace, (is that her name? Well it's as good as any?) who loves him for his purity, and nobilty, and long-suffering stupidity, I guess. But Willis also wants to marry Grace — for her money, and there's a slight hitch.
>
> He had got Hilda, the half-breed hired girl with child, and Hilda's French Canuck father is a mean old boy who'll stand for no hanky-panky. Also, Hilda is bound and determined Willis is going to marry her. If not, she'll tell on him about the money he's been stealing, and blaming Dave for.
>
> So one day in Dave's cabin (don't ask me what everybody has come to Dave's cabin for) when she's alone with Willis, she gives him her ultimatum. He tells her she'd better not talk if she knows what's good for her. But Hilda is stubborn.
>
> So Willis spots an axe handle that Dave's been whittling, and holding the axe handle behind him says, "Again I ask your silence." Hilda replies, "No." Willis: "Then you die" and he takes out after her with the axe handle. Hilda screams and runs around the center table with Willis in hot pursuit and she ducks into Dave's bedroom off Right, Willis and the lethal weapon right

on her heels. A loud offstage whack followed by a loud offstage scream. A loud offstage whack followed by a medium scream! A loud offstage whack followed by a low moan—and Willis comes backing onstage with the bloody axe handle in his guilty hand. He hears the others coming, attracted by the screams, and flings the handle away from him and hides. Dave arrives first and alone, picks up the bloody axe handle and stands there looking at it as the others dash in. They discover Hilda apparently dead and wonder who could have done such a dastardly deed. Willis, of course, points to Dave, standing there with the weapon, literally caught red-handed, and accuses him. Motive: Dave is the father of her unborn child."

On the night of the performance mentioned everything was going just fine up to the point where Willis begins to chase Hilda. She ran away from him, around the table, and over to the bedroom door, only to find it locked from offstage. In a fierce whisper she called offstage, "Open the door!" and madly took another turn around the table. Willis would gain on her on every step in spite of anything she or he could do. She ran back to the door shook it frantically, and whispered again as loud as she dared, "Open the door!" Willis bumped himself into chairs, stumbled over his own feet, and stopped finally "to glare at her in triumph but to no avail." At last he could do nothing else but catch up with her. She was still shaking the door and whispering desperate pleas to get the damn thing open. Everybody backstage must have been dead or asleep! Poor Willis! As an actor and character, there was nothing else he could do but hit her over the head with the axe handle. He must not have known how to fake his blow for the poor girl had a lump on her head for days.

For the sake of the record, Hilda was Diane Delaire (incorrect spelling, I'm sure) and Willis was Lit. Whitehouse. His brother Big was playing Dave. Made it a little confusing because they were twins and it was often hard to tell them apart unless one wore a crepe hair mustache. I don't know their real names, they were always called Big and Lit. For Little, of course. Lit happened to be bigger than Big, but you see . . . Oh, the hell with it!

Those inexperienced in theater should not be left without a resumé of the last act of the play. It is a classic finish to this fascinating and dramatic situation. Hilda recovers from the blow on her head but her mind is gone. She cannot tell who did the foul deed, or anything about Willis' constant thefts, or other kinds of perfidy.

It is the trial scene. Everyone is sitting in the anteroom outside the courtroom where Dave is being tried for the crime. Everyone is there except Hilda who is waiting in the buggy outside with her tiny, illegitimate baby in her arms.

Offstage, the jury returns and their verdict is heard, "We the gentlemen of the jury, find the defendant guilty!" Again offstage, Hilda screams, and the gallop of horses hooves is heard. The horses are running away with Hilda, and she will be thrown out. So runs the dialogue of the play. The writers of the rep shows were forced to such devices by the limitations of most of the stages the play would be produced on.

Hilda is thrown out! She is thrown out of the buggy, landing on her head. The blow restores her reason, and she rushes in to accuse Willis of all the vicious crimes, and clears Dave. Everybody, that is all the good, but mistaken people are restored to happiness in the last two and half pages of the script. A typically swift W. C. Herman denouement, with Eben (Toby) pushing the wicked Willis into a chair where he awaits further punishment. What happens to the blighted romance between Willis and Hilda is never told. It doesn't matter, for Dave and Grace (Doris) have been re-united, Dave's mother receives her good son back into the fold, and Eben (Toby) has given a kind of coup de grace to Willis. "It's just a real humdinger of a play, by Golly!" said Jim Parsons. In spite of the super melodrama of the situation the playwright, hack though he may be, manages, just as in *Clouds and Sunshine,* to make the serious parts of the ending acceptable by mixing in much comedy from Eben (Toby) and his father, Doc Quackenbush (the G-string comic).

The most tried and true saying in show business is "The show must go on!" The actors though in serious danger from frightening storms always kept the show going as long as possible. When catastrophe was inevitable the manager stopped the show. A reassuring force to the audience, he proceeded to get them safely outside the tent and on the way home. Even death, on the show itself, or among family or friends was not allowed to stop the performance.

Evan Evans and his wife Helen, a dancing act well established in the business, joined the Bud Hawkins show in 1929.[54] They brought along their twelve year old son Lester, and their sixteen year old daughter Maryette, billing themselves as the Evans Family. The Evans family had been operating a dancing school in Pittsburgh, semi-retired from vaudeville, before they joined the show. They stayed on the Hawkins show every season for several years. Maryette became an ingenue on that show.

She and a young man who played saxophone developed a very serious interest in each other. He came from a wealthy Lexington family, and often drove home on Sundays. He had taken Maryette with him several times to meet his family. They approved highly of her. The young couple was to be married at the end of the season.

One Monday evening just before showtime word came to the show that the young man had been killed in a car crash. Maryette went on with her performance which opened with a song. The piano player hit the introductory notes. No one had realized that her opening song that night was "I'm through with Love!" There was nothing she could do, but stand there and sing the song.

Blowdown, Aulger Brothers, at Jackson, Minnesota, 1928.

Snowdown,
L. Vern Slout
Players,
Vermontville,
Michigan.

Blowdown,
Savidge Shows.
Big Top is
O.K., Wisner,
Nebraska, 1930.

Blowdown,
Dramatic End
Tent, Walter
Savidge Players,
Winner, South
Dakota, 1917.

9. On the Lot

Canvas crews were indispensable, the unsung heros of the tent shows. Their position was humble, completely unglamorous, and so inferior that the women on the earlier shows were not allowed to speak to them.[55] The canvas crews did all the hard and dirty work and did not have adequate facilities for bathing or living. They were usually a crew of rough and dirty men. The smaller shows carried at least three crew members, and the larger shows had six to eight crewmen one of whom was in charge of the rest.

The average rep show organized to play week stands usually carried five men on their canvas crew. On many shows the musicians were paid to help set up and tear down. The top salary for canvasmen on a one-nigher was fifteen dollars a week, plus room and board.[56] These shows required continuous heavy work with no week-long rest period in between shows. The average working man made six dollars a week, plus "found." He was given one dollar a week bonus at the end of the season, a method managers used to keep their crews intact during the season.

When Jack Kelly ran away from home at the age of fifteen his first job in show business was as a canvasman on the McConkey

Circus. He recalled in an interview in the *Michigan State Journal* that it was a pretty tough assignment.[57] He had to do a man's work, often times two men's work; packing and unpacking the tent, shifting the equipment, and anything else there was to do until the outfit was set up. Unlike most youngsters he stuck it out. The bosses were big tough fellows who could keep the crew going. The crew had plenty of food, but they never got paid. Once in a while, Kelly would get up nerve to ask the big boss for a quarter. Whereupon the lofty brute would give the boy ten cents, the only money he ever saw.

When the show came into town, there were usually youngsters hanging around wanting to earn a pass to the show. Wallace Bruce told his boss canvasman that regardless of how many kids turned up wanting to carry chairs or do some other of the lighter tasks, he was to put them to work, even if there were more than a hundred. He said that this would lead to good will in the town. Even today the youngsters who bicycle to the circus lot the moment there is news of a show's arrival are indispensable for getting the tent up and ready for performance.

Every actor had his part in the set-up or tear-down. Today, most shows carry only one crewman. During the great days of the reps, the actors were not supposed to take any part in the manual labor. Mr. Bruce said that often an actor would help set chairs or do some of the lighter work. He added that if an actor did these things for the show he could always be counted on as a good trouper.

During World War I, Will Locke was playing with Leo Blondin's one-nighter, *Jesse James*.[58] The show traveled by train and played each night in a different town. During this war period men were scarce. Most of the male members of the cast were either too old, or ineligible for army service. These were the men that had to do the work of the crew putting up and taking down the tent.

In a Nebraska town, the show lot was on a corner, and was about a foot lower than the sidewalk around it. Next to the vacant lot was an old livery stable, behind which was a great heap of manure overflowing onto the back end of the show lot.

Blondin's troupe had just finished the after show concert one evening when a real gully-washer rainstorm came up. The crew tore down during the downpour although the wet canvas must have been impossible to properly roll up and sack. The lot was a lake, and a rising wind made it look like a storm at sea by the time the top was down and the canvas was unlaced and rolled.

The local drayman was a good fellow and helped the crew load the outfit on the dray. The crew gave up on the tent stakes, big wooden

The Footlights

ones, which stuck a foot above the water leaving them until morning. In the morning the water had not yet drained away from the lot. The crew, knee deep in water, had to push the stake puller around the flooded lot which was heavily flavored with manure. Locke said it made him think of the old actor who said, "When we would have a long, tough jump, a bum hotel, a barn of an opera house, or some other of the many discomforting vicissitudes of the road, we had to remember the old maxim: the public must be entertained!"

The tent reps were always at the mercy of the weather. The smallest shower kept the audience away, as did the threat of a summer storm. The tent shows flourished in the part of the country known as "Tornado Alley." A blowdown could turn a profitable season into a disaster.

The wind often blew steadily for several days. Ruby Bruce remembered this kind of wind, so strong that it bent small trees into right angles. The tent under storm would strain at every rope, loose pieces of canvas whipping wildly. Inside the tent, ropes and lighting equipment would dance about in a crazy way. During a performance the roar of the wind would make it difficult for the actors to be heard. The show would not be called off though unless absolute catastrophe threatened.

The prairie wind could come in great gusts, as it does ahead of a midwestern electrical storm. Everything is deadly quiet with lightning flashing through the sky in frightening zigzags, followed by the distant rumble of thunder. The rain has not begun to fall when comes a sudden gust of wind that never seems to stop. It can tear the tent from its mooring, and send it sailing. The wind tears at the weakest places, making rents here and there. The attack continues against the stronger parts of the fabric until the whole tent is in ribbons. If there is danger of the tent sailing away, or of being torn to shreds, the crew will try to drop it on the ground until morning. The canvas can then dry in the sun, the tears and rents be mended, and the tent raised again for the show to go on again as it should.

During the storm there is always danger of poles falling, electric wires being broken or canvas falling upon the people. Costumes are damaged or ruined, scenery torn and smudged, and lighting equipment broken beyond repair, all the result of summer storms.

Storms struck suddenly with little warning. When the McKennon Show was playing west Texas after World War II they had a terrifying experience with the wind and rain.[59] Mrs. McKennon's vivid description of what a storm like this can do to a tent show is worth recounting.

One instant it was so quiet, so humidly hot, that you unconsciously walked around with your mouth open like a panting dog. The next instant, the gale ballooned our top, lifting our side poles three feet in the air.

The wind struck the tent during the performance, about the middle of the first act. It was so fearfully strong that it made the quarter poles flap, and the center poles creak and sway. Some of the audience ran out the moment the wind hit the tent, but the rest, paralyzed with fear, sat frozen in their seats.

The extra help on the crew was gone; only the regular crew was on hand, led by a very cool and knowing canvasman called Heavy. The moment the wind struck he ran to let down the rolled up side walls in an effort to keep the wind from lifting the tent. Joe McKennon and the rest of the help frantically drove extra stakes on the windward side, to hold the tent down before the wind blew it over.

Inside the tent, the audience sat still paralyzed in their seats, as the actors yelled their lines above the noise of the screaming wind, whipping, shuddering tentpoles, the roar of the rain, thunder crashes, and the shouts of the crew men and the pounding of sledges on the stakes. Some of the actors had experienced blowdowns, but all of them knew the danger they were in. Nevertheless they went on with the play, sometimes "laughing hysterically," but always bravely yelling their lines.

McKennon had staked the windward side of the tent and all of the stage end, before he had a moment to think of the actors and the audience. He drew the tab curtain and stepped in front of it. Panting, he asked the audience not to be uneasy, "there is nothing to be alarmed about," and asked them to leave, stopping to pick up their rain checks. The audience filed out slowly, stopping momentarily to get their rain checks at the box office. The McKennon show survived this storm and many more during their summer rep tours.

After a big blowdown on the Charles Worthan's show the whole crew assembled on the lot and began repair work under the hot summer sun.[60] Some of the men had their shirts off and one of them was sunburned very badly. Since he had to play in the musical presentation his friends tried to help get him in shape. They put Unguentine ointment all over his back, over which they put his white shirt. After the music presentation when he took his shirt off he discovered that it was covered with blood.

On another occasion when the tent had been pitched at Greenview, Illinois, Charlie and his family had stopped over at Springfield for supper and a movie. When they came out of the movie it was storming.

The family drove to Greenview as fast as they could. When they got to the lot they found their tent in shreds. There was nothing to do that night so Charlie went to bed in his trailer parked right behind the damaged tent.

The next morning as Charlie and the leading man were looking at the tent a big strapping red-headed fellow came up to the lot. He had just jumped off a freight train. He said that it looked like they might need some help, and added, "so we might as well get busy." He began picking up the benches which had been scattered over the lot by the wind. Stopping a moment, he said, "Maybe you don't care to have me around. I just got out of state prison." Charlie answered, "Won't bother me, if you don't bother my people."

The Worthans gave the red-headed man his breakfast and he joined the rest of the crew cleaning up the wreckage from the blow-down. He did twice as much work as anybody else on the show. He stayed on the show for the rest of the season working the same way.

It was customary on this show for the boss canvasman to take over the box office while Mrs. Worthan went backstage to get ready for her part in the play. One night, for some reason, the job had to be delegated to Big Red, as he was known by this time. After he was finished with the task he came backstage to Charlie, and told him that the boss canvasman was not selling tickets off the regular roll, but was selling tickets of a different color. For each night, a different color of ticket was used. It turned out that the canvasman, who had been with the show for three years, a trusted employee, had been selling the tickets he had taken up on the previous night. Worthan didn't say anything about it immediately but when the canvasman tried the same trick on another night he caught him in the act. He accused the man of theft and asked, "How much have you robbed me of these last three years?" The canvasman turned livid, walked back to his living quarters, packed his things and left. Big Red, the ex-convict, had caught him cold.

Big Red stayed with the Worthan Show for the remainder of the season, but took offense at a chance remark and finally left. The radiator on the truck he was driving was leaky, and he took it to the garage to be fixed. While the mechanic was working on the truck Big Red went into the toilet; Charlie came into the garage and not knowing Big Red was anywhere about asked the mechanic if he had the radiator fixed. Receiving an affirmative answer, he added, "Maybe it'll do until he runs into something else!"

Big Red came out of the toilet and told Charlie he wouldn't work for him any more. Charlie had shown distrust of him and this was something he couldn't take. He felt he had shown Charlie that he was trustworthy and his feelings had been badly hurt by the boss' chance remark. Charlie tried to explain to him that it was only a careless remark motivated by temporary irritation. But this would not do. Big Red's integrity had been questioned. He left the show and was not seen again. Charlie Worthan bitterly regretted his angry tongue for men of Red's ability were all too rare.

Accidents always threatened the shows. Within a month's time the Tribley DeVere Company, playing the North Carolina countryside, suffered an auto accident, a fire which destroyed the light plant, and another fire which burnt down the cookhouse.[61]

Continuous travel about the country, even the short distance from one town to another, could be hazardous not only to the lives of the troupers, but to the financial security of the troupe. In *Bill Bruno's Bulletin*, May 15, 1930, a report of an accident which happened to the J. Doug Morgan Company on a move between Chillicothe, Missouri, and Indianola, Iowa showed how serious these accidents could be.

The daily papers of the region carried an item on May 8th stating that one man had been killed, and another seriously injured near Bethany, Missouri, by one of the Morgan show's trucks. The car in which the two men were riding was struck head on by one of the trucks at the bottom of a hill. The report further stated that the Morgan show property had been attached for damages and would have to close.

Both reports were partially true. In making the jump from Chillicothe to Indianola on Sunday, May 4th, the old ticket office truck which was being towed by the calliope became unhitched while the truck and the ticket truck were climbing the hill. An automobile coming from the other direction attempted to pass the calliope truck. The auto struck the unhooked Morgan truck with such force that the truck was thrown into the ditch. The auto crashed in the other ditch, and the wreckage of the demolished car pinned both occupants. The driver was killed but his companion was not badly injured.

The rest of the show caravan proceeded on its way, leaving behind the calliope and chair trucks, which were later attached. J. Doug Morgan was spending the Sunday at Cedar Rapids, when he was immediately notified of the accident. He got in touch with his insurance company who settled the case. No blame was attached to the show or the driver of the calliope truck, nor were any arrests made.

The traveling shows were not only at the mercy of the natural elements and accidents, but from human problems as well. The tent could never be left without someone on guard, for even the least valuable item, the most unlikely object of theft can have an attraction for some odd member of the human race. For example, what did the towner who tried to steal the chairs from the Jack and June Alfred Players, want them for? *Bill Bruno's Bulletin* headlined the incident:[62]

CRAVED CHAIRS
An Episode That Could Occur to Any Show

This item comes from the Lawn, Texas, *Echo*. On a Monday evening one Pete Atkinson, visited the show after the performance, telling the company that he was Pistol Pete, the city marshall of the town. The show people thought nothing of it, but when they returned to the auditorium, from the back of the tent, they found a few chairs missing. Also Pistol Pete.

Two members of the company, Pete Jones, and Cotton Moore had gone into the *Echo* office to inquire about some law concerning the show. When they returned to the tent, they found that their visitor had come back after another load of chairs. The two men hid near the entrance, and when the visitor came out, Cotton knocked him down. At that point, Jack Alfred returned and began to look for Wright, the night watchman. He fired a blank pistol into the air twice, trying to signal Wright. Failing to find Wright, Alfred got other help, and took Pistol Pete to Abilene, where he later was fined $60.80, and court expenses for the carload of chairs he had tried to steal.

The burglary of the Palace theater in Amarillo, Texas, in March, 1929, cost the Hazel Hurd Company about one thousand dollars worth of wardrobe, as well as the loss of valuable musical instruments.[63] The burglars stole two saxophones, two clarinets, twenty-five suits, ten evening gowns, guns, boots, and other articles. The Hurd Company, which had been out twenty-seven weeks, went on to play their next engagement a little light on gear.

When the Skeeter Kell show, playing Lancaster, Missouri, was held up in August, 1930, the report was at first not believed in the offices of Bill Bruno. The press dispatch was circulated in the state daily papers, but Bill did not believe it for two reasons: first, because the assertion that any manager of a show in the Midwest during that summer had nine hundred dollars seemed incredible since business had been very bad, and second, no tent show was reported to be exhibiting at Lancaster during the stated week.

Bill at last had to believe the story, however, even if confirming evidence reached him in a roundabout way; he does not elaborate on what he means by a roundabout way.

It seems that Colonel Dan McGougin, treasurer of the show, was in the company's car at the railroad yard on Friday afternoon, busily checking up the week's business, and preparing the salary envelopes for the following day. A masked youth, who looked to be about twenty years old, surprised the colonel and told him to hand over what money he had.

The colonel thought at first that some of the boys were playing a joke on him. He pushed the young fellow aside with the remark, "Don't try to kid me!" Right then two other men stepped through the door with leveled revolvers, and told McGougin to put up his hands, that they were not fooling. The Colonel finally realized that the holdup was genuine. At the command to hand over the money he produced thirty-five dollars of his own cash with the remark, "There it is!" and tossed it to the men.

The robbers apparently knew what they had come for. One of them snarled, "Don't stall! You know what we want—so hand it over!" When McGougin protested that he had no more the trio tied him up, and searched him. They found nine hundred dollars and left the rail car. They got into an automobile parked nearby, and fled in the direction of the Iowa line.

It didn't take McGougin long to free himself from the ropes. He went to the depot and telephoned Kell. They notified the sheriff who went after the men, accompanied by two deputies and McGougin, but the robbers were successful in their escape. They were obviously well-informed about the amount of money McGougin had. How they knew remains a mystery. The year before, Kell had been robbed of $2,400, by an ex-employee, but the company and crew were easily cleared of any part in the robbery this time.

In regard to this incident, Alex Pitcaithley had this to say: "McGougin was an ex-carnival man. I have heard that Kell called in detectives from St. Louis (who) after investigation said, "Why did you bother with us, YOU KNOW WHERE THE MONEY WENT!" I don't know which robbery, this, or the year before, was meant, but a character man on the show told me when I was on there (that) Kell wanted the money from his wife and arranged the stick-up!"[64]

These are the tales of the life on the shows. They are gathered from here and there, and from as many different periods as possible. They are typical and not typical, they are old and they are ordinary. But from them, a picture of life on the show may be reconstructed of how these people lived, people whose one great desire in life was to give a dramatic show.

Fred Wilson as "Toby."

Fred "Toby" Wilson at Tinker Air
Force Base, during World War II.

Fred Wilson, the original "Toby."

Plate VIII   144

Neil Schaffner as "Toby."

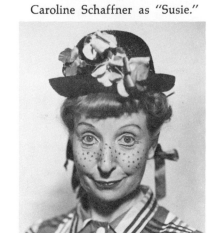

Caroline Schaffner as "Susie."

Charles Worthan as "Toby."

Lawrence "Boob" Brasfield
as "Toby."

V   WHEN TOBY CAME TO TOWN

1. The Genesis of Toby

The very nature of folklore usually precludes any possibility of watching the process of its development. If we know the actual creator of the work of folk art, this knowledge tends to forbid its classification as folklore. In an art of such public nature as theater, folk activity would be inhibited since theatrical effect is controlled by one or two professionals or a very small professional group.

Paradoxically, we have a good record of the ancestry, the knowledge of beginnings and the story of the development and modification of the theaterical character of Toby.

This extraordinary tale has been noticed and written about for the past thirty-five or forty years in Sunday newspapers, but it has been presented uncritically and inaccurately. Here is Toby's story, told as accurately as careful study of the printed records, the tradition handed down orally and through personal correspondence permits.

Theater historians have begun to take some notice of the tent repertoire companies.[1] As we have seen, their history along with that of the companies playing the small town theaters, or "opera houses" during an earlier period has been generally neglected. The creation of the Toby character either has been scorned or ignored. This attitude grew out of the contempt of the urban dweller for the small town culture and the resulting prejudice that the only theatrical activity worth writing about was that presented in the big cities.

Small town theater as shown in the preceding pages with its own traditions and techniques flourished completely independent of the metropolitan theater. In time, a distinctive literature of melodrama and comedy based on the tastes and attitudes of the audience was developed. Two distinctive comedy characters were originated: Toby, the red-headed, freckled youngster, who is smarter than he looks and the G-string, a garrulous and officious old man who is too easily gulled. The plays and these two characters have their roots in general theatrical tradition.

These buffoons are as old as dramatic literature. Each appears in the comedies of the early Roman Plautus, one as the impudent clown slave who is smarter than he looks, and the other as the tyrannical father who is not so clever as he thinks. In any discussion of the prototypes of Toby, William in *As You Like It*, and Abel Drugger in Jonson's *The Alchemist*, are always mentioned.

It was not until a little over a hundred years ago that the character of Toby in his typical American form of a comic rube youngster began to develop. Fifty years ago, Toby finally became his name once and for all time.

One of the earliest plays with a proto-Toby in the cast is the William Pratt version of *Ten Nights in a Barroom*.[2] It was first presented in Boston in 1847. In this play, Toby is called Sample Switchell. In a twentieth century version used by the L. Verne Slout Players of Vermontville, Michigan, he is described as "Comedy, Toby (or originally) New England Rube." The earlier version of the play describes him as a "Yankee tippler, very much alive..." These descriptions invite comparison with the famous Yankee character, very popular in the early American theatre.[3]

Yankee Robinson's great ambition was to play a Yankee comedian of the Dan Marble type.[4] Undoubtedly, his efforts at assuming this characterization gave him his nickname. After Fred Wilson's success as Toby, the character of Sample was played as Toby in the Midwest.

One proto-Toby appeared on stage at the Broadway Theater in New York, May 7, 1851. This character was called Toby Twinkles in the play *All That Glitters Is Not Gold*, by Thomas and J. M. Morton. The play is English in origin and had had a premiere performance at the Olympic Theater in London on January 13th, of that year.[5]

The Footlights

Toby's entrance is described thus, "he enters with his back to the audience sparring and hitting out violently with both hands." (This is an entrance characteristic of the later Toby.) His nose has just been broken in a fight at the mill. He was defending Martha Gibbs, a beautiful but poor mill worker. His costume for the first act is "blue vest, moleskin trousers, apron and sleeves (Brown Holland), paper cap." There is no mention of a red wig. Toby did not acquire this part of his dress until Fred Wilson's naturally red hair established the convention.

In these and many other plays of the time the rube comic was established as a convention in the American theater. He had special appeal for midwestern audiences. Toby's ancestors came from these rural characters. Toby, however, with his own name and characteristics separate from the usual rube comic, crystallized according to tradition from a definite incident.

The sudden popularity of Fred Wilson when he first played the conventional country boy began the development of the character. The audiences subsequently demanded that this role be played with the actor using red hair and freckles, the two features which Wilson naturally added. Actors, thereafter, had to appear under the name of Toby. This established the basic conventions of this part as future audiences learned to know them. According to rep show tradition the name Toby came from Tobe Haxton, the name of the country boy comic, or "first comedy," in the old melodrama *Clouds and Sunshine*, by W. C. Herman.

The generally accepted version of the adoption of this name is told by Robert Downing in *Theatre Arts*.[6] Mr. Downing said that he did four years of research, including personal interviews with Fred Wilson, in preparation for his article.

In one interview, Downing described the incident that prompted the adoption of Toby as the name for all future silly kid characters. This happened, according to Downing in Crawley, Louisiana, where Fred Wilson was playing with Murphy's Comedians. Wilson and Horace Murphy, the proprietor of the troupe, were strolling down the main street of the town. They were accosted by a ten-year old Cajun boy who had seen their show the previous night. He observed that Murphy was taking his clown out for a walk. When Murphy stopped to talk to him, he found that the youngster was puzzled by "the funny man," for he had seen Wilson as Toby Haxton in *Clouds and Sunshine* on Monday night, on Tuesday night as Toby Green in *Out of the Fold*, but on Wednesday as Bud in *Won By Waiting*. This was perplexing to the young fan for he could see no reason for the change in name from

Toby to Bud if the actor was to look, dress, talk, and act the same in all three parts. Murphy was a man wise in the ways of show business. Downing states: "He and Wilson applied Toby's name to all silly-kid parts in their repertory" from that time on. Downing dates the incident as 1909.

This is the legend, and indeed it is a legend. The principal items are founded on fact, but the details of the story are inaccurate and the dates and places certainly incorrect.

The title page of the copyrighted edition of *Clouds and Sunshine*, bears the date 1911.[7] It was published from the office of Alex Byers. The Library of Congress gives the date, September 5, 1911. Robert Sherman in *The Drama Cyclopedia* gives the date as 1911, but places the performance at Lafayette, Louisiana.[8] Since no such town as Crawley is listed in any atlas, quite probably Sherman's citation of Lafayette as the place of original performance is correct.

Horace Murphy added a mild corrective to the story Wilson told to Robert Downing.[9] He said, "regarding the boy asking about Toby, there was no such incident." When Murphy took Wilson to task for the story, Wilson replied that he had used "author's license." Actually, he explained, "it was an old man who met us in the street, and said, 'Hi, Mr. Murphy, I see you have your idiot out for some fresh air.'" When Murphy asked Fred why he had told the story as he did, he replied, "I'd rather be called a clown than an idiot."

Regardless of whether the questioner was a boy or an old man, or whether Wilson was called an idiot or a clown, the incident is of importance. Its significance lies in the first recorded suggestion by a member of the audience that the same name should be given to the character played the same way every night by the same man with never changing physical characteristic even though the plays were different.

Acting on this hint Murphy gave Wilson instructions to convert all the "first comedy" parts in their shows to the Toby character. Tobe Haxton of *Clouds and Sunshine* whose first name easily and naturally shifted to Toby must therefore be considered the first to emerge as Toby.

Most of the popular bills between the latter half of the nineteenth century, and the first ten years of the twentieth century had a silly-kid part. In *Out of the Fold*, he was Bobby Jenkins (in the version from Robert L. Sherman's collection; in the Broadway version he is listed as Toby Tompkins), in *Call of the Woods*, Eben Quackenbush; in *Way Down East*, Hi Holler; in *Lena Rivers*, Joel Slocum; and *Won By Waiting*, a re-written version of a much older play, *Marian Gray*, he is Bud Fisher. In *Over the Hill to the Poorhouse*, his name is Eben, and is listed as "b. f." or blackface comedy.[10] In other plays he is called Si, Zeb, Pete and Jake. All of these roles were given the name of Toby after Wilson's success as Tobe Haxton. The actor was required to wear a red wig and a freckled make-up. Even in such old and well-established plays as *St. Elmo*, in which the "first comedy" role is known as Van Jiggens, the name was sometimes changed to Toby and the make-up changed to red wig and freckles.

Horace Murphy added that when Alex Byers heard of Wilson's success, he ordered his staff to write plays with a similar comedy lead.[11] At this point the recent work of Dr. William Slout on Toby's origins should be noted.[12] In a taped interview with Horace Murphy on September 20, 1967, he raised some doubts about the facts of the foregoing investigations.[13] He said "important to the explanation of Toby origin are 1, the year, 2, the place, 3, the manner in which it came about, 4, the men responsible for the decision, and 5, the play that inspired the action."

In regard to the year this investigator and Dr. Slout are in agreement as being 1911. Sherman's reference and the Copyright Office have already been cited. In regard to the place, Crawley may well be Downing's or Wilson's misspelling of Crowley. Murphy confirms this as being the town in question. Murphy maintained that the play was not *Clouds and Sunshine*, but *Out of the Fold*, in which Toby Tompkins (not Bobby Jenkins) had been a favorite with many light comedians across the country.[14]

Neil Schaffner's version of his part in the creation of the Toby character is given in his autobiography. He placed the year of Toby's creation as 1912. His statements are substantiated in a letter from Horace Murphy of later date than those received by this writer. At the time when Murphy wrote his letter to Schaffner, and his interview with Dr. Slout, he was ninety years old or over. In his letters to this writer, he had at no time mentioned Neil Schaffner, or *Out of the Fold*. He did say however, "don't ask me for dates." The only firm fact in this bit of recent theater history is the information from the Copyright Office.

Neil Schaffner carried on the tradition of the Toby character, as well as that of the rep shows longer than any other midwestern actor-manager. He and his wife Caroline are responsible for the development of the Toby and Suzie team, originating from suggestions in both *Out of the Fold*, and *Clouds and Sunshine*.

It is quite possible that Fred Wilson came on the show bearing a copy of *Out of the Fold* but tent show tradition is strong in assigning the origin of the character to *Clouds and Sunshine*. Tent show tradition also credits the creation of Toby to the genius of Fred Wilson. His magnificent success in the creation of this role was due to his physical characteristics unmodified by makeup. Wilson said, "I came into this world with a shock of unruly red hair and later acquired a flock of freckles that all the makeup in Stein's laboratory couldn't have improved upon. The character was just myself plus a hickory shirt, patched jeans, boots with run-down heels, and a battered hat."[15]

Don Melrose, Kansas City actors' agent, in an article on Wilson in *Bill Bruno's Bulletin* said that Fred was a real comedian "who wowed them every Monday night with Toby."[16] Children and a great percentage of the adults in the audiences, did not remember the names of the other characters he played but they remembered Toby. They also remembered his red hair and freckles. Whenever Wilson played he was called Toby. When the boys and girls and even the grown-ups saw him off-stage they would invariably greet him as Toby. Toby's name and personal characteristics were stamped upon him forever by Fred Wilson's audiences.

Tobys proliferated all over the small town show world. In time Toby became the featured role instead of a conventional leading man. One of the earliest plays which featured Toby as the most important character is *Sputters*, by actor George Crawley. This play added stuttering to Toby's other social difficulties.

During the thirties, the Toby character became so indispensable to every tent company, that more than one company was thrown into difficulties when its comedian quit in a huff. Wallace Bruce said that Toby became one of the best loved characters ever written into a play.[17]

During the great years of the tent shows many managers continued to present what was called the standard repertoire, ignoring the Toby shows. If they did present a Toby they chose a Saturday night, when the show was about to be packed up and taken on the road to the next stand, and only a simple scenery set-up was needed. Toby shows usually did not require elaborate production, depending for their success on the abilities of the leading comic.

When financial troubles hit the shows in 1930, they were forced to go out of business or present Tobys. Their former audiences deserted them in favor of movies or the free entertainment offered by radio. Managers turned to the Toby shows in a desperate attempt to attract an audience. The audience by this time, however, was largely unacquainted with the living theater. A few of the managers were successful enough to keep their shows alive. Here again it is Toby, as a kind of people's hero, that makes him significant.

Toby came along during a period of crisis in American social life. The norm of American life as a fundamentally rural society had been changing rapidly since the Civil War.[18] It changed with even greater rapidity during the first thirty years of this century. City life became attractive because of its glamour and its promise of greater financial rewards. Progressive people deserted the small towns and the countryside for the possibilities offered by the city.

Those who stayed behind felt that they must somehow justify their unprogressive actions. They came to believe in certain myths, sometimes consciously, sometimes unconsciously; sometimes expressed, sometimes not. These myths that people lived by may be defined as "the images, gestures, and symbols which would objectify their experience and bring to their lives a simple and comprehensive meaning."[19]

Such was Toby. His country boy prototypes were homely and unattractive. It was Toby who had the additional homeliness of red hair and freckles. The small town audiences could identify themselves with him because in comparison with their city cousins they were uncouth and uncultivated. When Toby triumphed (it is a distinct advance in dramaturgy when the playwrights make the denouement depend upon some apparently foolish action of his), they themselves triumphed. Underneath, the rural folk felt that in spite of their simplicity, some overseeing power would in the end give them victory over the powerful but unjust.

The myth was already in the minds of the folk when Toby appeared to personify it. Its re-enactment became a ritual which to the people who saw it was virtual history. It represented what they wanted to believe to be the truth about life.

The audiences found their aesthetic satisfaction in the feelings aroused by the representation of the myth and purged by laughter. Their moral ideas were satisfied by the assurance that right had triumphed. The enactment of the plays became a kind of ritual in which the form never changed, although the words and events varied.

The people sustained the ritual once the plays began to be presented as Toby shows. Their applause from the very beginning and their eager inquiries about his coming to town showed their extraordinary approval and love for Toby. This approval created a popularity so great that he became the one outstanding character the rep shows produced and their one original contribution to the American theater.[20]

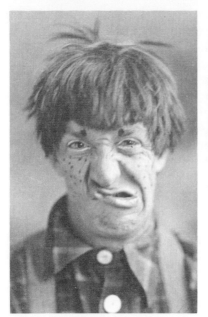

L. Verne Slout as "Toby."

Jack King as "Freckles," a name
he called himself most of the time.

"Speck" Leitch as "Toby."

Guy Hickman in G-string role, 1922.

2. Other Tobys

There were many other actors in the rep shows who became famous by playing Toby. The list following names several, but is by no means all inclusive: John J. Justus, Barrett Nevius, L. Verne Slout, Boob (Lawrence) Brasfield, Neil Schaffner, Donald Dixon, Harley Sadler, and Otto Imig. Evidence about how some of them played Toby has not been forthcoming. Toby remained a fixture in the small-town dramatic scene for the character never reached the metropolitan theater.

Neil Schaffner's Toby became nationally famous through TV presentations, magazine, and newspaper articles. Of all the established shows Schaffner's was the only one that survived. Mr. Schaffner and his wife retired from active performance in 1962. The show, under its old name, is still playing its old established territory under the management of James V. Davis, and his wife Juanita.[21]

Alex Pitcaithley, who worked for Mr. Schaffner in the mid-thirties said of him, "he was a fine fellow and one of the funniest Toby comedians I have ever seen. He was also outstanding in his delineations of G-strings or old men comedy characters. Schaffner was also a legitimate actor and his work as the Jewish father in *Abie's Irish Rose*

153

was flawless. He was also a prolific writer, and his bills, among them some of the best popular priced plays, were used by almost every rep show and some of the better stocks used them."[22]

In a review of the Schaffner show, an Iowa paper said:[23]

> He (Schaffner) proved himself a past master at ad libbing stopping the play now and then to chat with the audience, and also breaking into the rehearsal dialogue to toss off a bit of impromptu drollery. His fellow players didn't seem to mind— in fact, they evidently enjoyed it as much as he.
>
> And when one of the other characters got his tongue twisted over his lines, the whole cast joined the audience in howling over the miscue. It was partly this infectious informality and the evident enjoyment of their work that seemed to make the troupe so lovable.

Ad libbing became one of the principal characteristics of the Toby comedian. All actors are fond of ad libbing especially when they have just got a big laugh from the audience and feel sure that they can get another one by pushing just a little bit more. In a well-organized company ad libbing would be frowned on and stopped by most managers and directors. When the actor became the manager, however, he could do anything he pleased.

Donald Dixon was famous for ad libbing the Toby role. Monte Montrose, who worked with Dixon for a long time and was a close friend had some qualifications about Dixon's ad libbing. Montrose said that Dixon did ad lib at times and "when he'd established his rapport with his audience, he might leap down, seat himself beside some grande dame, slap her on the back, and engage her in brief conversation, which they seemed to love."[24] Dixon played an Ed Wynne-ish kind of character, both as to makeup and costume. "Above all," Mr. Montrose continued, "he was funny." He personally directed all his own scripts which were a "mass of gags, all of which were as meticulously directed as any of the lines in the play, so when you worked with him there was none of this wondering where you were, or what he'd do."

As Toby in *Clouds and Sunshine* his final line was, "Let him who is without sin among you cast the first stone. Then, during his curtain call, he would toss a huge boulder on the stage, heavy enough to shake the theater. Crude, of course, but it never failed to convulse the audience," said Mr. Montrose.

Boob Brasfield liked the comic situation show and would often ad lib business as well as lines.[25] "He was a natural comedian," praised his wife Neva. The feature story on which this material is based was inspired by their television show, Uncle Cyp (pronounced to rhyme with swipe) and Aunt Sap. Mrs. Brasfield said that his ability for being funny came from his mother who was never on the stage in her life, but who could mimic anything or anybody. Brasfield was a veteran performer with Broadway credits in his career, who like many other of his fellow actors returned to the small time which he loved so well. He stayed in the general vicinity of the script though he would toss in a new line whenever he saw fit. If on account of this an actor happened to miss a cue, Brasfield would be ready to cover with more ad libbing, and help the actor back to his place. He ended his career with Bisbee's Comedians.

His Toby was geared to the tastes of the Tennessee and Kentucky audiences to which the troupe played. Whether he was playing Toby, or Uncle Cyp, a character he invented when he felt that he was too old any longer to play Toby, he played in Grand Ole Op'ry style. He would often ad lib action. If he ran out of something to say, he would just hitch up his baggy breeches, stare stupidly across the foot-lights and the audience would scream with laughter.

The Toby comedians assumed the standard costume and makeup. Toby did become a different kind of bumpkin in different parts of the country. His witticisms in the west were the dry, cow-country type which would send the audiences rolling in the aisles with laughter, but would fall flat in another part of the country.[26]

As another example of how change in area could make an audience react to Toby differently, there is the experience of the Slout Company which in the forties tried trouping in the South. The show didn't fare very well, said Dr. Slout, "for Toby didn't speak with a southern accent."

In 1919, Otto Imig joined the Kinsey Komedy Company, "not as a Toby comedian, but . . . given the role after an amateur was taken to the bus after his first rehearsal."[27] This happened just before the opening of the spring season. Madge Kinsey gave Mr. Imig her father's red wig, and assigned him the part. "This I was told was a must" said Mr. Imig "and due to the fact that at that time I had black hair, I consented." But Mr. Imig was determined "not to follow in the footsteps of the Toby comics on the road or of those who preceded me with the Kinsey show." He trimmed the wig, used a straight makeup and "made my Toby intelligent, but sort of a backward human being just a little too intellectual for the villain to cope with." His purpose was to make Toby a lovable human being. He succeeded. He reflected that, "for fifteen years, I played this likeable person and made thou-sands of friends . . . No king could have been received more warmly and I'm glad I was able to accomplish my purpose . . . Believe me,

I can still hear the laughter and feel the love of the audience. I have been well repaid for my efforts." He commented on the love scenes which he had in some of the plays with the leading lady, saying, "I'm proud to say that I never received a laugh (for) the audience was always with me and felt sorry that I lost the girl. To be able to do this is an achievement and I was able to prove that Toby was a human being and a lovable character." In creating a human and lovable Toby, Mr. Imig kept the original quality of the character as it was first created. He was one of the few actors in the later years of the reps to make Toby a really believable character.

Les "Skeeter" Kell as "Toby."

Jimmy Davis: Outstanding contemporary "Toby."

3. What Happened to Toby?

Two completely opposite viewpoints come from the tent rep people concerning Toby. One states that he is the greatest comedy character ever invented, a belief held for the most part by the comedians who played the role. The other view is that he was the worst thing that could have happened to the reps and one of the real reasons for their passing as one of the major forms of show business. Dr. William Slout said, "Toby was just an afterthought, a move of desperation as the tent show outlasted its age."[28]

Slout thought that the playing of Toby in the latter days of the shows by burlesque comedians with their style of broad, ragged comedy, their ad libbing at the slightest sign of a laugh, was a bad influence on the development of the role. He cites the Rosalie Nash Players, in 1937, as an example. They hired a burlesque comic named Blackie Blackburn. He got away with "blue" comedy (dirty jokes, a type of thing always avoided by the reps), because the manager was deaf.

Toby was a temptation to the older men still in the business.[29] No actor likes to grow old, nor does he like to stop acting. The Toby character offered the older actor a chance to cover up the increasing signs of age. He could carry the makeup as far as he liked, clear over into clown makeup if he wished. Many men did just that. Instead of the bumbling boy, the uncouth yet charming silly kid with wit enough to outsmart the arrogance of the villain, he became at first, the older hired hand. From the hired hand, the character became hoked up even more until he faded into the clown, so grotesque that he lost the human characteristics which in the beginning had made him believable.

Bill Bruno had always resisted the trend toward Toby.[30] When in the late thirties, John Lawrence, a manager of long experience and good standing in the small-time show world, wrote an article, "Circles Like Tobys and G-strings," in the December, 1939 issue of the *Writer's Digest*, advising young and aspiring playwrights to supply the apparent demand for new plays, Bill took an opposite stand. Bruno said that from the number of subscriptions he had received following the publication of the article from embryo playwrights that Lawrence had really started something. He lamented the lack of new plays, a long-felt need, for at that time the rep shows were doing the same old plays over and over.

At this time, Lawrence had cited the figure of one hundred and fifty rural touring troupes that wanted new plays. Bruno praised his good advice to requirements of the managers, and how to market plays. He said:

> His best suggestion to playwrights about to attempt the market under discussion is that a melodrama is the best bet for their first offering to the circles. We have long contended that melodrama has been given too little attention by the shows. Instead the majority of the offerings have been a lot of twaddle with nothing happening. Except when Toby rushes on to save the curtain with a joke he has dug up out of the cemetery. Of course, we may be wrong in insisting that audiences want an occasional melodrama. But what do you see in nine cases out of ten when you go to the movies? You see "dressed-up" melodrama, unless it's clothes horse society sophistication, which usually flops. And even these have their melodramatic moments, as witness one of the cleverest pictures we have seen in months, *"The Women."*

Bruno disagreed violently with Lawrence on the subject of Toby, and G-string comedies.

> There is little doubt, however, that a certain type of manager who has become an addict to these most terrible baboons will gladly accept any play that will give him all the comedy and

allow him to hide his more or less natural talent under a red wig. These monstrosities are the real reason (of course we expect nobody to side with us when we make the statement) why show business is in its present pitiful condition. And the past summer has decisively proven that the Tobys ARE OUT! When the Tobys have been ousted, show business with its dignity will become popular once more.

Unfortunately, Tobys were definitely not out and show business, at least the small-time variety, did not recover. At the end of his editorial, Bill Bruno makes an interesting observation which further proves that tent rep was definitely not synonymous with Toby shows until the end of their existence. He noted, "The late Robert J. Sherman, most prolific writer of plays for repertoire, tent and circle shows, did not resort to Tobys. Instead, he wrote light comedy. His plays continue as the best sellers, even tho some of them are twenty years old." Bill Bruno reminded John Lawrence of his own play, *Hal O'The Hills*, another play popular twenty years or more after it was written, a play in which there is no Toby, "but plenty of action and an old man character who is human and naturally funny."

Just how many playwrights actually responded to these appeals is not known. There are lists, put out by Bob Feagin in Kansas City as late as 1940, in Alex Pitcaithley's collection, but there is no way to tell how many of these scripts were by new playwrights, or old scripts re-written and hoked up.

The only bills played by the few remaining companies today are light comedies written by older craftsmen such as Neil Schaffner, or the older plays re-written and dressed up under a new title. Of the first type, Mr. Schaffner's *Three in a Bed* is a good example of a good rousing comedy. It is original and suggestive in title, but utterly clean in its writing (a trick used often by the reps in their later days), and with a fairly minor role for Toby. Of the older type, there is *The Push*, re-written and set in a different locale, and *The Awakening of John Slater* under the title of *Toby Goes to Hollywood*.

Don Dixon was a great success in the Chicago area with Toby, this success was due not so much to Toby but to Dixon's abilities as a comedian. The rep managers in their last days thought of Toby as guaranteed box office. Toby needs a comedian to put him over in whatever guise he appears.

The city audiences were growing more and more limited with time. The small-town audience had almost disappeared. The city audience would not have known what to make of Toby unless he was played by a very skillful comedian. The small-town audience went to the movies in increasing numbers, and forgot their loyalties of the past.

Bill Bruno advised the writing of melodrama. The old-fashioned variety had by 1939 been hoked up and played too often for laughs. The idea of melodrama in these plays was no longer acceptable. Bruno rightly classified most serious movie dramas as melodramas. He overlooked the fact that they are so splendidly produced, in a way that the old opera house producer never could have achieved, that the artificiality of the plot and the falsehood in character and feeling are never seen by the audience.

Even the movies have begun to disappear from the small towns. For entertainment people can sit at home and watch TV free, even seeing Toby's contemporary counterpart in a character like Gomer Pyle. The free entertainment of radio and TV plus the auto and good roads finally killed the small-town audience.

The metropolitan theater audience at first diminished considerably in numbers by movies and TV has lately grown again. Plays, such as were written and produced in the thirties and before by some of the best playwrights in American theater are not really popular. To be a hit, it seems that a play must have some kind of blue comedy and be concerned solely with adult sexual life. The dramatic fare is extremely experimental, some of it so badly written and so badly done in terms of what used to be thought dramatic technique that the performers are not able to "give a good show."

There remains the musical, tremendously popular and sometimes called the only real theatrical expression of American culture. Many of these musicals, such as *Oklahoma*, are based on plays of the kind described in the preceding pages. These plays present ordinary human emotion in times of crisis, thus arousing similar emotions in the audience. If a playwright were to present this kind of dramatic fare to an audience today with the trimmings, the music, dancing, and splendour of productions, he would be accused of presenting corn.

Is it possible that what the theater needs to put it back into the healthy state it enjoyed before 1930 is more corn?

VI   OBIT

1. The Lights Dim

Three blows came, suddenly, and without warning. The threat of talking pictures, exemplified in the Vitaphone reels of 1927, was not taken seriously. In the first twenty years of the century, managers of troupes playing the small towns had met the challenge of the silent pictures and had triumphed. The metropolitan theater continued to flourish although the great period of road shows was past.

During the mid-twenties, the greatest number of productions in history was given on Broadway. In the hinterlands after 1926 every city large enough to claim itself a city had a flourishing stock company. In Chicago, fifteen to eighteen legitimate theaters operated in the Loop area. There were flourishing neighborhood stocks. When the record of Al Jolson singing "Sonny Boy" appeared in the local movie house, accompanying the picture of the same name, most of the managers offering circle stock fare paid little attention. They were drawing crowds. They could take to the tents in the summer and still make more money.

Some of the tent people realized that there was a threat of disaster. Mrs. Chick Boyes mentioned an experience she had during a visit she and Chick made to Chicago in the late twenties.[1] They visited the theater exhibiting one of the early sound reels as a feature attraction, a picture in which a dog barked. "That dog's bark may be the end of us," Chick told her.

Let us look at a typical small midwestern city in the season of 1927-28 in Hastings, Nebraska. There were two movie houses, one a long narrow hall used when the silents first began, and another of the more palatial, up-to-date variety. The old opera house was no longer used except for amateur theatricals. During the spring the Hazel McOwen Stock Company, one of the standard shows of southern Nebraska, played the palatial house, the Rivoli, two days a week, offering standard plays of the period. This troupe played circle stock two days each in Kearny, Grand Island, and Hastings. In mid-spring another company whose name has long since been forgotten, opened up in a long unused hall a few blocks from the main business section of town. This hall had a stage, but no other equipment to dignify it with the name of theater. The chairs were straight-backed, and the floor was level.

The threat of radio entertainment as competition was equally un-impressive. Throughout this decade the business of radio had grown by leaps and bounds. What in 1923 or 1924 was an interesting gadget had become by 1930 not only a respectable business but a great new addition to the amusement industry. The powerful stations and the great programs began to emerge as the national networks were in the process of development. All of these programs, good, mediocre, or bad, were free. Someone has said that it is very difficult to sell a product when your competitor down the street is giving it away. Live show business ignored this warning at first. Who could be adequately entertained by voices coming out of an electronic machine?

The threat of economic disaster was unthought of! We had been told time and again that economic prosperity was not only permanent but ever on the increase. The events of Black Tuesday, October, 1929, came as a real knock-out blow. Of the three threats to the living theater as a whole, this one can be said to have come without any real warning. A rumor went around the companies in the summer of 1929 that the season had been disastrous. No one took it very seriously. There had been bad seasons before and the troupes had re-covered.

Reasoning went similarly after the Wall Street debacle of the fall. There had been panics before and the country had recovered. Let a year or two pass and things would be as they had been perhaps even better. Well-managed and financially stable shows like other businesses run on similar lines would survive; the "fly-by-nights," the "hardly ables" and others would fail as they had always failed. No one dreamt that the good years before World War I, the fruition of pioneer growth and development, had gone forever. Very few realized that the apparent prosperity of the years during and after the first World War were economically unsound and deceptive. Everyone accepted the doctrine of the return to normalcy, little realizing that the whole civilized world was entering upon a long period of social and economic change, of difficult transitions, cruel and relentless upheaval.

These were the forces outside the shows that contributed to their decline and fall. There were equally strong forces within the shows working against them. Before we examine these, let us review in detail the outside competition, the free entertainment of radio and the glamour of talking pictures, and the financial pressures which made it difficult for the living theater to continue.

One of the first things the picture theater operators did was to try to get the city governments to increase the license fee charged the visiting tent shows. This began even before the appearance of the talkies, during the days of silent pictures. They based their tax argument on two propositions, namely, that the tent theaters would destroy their own livelihood, and that the tents were taking money out of town that should have stayed there. When the Taylor Players applied for a license to play in Boise in the summer of 1926 the picture theater men declared that their business should be protected.[2] They even summoned a Nazarene minister, the Reverend A. C. Tunnell, to their aid who deposed that the performances in the tent would disturb his congregation. *The Billboard* editorialized that "this is the old story of the fight between picture theater owners and the tents."

A week later, a Texas official was seeking repeal of an ordinance prohibiting tent shows in Waxahachie, Texas.[3] Under the date line of June 12, the *Billboard* carried the headline: ANONYMOUS OKLA DICTATOR SEEKS DEATH OF TENT SHOWS. The editorial goes on to say that in Pawhuska, a handbill was distributed to any person who could name the author of the trash being played in the tent, and called the show "Germified, Cut-throat Institutions."

During 1926, one of the peak years of the tents, several notices appeared in towns, attempting to restrict the tent shows by raising license fees or by barring them completely.[4] One headline read: KENTUCKY TRYING TO BAR TENT SHOWS. The article goes on to say that several towns which had been played regularly by the tents for years, were on the verge of being closed out since a license fee increase from ten dollars a day was being threatened.

On The Prairie   163

In Ravenna, Kentucky, the local legislators tried to pass a restrictive ordinance banning tent shows of all types but aimed at the Heffner-Vinson show. Heffner-Vinson won this bout with the law. Out in Utah, O. L. Farnsworth, head of the Imperial Stock Company sent a similar tale to the *Bill Bruno's Bulletin*.[5] A quotation from his letter sounded more ominous than he meant it to be:

> We, too, are having our fight with the high license proposition, after having been forced out of the houses by the picture interests. There is only one other company playing this territory under canvas and two other smaller organizations are playing the houses. Conditions are reported as very bad, but this may be due largely to the weather of the past month, which has been unusually severe.

Two incidents culled from the pages of the *Bill Bruno's Bulletin* of the season of 1930 illustrate how this running fight between the tent managers and the picture interests was carried on.[6] In these two stories the tent managers are successful even as late as 1930.

The Dude Arthur Comedians had billed Goliad, Texas, for the week of May 4th. The show arrived on Monday morning with no hint of trouble. The agent had arranged everything satisfactorily with the city officials during the previous week. Just as the top was in the air a committee of city officials arrived on the lot and told Dude that he couldn't show since there was an epidemic of scarlet fever in the town.

Dude wasn't quite satisfied with the story. He did some investigating and found out that it was the same trick that had been successfully worked before. He also found out that the picture house was going to operate that very evening. He made a call on the city officials and told them that he would show that night and every night unless both the movie house and the schools were closed. The movie house and the schools closed down immediately on the order of the city officials. On Thursday afternoon however, the movie manager had had enough. The tent show was told that it could open that night and the show ran for the balance of the week.

Dude decided to stand pat. He told the authorities that he would remain the following week to play the complete engagement. He insisted that for the good of the whole community as well as the show people the quarantine should continue the rest of the week. The city authorities agreed with him. The picture man lost an entire week of business. He gained a lot of undesirable publicity because the curiosity of the townspeople had been aroused, they wanted to see the Arthur show, especially when they found out that the picture man had tried to legislate the Comedians out of the town.

Bill Bruno said that this scored another point for the tent shows and proved that if managers did a bit of investigating in affairs of this kind, they had a good chance to successfully combat the picture house managers.

Les "Skeeter" Kell, during the same season of 1930, won a battle similar to Dude Arthur's encounter in Texas.[7] He succeeded in winning the town council and the business men of Nashville, Arkansas, over to his side. Nashville had for years been one of the best towns for this show. The agent had contracted for the license at the usual terms. He had billed the show for the week of April 28th. The week before the show was to open it was evident that the local picture man had brought considerable pressure on the city fathers. At a special session of the council, the license charge was raised to double what it had been. Kell found this situation when he reached Nashville on the Sunday before the show was to open.

Kell secured a lot just outside the city limits, raised his tent and on Monday night opened the show to an audience that packed the house. Throughout the week business continued at capacity. The comedian's friends throughout the countryside learned that he had been kept out of Nashville, and they flocked to the show. Kell encouraged this by offering a prize to anyone bringing the largest number of people from rural points. Wagons, trucks, and cars brought loads of people every night, but the five dollar prize was won on Wednesday night by a man who brought thirty-four people into the show on his truck.

The business men of Nashville soon realized that they were the losers for the show was keeping people out of the city. They complained bitterly to the council. On Wednesday morning an emissary begged Kell to move the outfit into town and play with no license charge. "Skeeter" decided that it was time to prove to all the townspeople that shows like his were a real benefit to the town. He refused to move, turning down the merchants' offer to stand the expense and finished his week on the lot outside the city limits.

"Skeeter" made his point. The city council invited him back for the next year at the old license fee. They promised that this agreement would hold indefinitely for all tent shows. Skeeter had not only won the battle over the license fee but he proved that the professional touring shows were a benefit to the business community. He had disproved the premise that a touring show took too much money out of a town. His own people, actors and crews, spent money for goods and services in the town. The show was bringing people into the town to spend money. There were people who ordinarily wouldn't have been there at all.

This business of educating the townspeople on the financial benefits to be derived from the tents was carried on vigorously by the Chase-Lister show during the same season.

This was the period in which the chain-stores began to flourish, bringing intense competition to small town businessmen.[8] It began to look as if they would be completely put out of business by the lower prices and greater financial backing of the chains. This threat raised the emotional temper of the merchants and many townspeople. The Chase-Lister show took full advantage of it.

The management of the show distributed a facts and figures sheet consisting of an open letter which they termed "Episode Number Two." This gave a comprehensive statement of the expenditures of the show, and its audience count for an average week in any town played. It concluded with this argument:

> We might add that the Chase-Lister company is not in any chain, nor in any circuit. It is not controlled or directed by any white-collared executive in New York or in the east. It is owned and operated by individuals who live in Iowa, who own property in Iowa, and pay taxes in Iowa; men who invest their earnings in Iowa, men who give their time, hard work and energy, in conjunction with yourselves, to the welfare and prosperity of your home and our own. Did any star from Hollywood ever leave any money with you?

Often the picture theater opposition did not hesitate to stoop to price cutting. Wallace Bruce reported in late May, 1930, that after his Number Two show under canvas opened to capacity at Wakeeney, Kansas, it finished the week to only fair business.[9] There were high school commencement exercises and other festivities, but the strongest opposition came from the picture house manager. He cut his weekend prices to five and fifteen cents, from the regular scale of fifteen and fifty cents. He did not have to meet a payroll on Saturday night as did Bruce.

Jim Parsons spoke of the antagonism of the movie theater owners and their attempts to keep the shows out of town.[10] He said that "often they would buy the local opera house and keep it closed or tear it down to keep the house shows out and do the same with the only available lots which a tent show could use. It wasn't always so. When I was small, it was taken for granted that the words, 'do you recognize the profession?' would admit us to the movies just as it would to any other theater."

Not only did the picture interests viciously fight any sort of competition but for many years they had been acquiring most of the theatrical real estate. They bought up the houses in the big cities in the twenties and during the thirties in the smaller cities and towns. Except where the houses were managed by men devoted to living theater such as Elbert "Slivers" Payton, who owned and operated the Drake Avenue Opera House in Centerville, Iowa, or where the hall was owned and operated by a lodge or club, most of the opera houses suitable for movies had been taken over even before this time. No owner of a building wanted to see his rents stop. When picture interests offered leases the owner accepted them. Thereafter the theater was managed according to the whims and policies of the picture interests.

When popular interest in silent pictures waned and the rep shows and vaudeville were of help in drawing a crowd, they were welcomed not only in the older theaters, but in the baroque palaces newly built by the picture interests. The new talkies zoomed attendance and the reps found themselves shut out of the newer houses as well as the older ones.

Mrs. Boyes has said that the company was suddenly refused bookings in theaters they had played in for years.[11] In the thirties, the McOwen company did not play the new Rivoli in Hastings but had to accept the facilities of the old and abandoned opera house.

The small town picture manager had been an independent business man throughout the period of the silent pictures. His investment for equipment was small, his rental for some unused building was not great, and his profits were excellent even at five or ten cents admission. The competition between the picture men and the tent operators was between equals no matter how vicious. When the pictures began to present sound films all of this changed.

Sound equipment was expensive. The low admissions prices charged for silent pictures could not possibly give the manager all of the gross income needed to assure him of a profit. In many of the smaller towns the picture house closed down permanently. In the larger towns the talkies flourished when the managers could see a return on their investment. The American people love new gadgets and this mechanical entertainment seemed in every way superior to the living theater. The rep shows were playing the same old bills in front of the same old scenery presented by the same old actors.

In another way the new talkie theaters represented unfair competition. Just as the local stores began to feel the competition of chain stores and give way to them, so did the local movie house because it became affiliated with some big complex system of theaters such as Publix, Twentieth Century Fox, or RKO. The threat to the local businesses was noticed by the townspeople, but the threat to the local amusement industry went unnoticed.

Better roads and more cars came along with the talkies and the radio. It was easy to get to the county seat town if there was no sound picture theater in one's own town. The rep shows, a novelty in the beginning, lost the greater part of their audiences to this contemporary novelty which offered a wider variety and choice of entertainment.

At the same time the great shows of the period of creative radio began to broadcast. People could sit at home and listen to free entertainment. Amos 'n' Andy, George Burns and Gracie Allen, Jack Benny and many others drew immense listening audiences. During the daytime there were ball games and soap operas. Any of these would lighten the routine tasks of ordinary people at the flick of a switch.

The reps tried to meet radio competition by using the medium as a way of getting free advertising for their shows. The story of the origins of Happy Bill's Radio Troupe is a wild one.[12]

The show, a combination radio band, rep show, and dance band, originated in a radio-dance outfit of the late thirties run by a Minnesota Swede named Big Ole. He had at one time been a Swede comic in vaudeville and he had a thick Swedish accent both offstage and on. He had been retired for several years and was running a tailor shop "somewhere in Minnesota—or maybe it was South Dakota," noted Jim Parsons, "and he had a nice little sideline; he booked a little old-time dance orchestra in neighboring towns and went along as the floor-show, doing his old vaudeville routine." He would do advance promotion on the local station's programs for his orchestra, and during the broadcast would advertise the upcoming dance. He filled the local station's need for live free music, and in return got free advertising for his dance band.

One day a "poor, little, hardly-able rep show came limping along and expired near Ole's headquarters. Eureka! and Inspiration! He took over the show adding it to his orchestra." Instead of presenting his act as an intermission feature of the dance Big Ole now offered a full-length play with vaudeville between the acts followed by a free dance. The audience had to pay a fifty cent admission fee for this bargain. Big Ole was an instant success, so much so that he hired a tailor to run his shop and returned to show business. He hired more musicians and more actors. They were a dime a dozen during the Depression.

Ole put out three road companies. All the companies stayed in the same hotel, and each evening would go out to three different towns. The troupers played the Grange Hall, or whatever hall was available. Any place that could possibly house a show-dance within a hundred miles was considered eligible. Each company was supposed to bring back more than a hundred dollars each night, i.e., a hundred dollars over and above all expenses, including salaries. Otherwise, Ole considered the show a flop.

Big Ole was rolling in prosperity and "knew about as much about show business as a hog knows about watchmaking." His idea was that the show had interchangeable parts. If he was playing a town for the first time he would put the best musicians and vaudeville acts from each show into one unit and send them there. If he happened to have a cast for a play, wonderful! If he didn't, he sent out a series of vaudeville acts to fill the bill.

The actors and musicians were paid about twenty dollars a week, a standard fee for the time. The entire "nut" for any of the shows for a week would not be above two hundred dollars plus car expenses.

Ole knew little about theater, and "would not have known a play if he fell over it." He knew nothing at all about where or how to get new plays. The actors anxious for work of any kind solved this problem for him, without any increase in pay.

When Big Ole had saturated his territory and there was no longer any interest in one of his shows he invented a novel way to get rid of the actors he no longer needed. He would send the no longer useful troupe "on the Death Trail to Duluth, and then refuse to have any more to do with them." He hired a truck driver named Bill Balthazar as manager for the troupe, furnished him with a ramshackle trailer, a tattered set of scenery, and sent the whole lot off to Duluth to starve, "with his blessings." The truck driver had proved a useful person as a booking agent in the past. Here was one last useful job for him.

Jim Parsons joined the Big Ole Radio Troupe in Duluth. Bill Balthazar, the former truck driver, "who had never even seen a show on any stage until a few weeks before," became the manager of the troupe. "But he was a good salesman, not to say con man." For a few weeks before Jim joined, getting the show started had been rough for Bill. He had sent frantic calls and telegrams to Big Ole for money to pay salaries. He was met by utter silence. If the show couldn't make expenses, Bill could worry, Big Ole wouldn't. Then for some unknown reason all the hard work that Bill had put into the show began to make it a success. It began to make a profit so that back salaries were paid up. Bill was always careful to see that at least some of the profits were used for some unexpected expense, such as hiring another actor-musician, in one instance Jim Parsons.

And now the calls and telegrams were coming from Ole: "send me the receipts each night, and *I'll* pay the salaries." "Send me the money today, or you're fired." "You're fired!" And now Ole was getting the silent treatment. The actors were getting paid, Bill was stealing the rest and Ole could go pound sand in a rathole. So Ole paid us a visit—in person. A fat, greasy and unctious person, showing us all what a nice, friendly fellow we were working for. Then, after the performance, closeted with Bill, Ole demanded his profits or else. And Bill chose else. He told Ole to take his trailer and his set of scenery and stick them up the most convenient location. The owner of the show was fired!

And thus Happy Bill and His Radio Troupe became a show. Jim said it was the worst sweatshop he ever worked on.

This was a typical day: Up at eight-thirty to be at the radio station and set up for our daily nine a.m. program—a half-hour of orchestra music, songs and other musical specialties with a long, long commercial boosting the show for that night, with the free dance, all for fifty cents, in the Grange Hall at the junction of Highway XX and old Corncracker Road, seventeen miles north of West Fartwhistle, Minnesota. Come one come all.

Then we were free for maybe four glorious hours (except every third or fourth week, when we had to rehearse a new show). About two, we'd clamber into the cars and hit out for the afore-said Grange Hall, perhaps a hundred miles away, over roads a foot deep in solid ice from December to April. Upon arriving, we unloaded the trailer and put up the set—often building a stage, or at least a proscenium, and nearly always having to rig some sort of front curtain. Then drive to a nearby farm where arrangements had been made to feed the animals, back to the hall, and get made up. Do the show and quick get out of makeup and pack the house while the chairs were being cleared out of the hall for the dance. About fifteen minutes after the third-act curtain, we'd be playing polkas, mazurkas and old-time waltzes like crazy, while the ladies took down the scenery and packed it away. At one a.m. we'd play Home Sweet Home (a touch bitterly), load up the trailer and away! Arrive back in Duluth about four a.m., a quick lunch a few hours sleep and back to the radio station to begin another glorious day in glamourous show biz. Seven days per week. I'm telling you!

Anyone questioning why actors would submit to such a life has forgotten the dear dead days of the Depression. Twenty dollars a week was a good salary when thousands of people had no job or salary at all.

Earlier attempts were made to meet the challenge of radio. These attempts were made to exploit the novelty, rather than to join the radio show and be a part of it. The H. B. Marshall Company in Iowa and the Jack and Maude Brooks Company in Wisconsin carried portable radio broadcasting stations during the summer of 1930.[13] They used the transmitter to broadcast their presentations. Presentations were a kind of glorified vaudeville used in the last days of silent pictures and even with the early talkies.

The Marshall company broadcast orchestra music "by the best organization in the country." Recorded music was played with the opening of the doors at 7:30 P.M. This music provided entertainment for the assembling audience until the rise of the curtain. Tommy and Helen, radio artists, were featured each night in the broadcast. Marshall broadcast Amos 'n' Andy, using a tie-up with a nationally known advertising firm.

Jack Brooks followed the plan of broadcasting music every night preceding the show but he took advantage of the opportunity to broadcast to the audience, arguments in favor of the superiority of the living drama over the mechanical medium.[14]

Often the rep shows throughout the important period of commercial radio associated themselves with a radio station as program producers. The Herschell Radio Players, composed of Kansas City rep actors, announced their successful appearances on the air over station KMBC in Kansas City in September, 1930.[15]

All of the troupe's thirty minute dramas and comedies were written by Herschell Weiss, Kansas City playbroker and playwright. The first offering was a railroad drama with music, *The Wreck of the Old 97*. This was followed by a comedy crook drama, *On the Level*, and a tabloid version of Weiss's successful play, *A Kentucky Thoroughbred*. Among those appearing on the program who are already familiar figures to the reader were Bill Bruno and Bush Burrichter.

The attempt to use radio during the thirties for the benefit of the rep shows, and in a small way to be a part of the radio business proved to be a failure. The national economy although improved was still in a period of deflation.

The rep shows had lost their aura of glamour to Hollywood. This loss of image combined with the hard and grueling life on the road made them unattractive to young people who might have wanted to start out in rep show business. Only young people like Jim Parsons who had grown up in the business were willing to continue with the rep theater.

Offerings of presentations was another device used to meet the heavy competition which had fully developed in 1930. This was not a new idea in show business. Presentations were musical tabloids, which in their beginning were used by the silent picture houses to add live interest to movie programs. They were continued by the houses presenting talking pictures to add the element of living theater to their performances. It was an element their audiences were used to. It was an attempt on the part of such organizations as RKO to provide employment for the performers in vaudeville, a waning part of show business. As used by the rep shows, presentations were staged to create for themselves and their audiences some of the growing glamour of the shows produced in Hollywood.

Presentations failed in this case because they were different from the acts used by the rep shows to successfully meet competition — shows generating their own originality and business creativity through the skill of the managers. They failed because they were being imitative. They were trying to modernize the show in terms of other aspects of show business. Rep shows were really ceasing to be themselves.

The kind of show they put on is described by Jim Parsons.[16] He described them as a "sort of brief revue built around a single theme" presented before the main show. "This was when," recalled Jim, "they started putting big orchestras on the stage with acts, etc." Dick Powell and Jack Carson, later well-known movie performers, started their careers as resident M.C.'s in movie presentation houses.

Neale Helvey, who had taken over the J. Doug Morgan show after the original owner's death, (this was first known as the Morgan-Helvey Show and later as the Helvey Show) was the most successful producer of this theatrical novelty. Neale had a big show and good show. He had had an interesting career. "From all reports, he was an excellent pianist, an imaginative producer, a very handsome leading man, and an awful actor," said Jim Parsons. He had started in show business as Eva Tanguay's accompanist. How he got into the rep business is unknown.

Neale adopted the idea of presentations and started a trend that lasted for years. He would take a single theme, find songs that fitted it and build a very elaborate set with some sort of theatrical effect for the climax. He would fit what talents he had on his show into the act. He was very successful with this kind of production number.

Jim Parsons described Neale's "Holland presentation, which he knew because it was stolen by two shows he worked on."

Neale had painted a special back drop with fields of tulips on it. Also a bed of artificial tulips running the width of the stage were planted near the footlights. There was a large windmill set piece at the rear.

The company, both men and women, were costumed in special Dutch boy and Dutch girl costumes. The tabloid musical was extremely well done. It was all singing and dancing, wooden shoe dancing with both serious and comic numbers.

At the end to the tune of "Tulip Time in Holland," the full cast was on stage. They would come downstage on the second chorus, the lights would dim and "all the little Dutch girls would advance on the artificial tulip beds with watering cans as the windmill began to turn and lights inside the artificial tulip beds went on and off in time to the music and the swinging of the watering cans.

The shows were generally produced with a fairly small cast, and the little Dutch girls could include the juvenile man, heavy and character man!

This was an elaborate kind of act for a tent show. It sounds corny to us today, but we should remember similar shows on television which in perspective would make the rep shows look less old-fashioned.

Neale was a very talented man. After the end of tent shows he took three of his people who doubled on instruments and singing, "and made a cocktail lounge combo of them, using lots of tent show material and dressing it up in his own way—which was pretty good." Neale's combo was such a hit at the Dome Room of the Sherman Hotel in Chicago that they stayed there for three years. They were just as successful in other similar night spots. Neale died as a fairly young man during the forties.

The presentations did the tent shows no good. They were effective only under the direction of an expert. They were expensive to produce and called for expensive talent which added to the financial burden of the shows. If the small towners wanted to see such presentations they were always available in the nearest city where they could be easily and glamourously produced.

It should be noted here that the practice of cutting down the feature play of the evening to allow the presentation of other kinds of amusement had been going on for years. This practice began when the vaudeville portion of the entertainment was thought to attract more customers than the play. Specialties had originally been done to keep the audiences in their seats during scene changes by presenting a continuous show. We have noted that the J. Doug Morgan Show in its later years, as advertised in *Bill Bruno's Bulletin* does not feature the plays at all, but rather the number and variety of its vaudeville acts. This illustrated the tendency during the later years for the managers to think that their audiences would come to see an elaborate stage show instead of a play. Often the vaudeville actually cheapened the rest of the show.

Bill Bruno presented his argument for dramatic shows thus:[17]

It ought not to take much argument to convince any manager that presentations were done to death by the silent movies two years ago, and we call their attention to the fact that none of the large theaters and a very few of the smaller ones are using this form of entertainment at present. The midwest managers of tent shows cannot lay much claim to originality when they go wild over something that passed two years ago. Just now the talkies are killing themselves by too much presentation in the big pictures. It is entirely probable when a tent show comes to town, that the amusement seeker will say to himself "Thank God, HERE IS SOMETHING DIFFERENT." Then he attends the first night—and gets exactly what he ran away from at the picture theatre.

These attempts to meet competition were of no help to the shows. Business went downhill steadily. Conditions worsened and finally reached a hopeless low signified by the bank holiday of 1933. The shows could do nothing but disband, or go on as best they could. Since in all other business and professions thousands of people were out of work, the best thing to do seemed to be to go on.

Actors' Equity Association was the one element in show business that could give both actors and managers some feeling of security. Soon after the Actors' strike in New York City in 1919 the news of the strike and its success traveled to every actor in the country. Intense recruiting activity was carried on by actors out of Kansas City to get their fellow performers to join the union. A central Equity office was established in Kansas City, officered by Ruth and Frank Delmaine, in 1920.

During the twenties the Kansas City Equity office was the third largest in the country, with New York first, and Chicago second. Equity offered protection to the actor by establishing standard salary rates and help in collecting his salary from unscrupulous managers. It also bound the actors to observe certain standards of professional conduct toward the manager and the show. As far as the midwestern actor and manager were concerned when it came to a showdown Equity failed them.

Bill Bruno estimated that late in the season of 1930 salary claims filed in the Kansas City Equity office had reached a total of $5,000.[18]

The Footlights

"Enough salary claims were filed to worry the K. C. representative and even more so when added to the claims uncollected during the past five years."

The preceding five years had been most prosperous for the rep shows. Bill asked, "Does anyone of our readers know one authentic case where salary due an actor in the midwest has been collected? If so, we promise to print such an astounding piece of news in bright red ink on our first page."

Elwin Strong reported in the *Bill Bruno's Bulletin* that he had received very unfair treatment from two members of his company, Rupert Clark and Trevor Bardette. They had signed Equity contracts for the run of the tent season. These two men decided to leave the show without notice apparently to take engagements elsewhere. Strong in his report claimed that both had defied Equity's demand that they remain and fulfill their contracts. They refused to honor their contracts in spite of letters and wires from Chicago and New York.

This left Mr. Strong in an unpleasant position for he had some excellent fair dates ahead. He hurriedly got two actors and had them 'get up' in a strong line of parts on short notice. He did this rather then cancel his fair dates and throw the company out of work. Strong had filed his claims with the New York office. Nothing ever came of his protests.

Frank Gilmore, according to the *Bill Bruno's Bulletin*, was much more interested in organizing the screen actors of Hollywood.[19] Funds which might have been used to help out the actors and managers in the Midwest were used futilely for this purpose.

Editorially, Bill Bruno commented vividly on this situation:

> One cannot but wonder why Equity, after having proven itself most generous in the Hollywood affair (in spending money to try to organize picture actors), doesn't use some of this acknowledged large surplus in fighting the picture interest in their continued agitation for higher licenses for the western tent shows. These shows are in danger of being completely legislated out of business and they provide employment for many hundreds of Equity members who pay their dues.
>
> Wouldn't the amount sluffed away in the misguided attempt at organizing the picture actors have been put to far greater constructive use had the sum been spent in assisting a fight against the high licenses in the western territory.

Actors gradually dropped out of the organization and managers ceased to pay any attention to it. It is doubtful that Equity could have done anything much about the situation even if the New York oriented organization had wanted to. The bottom was dropping out of show business even on Broadway. The attitude had to be "get work where and when you can and for however much you can get." Bill Bruno throughout the pages of his little sheet reflected the resentment of the actors toward a union they had supported loyally with their small salaries. Unions made up of members associated with the theatrical arts, musicians and stage hands did not support their associates in theater acting during their efforts to survive.

Clyde Gordinier wrote in the *Bill Bruno's Bulletin* of September 4, 1930, of his futile attempt to open a popular-priced stock company in Des Moines. The demands of the stage hands and the musicians were so excessive that Gordinier thought it foolish to try the season. He said, "Equity should have started to battle these conditions ten years ago. Instead they battled the managers and made buddies of the stage hands. And now many actors are out of work on account of the stage hands trying to get more salary than bankers." Bill Bruno asked the show folks what they thought about the situation, saying, "Them's our sentiments, also."

During the same month, the Shubert Theatre in Kansas City had announced that it would probably be forced to remain dark during the upcoming season because of the demands made by the stage hands. The stock company billed for the Orpheum had been called off. Loie Bridges' opening at the Globe was being delayed for the same reason.

All of these difficulties only accelerated a steadily deteriorating situation. Difficulties of some kind or other always beset people in any kind of show business. The inability of the rep people to battle these external forces successfully can not only be laid to the severe economic depression, but to the forces working within the shows toward their eventual failure.

The shows were intensely individualistic institutions. The managers of the older shows had brought them to great financial success through their own efforts without anyone's assistance.

Their successors worked along the same tradition. Any efforts at organization had no effect on account of this attitude.

As early as 1926, an attempt was made to organize a Tent Rep Managers Protective Association.[20] The managers met from time to time but never really got together on any program of cooperation.

The same problem had been presented to many other small town businesses, especially the grocery stores with the coming of the major grocery chain stores. The grocery and drug stores eventually met this kind of competition by using cooperative buying organizations, but the rep shows never achieved any cooperation such as that.

As early as 1929, the manager's organization began to fail. At a Kansas City meeting in March Paul English, one of the foremost of the managers, resigned from the presidency of the organization after two years in office.[21] Mr. English had been a conscientious president. Two factors had contributed to the downfall of the Association: English wasn't a fighter, and the removal of the secretarial office to the South had put it out of the reach of the managers who wanted to make the organization a success. Bill Bruno thought that a third factor was the biggest obstacle — the showmen as a whole refused to co-operate. Successful organization of the showmen appeared to be hopeless whether in the West or in the East.

English upon his resignation made earnest pleas for continuing T. R. M. P. A. He suggested Colonel W. I. Swain for the presidency. Bill Bruno agreed with the choice, but thought there was something more fundamentally wrong. The organization lacked punch. Originally Equity had been a member of the Association but following objection by smaller members the Actors' Union withdrew. To quote Bill, "Every manager of a show of any kind was needed to give the organization the membership needed and the funds required to successfully function."

Some kind of class distinction was made. The smaller managers came in but they were not welcomed into the organization although they were enthusiastic about it. They wanted Colonel Swain for president, but time was wasted over some kind of referendum and their enthusiasm waned.

First, the managers wanted Equity out of the organization and they got that action. Then they wanted Colonel Swain, but above all else they wanted action. They didn't get it at any time. One manager's opinion written to the *Bill Bruno's Bulletin* expressed the feeling of most of the managers:

> I am ready to join T. R. M. P. A. just as soon as they show that they can DO something for the managers whom they expect to contribute to its support. But I am not interested in or am I going to pay for a banquet or two and a lot of speeches that don't interest me. When they show me that they can win just ONE legislative case anywhere, then I will say the organization is a success and will be only too anxious to join the association. I'll pay my money for action any time, and I'll bet there are a lot of managers who feel like I do.

English had made a statement regarding Equity's membership in the organization insisting that "with Equity we have proved a struggling, straggling, unsuccessful group." Bill Bruno felt that if showmen could not manage their own organization to success it would be better never to attempt it. Frank Delmaine of Kansas City Equity had done a great deal for the organization. Even so no outside assistance should have been necessary. He felt that a strong organization including everyone in the business was necessary.

Will Lister predicted that all tent shows would be legislated out of existence within five years unless some action was taken. An organization would be one way of fighting the interests against them. Bill Bruno saw little hope of accomplishing any such thing, although he agreed thoroughly with Lister. Time proved he was right; all the effort came to naught.

The managers never got together to pool their financial resources so as to meet the movie money that was buying up and leasing theatrical real estate all over the country. They could not fight the legislation against them. They were still an individualistic small town product trying to meet a huge combined force, each manager fighting on his own.

Worst of all, some of them began to fight one another. Bill Bruno reported a wholesale fight for territory by a number of Iowa shows. They are "day and date playing." Several shows had their advance billing covered up by another show competing in the same town on the same date. Billings were being posted three and four weeks in advance of the playing date. Bruno said, "It cannot have a good effect on reasonable license charges. Shows write to city mayors far in advance of the date to be played and offer an increase in fees if another show is barred out." The picture competition had not only used cut throat practices toward the tents but among themselves. Bill thought that the picture managers had never gone as far as some of the tent managers had in competing with one another. The shows could not possibly gain by all this fighting. He suggested, sardonically, that "after the League at Geneva has succeeded in establishing world peace, they then try their hand at a real peace pact by getting the tent show managers of the central territory into something of that sort." He saw that the latter was as impossible as the establishment of world peace.

There were no really new plays. Hundreds of plays were being ground out yearly by playwrights in places like Kansas City. These plays were always written to a formula as old as the earliest original rep play. The only thing new about most of them was that they were written as Toby shows, each one no different from the last except that it showed Toby in another adventure.

Bill Bruno commented that one thing killing the reps was the emphasis on Toby. The earlier audiences of the reps had been interested in theater to the point of attending tent productions of metropolitan successes such as Elwin Strong and the Aulger Brothers presented. These audiences had been lost to talkies and radio. In a desperate attempt to attract an audience of any kind, the managers presented the Tobys. These seemed to be a popular success with a certain kind of audience, but they down-graded the quality of the shows. Every rep person interviewed has expressed strong feelings against the Tobys. For the most part they thought that the emphasis on Toby distorted the dramatic values of the play. These people had been very proud of the work that they had done. They resented being forced to go along with the Toby trend.

Jim Parsons felt that Toby "was an important contributing factor in the Decline and Fall."[22] The earlier shows, as has been pointed out, generally played the standard repertoire or plays especially written to appeal to a midwestern audience. After Toby came along there were usually only two Toby performances a week. When the competition of talkies and radio arrived, the reps lost the intellectual audiences to this entertainment and began to emphasize the hokum "to bring in more of the audiences from the bottom." And what Jim called the vicious circle began. "At first, Toby had been a reasonably legitimate country bumpkin, but now came the preposterous red wigs, ridiculous wardrobe and makeups, any grotesquerie that might get a laugh. And now came the Tobys who were not and never could be comedians."

As competing entertainment improved, tent show comedy deteriorated. "Many tent shows—eventually almost all—stopped presenting plays and concentrated on three-act vaudeville skits starring a burlesque-type comedian." Eventually even the most ignorant members of the public became educated to something better and there were not enough "last-standers left to fill the tent."

Some of the Tobys were good. Jim Parsons mentioned among others Bush Burrichter, and Rod and Boob Brasfield. In fact, Rod Brasfield was the idol of the entire territory played by J. C. Bisbee, owner-manager of Bisbee's Comedians. Rod became a member of the Grand Ole Opry radio troupe, featured for many years. He also made one movie, *A Face in the Crowd*.

To return to the subject of plays, Jim considered most of the old plays written for the reps as good workmanlike jobs of play writing. Some of the efforts of Robert J. Sherman, although pretty stale, were still presentable as plays. The plays of the thirties consisted of all the old Toby gags anybody could think of surrounding any kind of plot.

"Many were so bad that I doubt if anyone ever played them and others which were played shouldn't have been," said Parsons. The playwrights tried to take advantage of timely topics. Only a few weeks after Pearl Harbor, *Toby at Pearl Harbor* appeared on the market. Jim played the Japanese heavy in this with the Roberson Troupe in 1942.

The Toby shows were definitely not a life-saver for the reps. They gave the rep shows the reputation of being a substitute for the dead burlesque shows. The shows that survived Worald War II were all Tobys. Their long life and success have been due to the popularity of certain actors, such as Neil Schaffner. His successor Jimmy Davis has continued the Schaffner show to the present time. He has modernized his approach and is making a greater and greater success of his operation.

The shows were also growing old. Neil Schaffner had begun his career in show business early in the century. He had organized his own show in 1926, and played it with great success throughout the Depression, through World War II and into the sixties, making his final farewell tour in 1962. He was fortunate in finding a young man such as Jimmy Davis who had the right mental attitude toward this aspect of show business.

At the present time and during the thirties and forties young men with a real interest in this kind of show were few and far between. Business conditions improved considerably in the late thirties but the rep shows did not seem to be able to attract young people or keep the ones they had.

Too many of the troupers were old, leading men as well as leading ladies. Some of the ladies who were past their prime were perhaps only a bit hippy, but their general demeanor made the love-making of a young leading man seem ridiculous. Papa could hide behind the grotesque Toby makeup, but Mama had to go on with straight makeup. Even a Surprise Pink gelatine over the glaring footlights could not tone her worn look down.

The old-timers still believed that the life they loved and the business that had proved so profitable to them would some day return in all its former glory. The troupes fought the wind, the rain, and the dust; they patched up the old tent instead of buying a new one, and they made do with worn and faded scenery and the simplest of props. They bought second hand clothes all in the hope of a return to show business prosperity.

It is cruel to be too critical of these people. Many of them had to go on. There was nothing else for them to do and no one to take their place. Many times their children had an intense dislike for the business and left it as soon as they could. Too many times the per-

The Footlights

sonnel had to be made up of people who were essentially adventurers and fly-by-nights, not really show business people at all.

The scenery was old and there was little money to fancy up the productions. The tents got old, increasingly hard to get, and were more expensive than they had been with the advent of post-war prosperity. The companies which had been in the habit of making scenery turned to other activities with the decrease of orders from the reps. Henry Wodetzki of the Danville Tent and Awning Company said that he made Roberson-Gifford's last tent in 1943.[23] A dramatic end tent would have to be specially made at present. It is very doubtful that anyone except a person like Mr. Wodetzki with the proper experience would know how to make it.

Bill Bruno wrote words of encouragement and hope until the day he went into the hospital to be treated for his final illness. He felt that the dramatic shows were the potential money-makers and the presentations, the musical tabs, the Toby shows, were all vain efforts to bring a dying business back to life, and would in the end be the destruction of the reps.

His comments in the late thirties were vivid resumés of the whole situation mixed with hopeful words for the future:[24]

> You remember 1929, don't you? That was the peak summer of tent show business. When any sort of show under a tent could get business; when salaries were up to a high which perhaps never again will be reached in the industry; when Equity was in the height of its power; when actors bought only the better cars; when trailer homes were unknown; when show business was a business. At the end of that year the Depression and the Tobies hit us in full force. The following year, the never to be forgotten 1930, saw the tent shows slide slowly but surely to a low that wasn't reached even during the war days. From which they are still battling to recover, and putting up a mighty good fight.
>
> It needs only a return of conditions that are even fairly normal for a complete recovery. Because people still want the dramatic shows. No greater proof of this can be found than the fact that with the exception of two shows, companies have been able to pull through two months of the most abominable weather they have ever fought against. And if latest predictions of the business powers of the country can be given credence, the upturn in business will start July first and with it will begin the upturn in show business in this territory. Let's hope so.

Every year in the spring or early summer, Bill Bruno would present a roster of the companies out during the season. No claim was made that the list was complete and there was certainly nothing official about it. Bill put out the first roster in early May of 1929. He wrote an article for the front page of his June 23, 1938, issue on the changes in ten years.

He said that it is safe to say that the fifty-eight companies who presented their rosters for the season represented about half the companies on the road during that summer. Aside from the shows represented by the rosters, other shows from earlier issues are mentioned throughout the rest of the magazine. Of the hundred shows or so listed in 1929 less than half were operating in 1938. Bill went on to say, in his optimistic way, that other shows have appeared to take their place.

Nevertheless in his road roster number of June 13, 1940, Bill had to admit that things were bad. In comparing the list of shows from the May, 1929 issue he noted that many of the old-time shows had disappeared from the road. Most of them were standard shows and had been pioneers in the tent business.

Among those shows which had disappeared by 1940, were: Brunk's Comedians, Chase-Lister Company, two of the companies owned by Hazel Cass, the Jessie Colton Company, Neale Helvey Players, McOwen Stock Company, R. J. McOwen, manager, the Hazel McOwen Stock Company, Ralph Moody manager, Savidge Players, Slout Players (revived after World War II), Elwin Strong Company, and the Wight Theatre Company.

The rep shows continued after World War II and there are two or three operating today. Let us look at Bill Bruno's final editions of June 13, 1940, and the last issue of August 22, 1940, as marking the end of the era of the rep shows.

In the Christmas number of December, 1939, the *Bill Bruno's Bulletin* counted 150 shows still on the road. The June 13, 1940, issue lists seventy-eight shows. It is likely that this list had a high degree of accuracy. Bob Hofeller Products Company of Chicago was advertising prize candy packages and popcorn and supplies. Mrs. G. H. Perrin is still running her re-sale shop in Kansas City. Wayne's Theatrical Agency, Schnitz Seymoure, and Mrs. Agnes Simpson are still advertising plays. The *Bill Bruno's Bulletin* has also established a play bureau.

People are still optimistic about the rep business, because there is an ad, "Want to Rent or Lease a Small Top," complete and large enough to seat about 700, as well as several hundred folding chairs for a season to start September first. The ad also states that the person wants a good canvas man to take care of the outfit who must live on the lot, be absolutely sober, and be generally useful.

The usual editorial comment on the bad weather of the spring is there and Bill reminded the actors to be as loyal as possible to any manager having troubles. He also commented on opposition to flesh shows and said that it is not confined to the small towns. In Kansas City, Doc Franklin Street, who was operating a "Mighty good medicine show, was forced off a suburban lot by a picture man whose theatre was situated a couple of blocks away." After the picture man's bait of a free present to everyone attending was unsuccessful, he apparently appealed to "Higher powers, and Street was refused further license."

Wallace Bruce had run into picture opposition in St. John, Kansas, where the "picture baron of that wide spot in the road" advertised throughout the county, "that old line of tripe about 'spend your money in Stafford County. Spend your money where it will return to you.'" Bruce said he saw no evidence of screen actors in any of the local restaurants or any sign that Hollywood had moved its studios to "that blot on the landscape."

Kansas City show business was not above using Hollywood as a means of box office drawing power. Al C. Wilson's ad for plays listed six new plays only one of which had a Toby possibility. He featured "late modern plays with box office draw; plays by recognized Hollywood writers," and farther down in the one column ad, "Plays by Grace Hayward. All plays formerly handled by the Unity Play Company of Hollywood are now leased through this office." Some of the shows such as the Walters Amusement Company are playing pictures under a tent. Walters was featuring, "Hitler, the Beast of Berlin," and was playing the picture under American Legion auspices.

A new kind of opposition emerged. The *Bill Bruno's Bulletin* said that "every radio station, no matter how small, is booking its entertainers for fair, celebration and vaudeville dates." A trend began which continued and grew into a new and big aspect of show business. At the present time the appearance of radio and television name stars in the grandstand show at the big state fairs is one of the most attractive features of the fairs. The county fair dates after World War I were big money makers for the tent shows. Even this financial life-saver after a bad box office summer was beginning to be taken away from them.

Another ominous cloud appeared on the horizon. Bill Bruno reported that "we have been receiving letters from managers in every section asking if in our poor opinion, the war is responsible for their poor business. As all complained of rain, it is difficult to place the blame. War or weather, all lines of business are complaining about present business conditions."

The most startling discovery made in those last issues is an advertisement by Ted North. Ted North and the North Brothers Companies had been for over thirty years the leading show of the business, playing city stock, circles, and tent shows from Saskatchewan to Texas with a wide reputation for excellent productions. Genevieve Russel (North) had been the most prominent leading lady throughout this wide area.

In 1937, the *Bill Bruno's Bulletin* reported the last appearance of this grand leading lady as guest star with her son Ted's stock company.[25] It was her first appearance on a Topeka stage in twenty-five years. At that time she had been a leading woman of C. Chapin North's stock company for five years. During this run of her husband's company she had appeared in 194 plays. People who had been brought up as children to see her and the supporting company brought their own children to see "Jenny" North, their favorite, to see what real acting was like. As a climax to the two week engagement of sold-out houses she was guest of honor at a big party on the final Saturday night, a party celebrating her sixty-second birthday.

Three years later, Ted North is offering:[26]

> For Sale Cheap, Tent, 65 x 115 feet, with poles and nearly new ten foot wall, $500.00. 75 dozen best B-L circus flat folding chairs at $10.50 per dozen, Cost $18.00 per dozen new; Seven lengths seven-high heavy built Blues, $50.00; 32 x 24 stage, forty feet high, with jacks and stringers, $75.00; Palace style Marquee, 20 x 30, $25.00; Good Proscenium, 28 x 65, $50.00, or goes with top; all kinds of good flat and hanging scenery from $10.00 to $50.00 a set; Prop Trunks, Picture frames, Ticket Boxes and good switchboard and wiring cheap; Flood lights at $10.00 each. Come and look this over in Topeka, or write 'Ted' North, 2800 Kentucky Avenue, Topeka, Kansas.

The end of the story of the great North Brothers is reported in the *Billboard:*[27]

> Ted North Sr., in Kansas from Texas last month to dispose of all his property in connection with the Ted North Players, walked out of his storage house, in Topeka, Kansas, the other day with four 8 x 10 photographs, and that was all that was left of the North rep shows in the midwest. He sold his top and sidewalls some time ago; let the City of Topeka have his blues, and gave a farmer his center poles, stakes, ticket boxes, and side poles. As he left, he spotted a lobby display board with four photographs of himself, his wife, Arthur Kelly, and Ethel Regan. He removed the photos and threw the lobby board into the alley and thus disappeared for all time a show that was a tradition in Kansas for half a century.

The Footlights

Ted North went to Hollywood. He managed a big picture theater there for many years. His son Ted North Jr., known professionally as Michael North, operates a large and very successful theatrical agency, booking Hollywood starts for big state fair dates.

This incident reported in the *Billboard* could be used as a dramatic finale for the tents. The shows continued as best they could even when World War II suddenly changed life in America.

Let us return to the final issue of *Bill Bruno's Bulletin*. The big news is that Harley Sadler planned to take out his show even though his plans to unite with the Gene Austin Show to make a really big show did not seem advisable. "The king of Texas will continue giving his many patrons exactly what they want to see—Harley Sadler and his Own Show." The company planned to open early in September playing northwestern Texas with one and two night stands using a twelve hundred seat outfit and presenting thirty-five people, a strong cast in the dramatic line, with special vaudeville acts new to the territory.

The Frank Ginnivan Show had closed and the manager had gone fishing. J. Doug Morgan will try an indefinite engagement of stock at Ottumwa, Iowa, featuring Don Dixon, "a terrific favorite in the Iowa city." Swanson's "Big Ole" company opened on a Wisconsin route the week of the issue. We have already had a considerable description of what life on this company was like. Ben Wilkes, Wallace Bruce, Brunk's Comedians, Harley Sadler, and the Hugo Players, among the tried, true and unbeaten rep shows, are advertising for talent. Bill is offering the plays from his new bureau to circle stock companies for the winter.

The only editorial comment in this issue is on the front page in a box:

PLEASE NOTE

Following mailing of this issue, your editor enters Bell Memorial Hospital, Kansas City, Kansas, for two weeks observation and build up. We are again obliged to suspend publication for that time and ask the indulgence of our subscribers.

This point marks the real end of the business. It only remains to chronicle the events after World War II, a slow determined struggle to put off the actual end of the rep shows.

A notice in the *Billboard*, from L. Verne Slout, written from his headquarters in Vermontville, Michigan, described the state of the reps after the war.[28] Slout had been among the missing in the late thirties numbers of *Bill Bruno's Bulletin*. He had revived his show and continued playing until the early sixties.

He began by commenting on the letters from old performers and show fans bemoaning the death of tent rep theater. He said that poor business, radio, motion pictures, television, and even the New Deal had killed the rep shows off. He said:

> In these days one show doesn't have to wait to get onto a lot until the show there the week before moves off; I admit that the old-time professional . . . performer is getting scarce, but I do not admit that the shows are dying or that there isn't a place for them. The few shows that still exist are standard, dependable name shows. Their equipment is better than it ever has been. Instead of transporting an outfit in a baggage car or cross country on farmer's wagons, they all have their own trucks, trailers, and house cars . . . their own orchestras, sound systems, and bally trucks.

He believed that the plays presented were more modern and attractive with the result that most managers are ending up on the "right side of the ledger." No one ever heard gossip about actors not receiving salaries, and he said wryly,

> This isn't because of Equity shows. Equity forgot about tent shows when the shows shrunk in number and a representative couldn't go out and collect enough dues to more than pay his salary and expenses much less leave something for Equity.

All tent show managers when interviewed were equally bitter about Equity. Nevertheless, Slout and other managers at this time are using a contract modeled on the old Equity form.

He mentioned in addition to his own show, the Toby and Ora Slout Players, and a dozen of the old shows still playing as a proof that the public still does want the tent show. Among these still playing are Bisbee's Comedians, Neil and Caroline Schaffner, the Plunkett Family Show, Hugo Players, Chick Boyes Players, Dennis Players, Tilton Players, Manhattan Players, Roberson Players, Jack Collier Players, Brooks Stock Company, and Brunk's Comedians. A new name appears on this list; the Sund Players. Jess and Dot Sund began the new show, one of the two new shows after World War II. The other new show is the McKennon Players.

Slout had not listed his show in the 1940 roster of the *Bill Bruno's Bulletin*. Notices in *The Billboard* during the war years show that Slout was operating out of his home town during the 1940's. He toured his show for the last time in 1953. Slout retired after a final performance in the old Vermontville Opera house. He died in retirement on April 13, 1954. Among other shows not mentioned by

Slout which continued during the war years and were active afterwards were the Norma Ginnivan Show, and the Madge Kinsey Company. There were probably others whose records were not available.

Harley Sadler stored his outfit during the war years and became interested in business and politics. He was a member of the Texas Senate when he died, October 14, 1954, after being stricken with a heart attack while emceeing a benefit show for the Boy Scouts.[29] He had served three terms in the Texas House of Representatives before his election to the Senate. During this period he spent one season back in show business with the McKennon Players.

By 1963, all but three of these shows had disappeared. Henry Brunk had stored his show in 1958 on his farm near Boise City, Oklahoma. After closing his rep show, Brunk started to work for a circus.

By 1973 he had completely retired, making his home in Wichita, Kansas, except for the cold months of the winter which he and his wife spend in Florida.

Jack Collier stored his show in Farmer City, Illinois, where he worked as City Clerk. Later in 1966, he sold the show to Harold Rosier of Jackson, Michigan, who for several years has been operating an "Old Time Stock Company" near Jackson. The Schaffner Players have operated from their beginnings in 1926 and are still going under the direction of Jimmy and Juanita Davis. Billy Choate, one of the family who formerly operated Choate's Comedians, operated Bisbee's Comedians until 1966. This was the show on which Boob Brasfield made his final appearances before he died in 1966. Dot and Jess Sund operated their show out of Maryville, Missouri. They played southern Iowa and northern Missouri until 1967. On their show were such old timers as Ralph Blackwell, Bob Fisher, and George and Margaret Kleber. Laura Guthrie, of the old Tilton-Guthrie show, Leo Lacy, Ethan Allen, and grand old Bert Dexter have worked with Jimmy Davis on the Schaffner Show.

Here ends the story of the small town theater. This is the story of the tent rep shows and the repertory companies and one-nighters playing the old-time opera houses. Even to the very end the older men in the business were hopeful that the great days would return. The need for such shows seemed to pass away. Bill Bruno could look back in 1930, to the list of over fifteen attractions which had been booked by the middle of July, 1900, for the winter season at the Atlantic, Iowa, Opera House.[30] Viewed from a perspective of over seventy years the list is still impressive even in these days when there is an upswing of interest in living theater.

Bill's list includes such favorites as Jolly Della Pringle's *Quo Vadis*, Sol Smith Russell's *A Poor Relation* and *The Woman in the Case*, and the perennial *Uncle Tom's Cabin*. In addition, the manager has announced dates for six lyceum attractions appealing to the intellectual element in the town.

"Thirty years is a long stretch," said Bill, and the seventy years is even longer. During these years, the great roadshows reached their greatest period of development, declined, and almost disappeared. The silent pictures became popular entertainment, but were challenged and defeated by the rep shows in the country. The stock companies in the big and smaller cities, and on Broadway reached their highest peak in numbers of shows produced, theaters operating, and in dramatic activity. After all these fabulous years, radio and talking pictures changed the world of entertainment only to be defeated in their own turn by television. All of these aspects of show business are much more important commercially than artistically.

As for the rep shows, they not only grew old in their personnel, but they no longer filled a need. The small towns, though still rural, did not exist in such great contrast to the big cities very close to them by automobile. Rural culture as a distinct element in our civilization, declined. A thin veneer of Hollywood and television sophistication took its place. The individualism, the strong mores gave way to this commercialized culture. The tents attempted to meet this challenge by imitation, but the imitation was obvious and it failed. The myth on which the rural audiences based their opinions and tastes, they now no longer believed. With the disappearance of belief in the myth there was no longer any need for the ritual. E. L. Paul lamented in the pages of *The Billboard* twenty-five years ago:[31]

> When one thinks of the activity that used to keep everyone on his toes around the booking offices and hotel lobbies in Chicago and Kansas City, Mo., just a few years ago, with more than 200 managers hustling to fill their casts, lease plays, buy tents and all the other activities that went with the organizing of a summer dramatic company, it is a little disheartening to have to report that not one dramatic show was organized this spring in this, the heart of America, which also was the heart of the tent show and airdome business.

Will Locke, E. L. Paul, and others in their contributions to the story of the rep shows printed from time to time in *The Billboard* are fond of listing the many graduates from the rep shows to the metropolitan stage. Although there are many, Jeanne Eagles with her tempestuous playing of Sadie Thompson in *Rain* is probably most easily remembered. Belle Bennett, daughter of Billy Bennett who ran a show out of Milaca, Minnesota; Spencer Tracy, who was once leading man of William Wright's Players; Melvyn Douglas, who started as prop man with the George Roberson Players; and one of the most glamourous of the silent film stars, John Gilbert, stepson of Jolly Della Pringle, are movie stars who got their start in the rep business. Walter D. Nealand said that Melvyn Douglas, then Mel Hesselberger, persuaded his college chum Ralph Bellamy to join him on the Roberson Show. Bellamy played general business, juggled trunks and helped put up and take down the tent for a small salary. For contemporary audiences who may have forgotten or never known some of the stars of the past, there is one actor of stellar quality who started with the rep shows. Milburn Stone, the "Doc" of the TV show, *Gunsmoke*, was a very popular leading man with various shows. His name appeared often in the pages of *Bill Bruno's Bulletin*.

Today it is still more disheartening to have to report that Kansas City is so dead theatrically that it has not one legitimate theater in operation. *The Billboard* no longer exists as the show folks' bible, but is now a phonograph record review.

On the other hand there are now stock companies in locations where they have never been before or have not been for a long time. Show business has also given birth to that sub-branch of theatrical presentations, the dinner theater. There are new resident companies in the larger cities, although their repertory consists of foreign, classical and New York-born plays. There is a thriving Equity office in Chicago, where not too many years ago all of the union's business was done in the Equity representative's apartment.

There is only one show left that operates in the manner of the old tent reps. The Schaffner Players, owned and operated by Jimmy and Juanita Davis, still tours. They travel the show in the old-time way of fighting mud, rain, wind and dust, successfully playing in small towns in southeastern Iowa, western Illinois, and northern Missouri.

Mr. Davis has tried to blend the old with the new. He has had week-long engagements at the Iowa State Fair, the Nebraska State Fair, the Spirit of America Fair at Saratoga, New York, and the Smithsonian Institution at Washington, D.C. His is a big attraction at the Old Settlers' and Threshers' Re-union at Mt. Pleasant, Iowa, where a theater has been built for rep shows. One floor of the building is devoted to a museum of the rep shows which should provide a vast amount of theater memorabilia for future research.

Another show has continued the tradition of the reps although it did not travel.[32] Harold Rosier of Jackson, Michigan, is a person long familiar with the rep show business. In 1966 he bought Jack Collier's tent which was in storage in Farmer City, Illinois, and set it up in Michigan. For several years he presented his Rosier Players at History Town between Brighton and Detroit.

In 1973 Mr. Rosier received a grant from the Michigan Arts Council and resumed production in 1974. His method of producing the old plays would give anyone interested an opportunity to see how they were acted in the heyday of the rep shows. Many people have a complete misunderstanding of the term Melodrama. A good deal of this misunderstanding is due to the saloon theater of the recent past, where the plays were presented with their worst qualities emphasized. The villain flying about in a black cape, twirling a huge mustachio, and the heroine beautiful but mentally deficient. The lines in such plays as *Ten Nights in a Barroom*, are stilted, old-fashioned and are hardly funny.

Rosier bases his theory of presentation on his own experience—that the rep shows were presented in just as natural a fashion as any contemporary realistic play. He has steadfastly refused to burlesque the old shows in any way.

Can one, then, indulge in the hopes of Bill Bruno and Verne Slout? Is there a hope at all that living theater will become once more a part of the lives of the population as it once was, not a thing of imposed culture from outside, but creative, and really responsive to the thoughts and feeling of the American people, a genuine American popular culture?

Two Rep Veterans: Bert Dexter, fifty one years in the business (center) with Milburn Stone (Doc of "Gunsmoke") a famous leading man of the reps in his younger days, along with Ken Curtis (Festus).

190

APPENDIX

Pearle Wilson as "Polly," 1914.

Fred Wilson in *Polly of the Circus*, 1914.

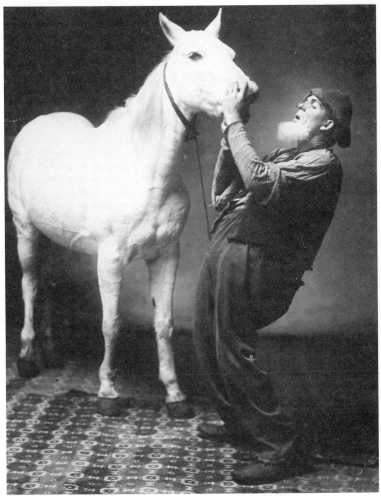

193

Fred Wilson as G-string.

Fred (Toby) Wilson

Some of Fred Wilson's character and personality come forth out of the anecdotes related of him and his family in previous pages.[1] Born at Blue Rapids, Kansas, on August 16, 1879, he had made his first stage appearance at Hannibal, Missouri, at the age of fourteen.

He had completed two years of high school, the usual education of his time. In those days graduation from high school was the equivalent of a college degree today. In many small towns the high school curriculum extended no further than the tenth grade. Many midwestern towns did not even have a high school. Fred attended elementary and the first year of high school at California, Missouri, ending his education in the tenth grade at Independence, Missouri.

Fred realized the importance of education. His own children received the best education his salary could afford. For show folks the education of their children was a major problem because the show was always on the move. The Wilson children accompanied their parents on the show only during the summer.

Fred could always be counted upon to help anyone who wanted to learn. He taught Joe Sola, one of the canvasmen on his shows to read and write. Joe later became head property man for many big shows out of New York.

The letters he wrote to his daughter Evelyn Barrick really demonstrate both his comic genius and his lovable personality. Mrs. Barrick said that he wrote only one or two letters a year. These letters usually contained trivia on his view of life, and nothing of any great importance. This trivia showed what he thought about and what he felt about show business which is important to us.[2]

He used the telephone to communicate with his daughter more often than writing. (His son, Neil, had been killed in an accident at the age of fourteen.) At one time, he did not have his daughter's phone number and wrote asking her if she was using smoke signals to talk to people.

A tough-minded severity toward his family and their activities coming from his old-fashioned up bringing along with some remaining puritan prejudices was the cause of his separation from his first wife Pearle. The separation was undoubtedly very unhappy for both of them. After his separation from Pearle in 1921, he went into vaudeville. He began an act with a company of twenty people playing the Orpheum circuit. He played at the Palace Theater in New York, as the culmination of his vaudeville career. From September 30, 1924 until June, 1930 he worked as an actor and producer for the Harry Rogers Enterprises.

Mentioning these big-time engagements should substantiate his reputation as an excellent performer. Too many people have looked down on the performers in the small-time shows, considering them unskilled hams. This is a very unfair estimate. Many of the small-time actors did play the big-time, gaining fame and fortune. Many of them freely left the big-time to return to the country. Fred in a letter to Evelyn said that he preferred playing Arkansas to New York City.

Fred Wilson's later career included engagements as a director and featured performer at the Music Box Theater in Hollywood. Before he took this engagement he had returned to Oklahoma from New York. Oklahoma was evidently his favorite spot in the country. In 1930 he was making an appearance with a tent stock in Oklahoma City.[3] His entry into the company had been on short notice but his reputation was so great that business began to pick up immediately. He was playing such bills as *Oscar's Wild*, and an old success of his, *The Hired Hand*. He returned to Oklahoma City after the Chicago closing of the play he starred in, Joe Howard's production *The Time, The Place, and the Girl*.

He owned and operated a cafe from his return to Oklahoma City until 1936 when he began managing movie theaters. This job included writing and producing stage shows as well as supervising employees and designing publicity for the theaters.

On November 27, 1942 he ended his career in the theater. At that time he began to work as an employee counselor at Tinker Air Force Base.[4] Fred had spent fifty-two years on the stage, the movie lot, and before the microphone. Even at Tinker Air Force Base he was called on to perform again. He played Pop Warren in *The Warrens at War*, a propaganda broadcast carried over the Columbia network. He also assisted in the writing of the series.

The Take-Off, A Tinker Air Force Base publication said of him:

This base was a mammoth stage where real things were being dramatized. During his almost ten years of service, Toby's heart kept pace with the rhythmic pulsing of the riveter, the

The Footlights

grinding of the lathe, and the whirling of the aircraft motor. In many respects, Toby's life resembled that of the great Will Rogers. He never met a man he didn't like, and like Will, Toby would talk with kings and never lose the common touch.

Fred died sleeping peacefully in his favorite chair at the family home in Oklahoma City on June 10, 1952. He had become chief of Special Events section, Liason Office, and was Tinker's best known and most loved civilian employee. He had done a full day's work on the day before he died. Before he went home on the last day he had performed a comic impression of two drunks for fellow employees. This was a favorite comedy subject at that time for him. This last performance was a fitting climax to a life filled with the adventure and wanderlust of the stage and the bright lights.

Fred Wilson loved people, audiences and performing. Although he reached the pinnacle of success for any performer he never lost his love for the people, towns, and countryside of the Midwest.

Fred Wilson shortly before his death in 1952.

I. SECTION NOTES

1 It has been impossible to positively identify this show. The only company which consistently carried a carnival as a ballyhoo to the dramatic show was the Walter Savidge Co. In 1906 Walter Savidge and his brother Elwin Strong (Ray Savidge) of Wayne, Nebraska, began trouping a show of this kind. Later the two brothers dissolved their partnership and each one trouped his own show, Walter continuing with the carnival ballyhoo. Programs in my possession (courtesy LeRoy Overstreet, Mallard, Iowa) of the Walter Savidge Co. show the Savidge Co. in 1915 playing *The Heart of Wetona*, a play undoubtedly like *Red Feather and His Squaw* derivative from such metropolitan successes as *Strongheart* or *The Squawman*.

I do not remember the name of the company on the show print displayed in Niobrara. Memory can play one false, but I remember looking for it as a child of ten who had suddenly been seized with the fever of show business. The dramatic company, I do not remember that the carnival was advertised, was publicized under the name of its featured play, *Red Feather and His Squaw*. Neither LeRoy Overstreet, at that time public relations man with the Savidge Co., nor Mrs. Walter Savidge remember the play. Thus, whether this was the Strong troupe with a carnival, the Savidge-Strong troupe, or another totally different show carrying a carnival, I do not know and have found no way of getting accurate information. Traditionally, the Savidge troupe was the only tent rep show carrying a carnival as a ballyhoo. The territory being played at the time was that played by both Strong and Savidge throughout their careers.

2 See Susanne K. Langer, *Feeling and Form* (New York, 1953), pp. 306-325.

3 K. C. Young, "Tent Shows," *New York Times*, April 21, 1927, IV, p. 18. D. C. Gillette, "Tent Shows," October 16, 1927, IX, 2:1. George Eels, "Barnstormers," *Signature*, June 1965.

4 pp. 50 ff.

5 A fine example of one of these small town theaters can be seen today in Shelbina, Missouri. It occupies the second floor of an old building (today the first floor is a modern market) and is just as it was when the last show played it some forty years ago. Some of the scenery is still in place. The hall held about 1,000 people.

6 Clarence Darrow, *The Story of My Life* (New York, 1934) p. 33.

II. SECTION NOTES

1 Noah Ludlow, *Dramatic Life as I Found It* (St. Louis, 1880).

2 Robert L. Sherman, *Chicago Stage: Its Record and Achievement* (Chicago, 1932) p. 110.

3 *The Billboard*, January 3, 1947.

4 Sol Smith, *Theatrical Management in the West and South for Thirty Years* (New York, 1869).

5 (Chicago, 1939).

6 (Hollywood, 1952).

7 (Newton, Iowa n. d.).

8 (New York, 1937).

9 Personal experience.

10 p. 40.

11 p. 260; Sherman's dates, although often open to question, seem to be verified in T. Allston Brown, *History of the American Stage* (New York, 1870, p. 370) who states that about 1848 or 1849 Robinson located in Rock Island, Illinois, just across the river from Davenport, and there "made a tent with his own hands . . . and started the Robinson Athenaeum, playing *The Drunkard*,

and like pieces, and as each tent was worn out, its successor would be much larger." See his own words, *New York Clipper*, November 17, 1872, p. 384. Reference courtesy Dr. William Slout.

Yankee Robinson was born Fayette Lodavik Robinson, May 2, 1818, Avon Mineral Springs, New York. (*New York Clipper*, December 30, 1865.) Possibly his name, Yankee, came from his desire and his attempts to play the Yankee character, popular at this time. (See Slout, *The Repertoire Tent Show from Its Beginnings to 1920*, Dissertation, University of California at Los Angeles, 1970) p. 147.

[12] T. Allston Brown, *History of the American Stage* (New York, 1870) p. 317.

[13] Schick, pp. 8-9; also Calkins, p. 242 for performances of Robinson's company in Galesburg, Illinois.

[14] *New York Clipper*, November 17, 1872, p. 384.

[15] Sherman, p. 658.

[16] p. 24.

[17] *The Billboard*, December 25, 1926.

[18] *The Billboard*, December 6, 1959: "Ginnivan, Frank, 80, in Ashley, Ind., it has just been learned. He operated the Ginnivan Dramatic Company for 30 years prior to 1942, the show's last year on the road. The show name dated back to 1897, when it was operated by Ginnivan's father, probably making it the oldest such attraction in history. His sister, Norma, who died in 1953, also had been connected with the show."

[19] *The Billboard*, December 25, 1926.

[20] *The Billboard*, July 15, 1950.

[21] *The Billboard*, "The Repertoire Show of Today," December 12, 1925, p. 18.

[22] William L. Slout, *The Repertoire Tent Show from Its Beginning to 1920*. (University of California, Los Angeles, Dissertation, 1970) p. 68.

[23] *The Billboard*, statement by J. B. Richardson of Orion, Illinois, December 25, 1926.

[24] *Bill Bruno's Bulletin*, December 17, 1937.

[25] Louis Verneuil, *La Vie Merveilleuse de Sarah Bernhardt* (New York, 1942) p. 255. In translation by Ernest Boyd (New York, 1942) p. 251.

[26] *The Billboard*, January 15, 1949.

[27] *Bill Bruno's Bulletin*, "Circle Stock Grew Out of Rep," Dec. 17, 1936. All references to circle stock come from this article or my own experience.

[28] p. 77.

III. SECTION NOTES

[1] "Our Canvas Broadway," Country Gentleman, May, 1931.

[2] Calkins, *passim*.

[3] Schick, p. 81; interview, July 15, 1965, Miss Lucille Spooner, Centerville, Iowa.

[4] May.

[5] *The Billboard*, January 29, 1927, and March 27, 1948.

[6] Letter, May 18, 1965.

[7] Clipping in Alex Pitcaithley's collection from *The Billboard*, by Bruce Rinaldo, specific date missing.

[8] Peggy Dern's novel, *Tent Show* (New York, 1944), is based on the activities and experiences of the Lazone Co.

[9] *The Billboard*, "10-20-30 and Up the Ladder," by Walter D. Nealand, November 30, 1940. Also information on the Paytons and the Spooners from interview with Miss Lucille Spooner, July 15, 1965, and her personal memorabilia of the two families.

[10] Interview, March 29, 1965.

[11] Interview, March 20, 1965.

[12] June 13, 1960.

[13] Sources withheld.

[14] Unpublished notes.

[15] May

[16] See Section VI, The Lights Dim.

[17] pp. 69 ff., also 35.

[18] Gil Robinson, *Old Wagon Show Days* (Cincinnati, 1925) pp. 30 f.

[19] Ernest Jack Sharp (Sharpsteen) *One Life* (Grand Rapids, Michigan, 1950) p. 38.

[20] The Autobiography of Herbert Walters (Channell) *Fifty Years Under Canvas*, transcribed and co-authored by Velma E. Lowry, edited by Miron A. Morrill, Division of Languages and Literature, Southwestern College, Winfield, Kansas (Hugo, Oklahoma, 1962).

[21] *The Billboard*, November 6, 1954.

[22] Interview, July 13, 1965, La Plata, Missouri, with Addison Aulger. Alex Pitcaithley, letter, October 31, 1970, has this to add: This sounds like TUNNEL cars now used by Ringling—small wagons several of which are hooked together and pulled to loading (ramp) and rolled right in. They are small, of course, more like trailers. Now I know on Tom show one-nighters I have seen small wagons that knocked down or folded and were put on a baggage car like the ticket wagon in the shape of a cabin—but one large enough to carry the POLES?"

[23] Omaha, Nebraska, *World-Herald*, July 21, 1929.

[24] Mrs. Savidge.

[25] *The Billboard*, December 12, 1925.

[26] p. 36.

[27] Chicago *Sun-Times*, "Theatre Trunk Firm Locks Up After 92 Years," April 25, 1951.

[28] Carson, *The Theatre on the Frontier*, p. 1.

[29] p. 6.

[30] *The Autobiography of Joseph Jefferson* (New York, 1889) p. 31.

[31] *The Billboard*, August 28, 1948.

[32] For instance, the opera house at Shelbina, Missouri.

[33] Schick, p. 63.

[34] *Signs of the Times*, "The Sign Business Evolved from Scenery Painting," by Eugene Lockhart, March, 1957, p. 40.

[35] Interview, March 9, 1965.

[36] Interview.

[37] Schick, pp. 73, 74.

[38] E. L. Paul. "The Airdomes Come and Go," undated clipping (probably 1949), in Pitcaithley collection; also undated clipping "Gay 90's Airdomes Ace Summer Spots for Repsters" in Pitcaithley collection.

[39] Personal experience.

[40] Nealand.

[41] Hank Hurley in *The Billboard*, October 29, 1949; corrected by letter from H. C. Somerville, Mission, Kansas, April 29, 1965, grandson of C. J. Baker.

[42] *Bill Bruno's Bulletin*, May 15, 1930.

[43] Letter, April 29, 1965.

[44] Bert Dexter, July 12, 1965.

[45] Ernest Chandler, *Awnings and Tents: Construction and Design* (published by the author, New York, 1914, p. 319; lent by Rogers Tent and Awning Co., Fremont, Nebraska, 1965.

[46] Vermontville, Michigan, Echo, May 2, 1929. Furnished by Dr. William Slout, California State College at San Bernardino, San Bernardino, California.

[47] Aulger.

48 Miss Lodema Corey, Interview, March 24, 1965.
49 Unpublished notes.
50 Letter, May 11, 1965.
51 May.
52 Mrs. Barrick, Letter, April 8, 1965.
53 November 16, 1960.
54 Vermontville, Michigan, *Echo*, May 2, 1929.
55 Letter, May 31, 1965.
56 Date on picture furnished by Mrs. Barrick, April 20, 1965.
57 p. 87.
58 Pitcaithley, interview, March 14, 1965.
59 *The Billboard*, December 11, 1926.
60 Albert F. McLean, Jr., *American Vaudeville as Ritual* (Lexington, Kentucky, 1965).
61 L. H. Wight, interview, April 22, 1965.
62 Not to be confused with Robert L. Sherman, actor, playbroker, manager, successor to Alex Byers.
63 *Bill Bruno's Bulletin*, March 21, 1929.
64 Mrs. Barrick, letter, July 4, 1965.
65 See McLean.
66 *Bill Bruno's Bulletin*, May 29, 1930.
67 Letter, Sept. 10, 1965.
68 *Bill Bruno's Bulletin*, March 21, 1929.
69 Autobiography.
70 November 11, 1905.
71 Trixie Maskew, Kansas City, Missouri, interview, March 23, 1965; substantiated by Mrs. Pringle's niece, Mrs. Crawford Eagle, Los Angeles, California, letter, November 11, 1970.
72 Edward J. Ewing, interview, Feb. 12, 1965, Decatur, Illinois.
73 March 21, 1929.
74 Unpublished notes.
75 Unpublished notes.
76 Vance Johnson, "Hits in the Tall Corn," *Colliers*, August 20, 1949.
77 Interview, H. R. Brandt, Kansas City, Missouri, July 27, 1965; *Bill Bruno's Bulletin*, December 17, 1936 and advertisement.

IV. SECTION NOTES

1 May.
2 Interview, March 21.
3 In 1965 the Capital.
4 Henry C. Haskell, Jr., and Richard B. Fowler, *City of the Future, A Narrative History of Kansas City, 1850-1890* (Kansas City, Missouri, 1950).
5 William Allen White, *Autobiography* (New York, 1946) p. 205.
6 Letter, May 21, 1965.
7 Will Locke, "Happy Hectic K. C.," *The Billboard*, undated clipping in Pitcaithley collection.
8 p. 117.
9 Interview, March 3, 1965.
10 Alex Pitcaithley says that he thinks Mr. Simpson was either exaggerating or forgetful when he talked about a quarter page advertisement in *The Billboard* each week. "Maybe," says Alex, "he meant the *Bulletin* which sounds more like it. A quarter page ad in *Billboard* would have been most expensive even in Simpson's heyday. I myself have never seen this kind of ad in all the issues of *The Billboard* I have gone through." Interview, March 14, 1965.

[11] Letter, October 14, 1965.

[12] Interview, April 22, 1965, Chicago, Illinois.

[13] May.

[14] Autobiography.

[15] Interview, Kansas City, Missouri, March 23, 1965.

[16] *The Billboard*, December 29, 1934.

[17] Copy of magazine from LeRoy Overstreet, Mallard, Iowa.

[18] Much of the information on Bill Bruno comes from E. T. Conley of Monango, N. D. who knew him well, and from a column in a Kansas City newspaper (name of paper and date cut off—correspondence with the *Star* gives no further enlightenment) in Mr. Conley's collection of memorabilia, a column entitled "About Town" by Landon Laird. The date would necessarily be during the late summer or early fall of 1940, shortly after Mr. Bruno's death since it is written in the form of a eulogy of the kind used popularly at funerals.

[19] p. 4.

[20] June 5, 1930, p. 8.

[21] R. D. Klassen, *The Tent-Repertoire Theatre: A Rural American Institution*, p. 32 (Michigan State University Dissertation, East Lansing, Michigan, 1969).

[22] Masthead in *Bulletin* of any issue carries the name Will H. Bruno.

[23] May.

[24] Letter, April 18, 1965.

[25] Letter, September 23, 1965.

[26] "Bill Ladd's Almanac," *Courier-Journal*, Louisville, Kentucky, July 26, 1965.

[27] March 24, 1965.

[28] Monte Montrose, interview, July 23, 1965.

[29] Interviews with Mrs. Savidge, Mrs. Boyes, and Miss Corey, 1965.

[30] Interview, Ralph Blackwell, New Virginia, Iowa, July 16, 1965.

[31] *Christian Science Monitor*, January 15, 1951.

[32] Interview with Ward Hatcher, *Courier-Journal*, Louisville, Kentucky, October 28, 1948.

[33] *Ibid.*

[34] Parsons, Letter, October 14, 1965.

[35] *The Billboard*, July 10, 1948.

[36] Autobiography.

[37] *Ibid.*

[38] *The Billboard*, December 13, 1947.

[39] Letter, September 23, 1965.

[40] Letter, September 14, 1965.

[41] Letter, April 27, 1965.

[42] Letter, September 14, 1965.

[43] Unpublished notes.

[44] Letter, May 21, 1965.

[45] Letter, April 20, 1965.

[46] *Ibid.*

[47] *Ibid.*

[48] Letter, September 14, 1965.

[49] Letter, September 14, 1965.

[50] Unpublished notes.

[51] Parsons, Letter, September 23, 1965.
September 23, 1965.

[52] *Ibid.*

[53] *Ibid.*

[54] *Ibid.*

[55] Mrs. Chick Boyes, August 12, 1966.

[56] Addison Aulger.

202

57 November 29, 1936.
58 *The Billboard*, January 15, 1949.
59 McKennon, p. 112.
60 Interview, March 21, 1965.
61 *Bill Bruno's Bulletin*, March 21, 1930.
62 *Bill Bruno's Bulletin*, August 14, 1929.
63 *Bill Bruno's Bulletin*, March 21, 1929.
64 Pitcaithley, letter, October 30, 1970.

V. SECTION NOTES

1 For instance, Larry Dale Clark, *Toby Shows: A Form of American Popular Theatre* (University of Illinois Dissertation 1963); Sherwood Snyder III, *The Toby Shows* (University of Minnesota Dissertation, 1966); Robert Dean Klassen, *The Tent-Repertoire Theatre: A Rural American Institution* (Michigan State University Dissertation, 1969); *The Repertoire Tent Show from its Beginning to 1920*, William Lawrence Slout (University of California at Los Angeles Dissertation, 1970); The last is published as *Theatre in a Tent* (Popular Press, Bowling Green, Ohio 1972). This writer is much indebted to both Dr. Clark's and Dr. Slout's work.

2 (New York, n. d.)

3 See Francis Hodge, *Yankee Theatre: The Image of America on the Stage, 1825-1850* (Austin, Texas, 1964).

4 Sherman, *Chicago Stage: Its Record and Achievement*, p. 260.

5 (New York, 1889) copy from Dr. William L. Slout, San Bernardino State College, San Bernardino, California.

6 XXX, November, 1946, pp. 653 ff.

7 The notice from the Copyright Office reads: "CLOUDS AND SUNSHINE, by W. C. Herman. Registered in the name of Alexander Byers, under D25244, following publication September 5, 1911. No renewal found." Copyrighted version of the play lent by Hilliard Wight.

8 p. 102.

9 Letter, April 13, 1965.

10 There are two plays based on this poem of Will Carleton's, *Over the Hills to the Poorhouse* by A. O. Miller, and *Over the Hill to the Poorhouse* by J. L. Polk, each presented for the first time in 1889, the first in Blissfield, Michigan, and the second in Syracuse, New York. See *Drama Cyclopedia* p. 416. A film with the latter title and the same subject matter was made about 1922 by the Fox Film Co.

11 Letter, April 8, 1965.

12 Dr. Slout's argument is given in full on pp. 92-97 of *Theatre in a Tent*.

13 September 20, 1967.

14 Slout, p. 122, footnote 35 (c. VIII), "American Theatre program for week commencing March 14, 1904; New York *Dramatic Mirror*, March 19, 1904, p. 16; New York *Herald*, March 9, 1904."

15 Downing, p. 653.

16 December 17, 1936.

17 Unpublished notes.

18 McLean, pp. 1-15.

19 Ibid., p. 2.

20 For an expanded treatment of the material in this article see Jere C. Mickel "The Genesis of Toby" *Journal of American Folklore* v. 8 #318, October-December 1967.

21 Mr. Schaffner died in the summer of 1969.

22 Autobiography.

23 Oskaloosa, Iowa, *Daily Herald*, June 10, 1958.

24 Letter, August 24, 1965.

[25] Elmer Hinton, "Along the Sawdust Trail," Hasville, Tennessee, *Tennesseean*, July 6, 1958.
[26] Vance Johnson, "Hits in the Tall Corn," *Colliers*, August 10, 1949.
[27] Letter, September 28, 1965.
[28] Letter, October 8, 1965.
[29] Letter, November 24, 1965.
[30] Christmas number, 1939.

VI. SECTION NOTES

[1] Interview, August 12, 1966.
[2] *The Billboard*, April 10, 1926.
[3] April 17, 1926.
[4] *The Billboard*, June 19, July 3 and July 10.
[5] May 29, 1930.
[6] May 22 and May 15.
[7] *Bill Bruno's Bulletin*, May 15, 1930.
[8] *Ibid.*, May 22, 1930.
[9] *Ibid.*, May 22, 1930.
[10] Letter, September 14, 1965.
[11] Interview, August 12, 1966.
[12] Letter, September 23, 1965.
[13] *Bill Bruno's Bulletin*, May 29, 1930.
[14] *Ibid.*, June 13, 1940.
[15] *Ibid.*, September 4, 1930.
[16] Letter, September 23, 1965.
[17] May 22, 1930.
[18] August 21, 1930.
[19] *Bill Bruno's Bulletin*, March 21, 1929.
[20] *Ibid.*, May 22, 1930.
[21] *Bill Bruno's Bulletin*, March 21, 1929, and *The Billboard*, April 3, 1926. See also *Equity Magazine* during the period 1920-37 for details. It always carried an annual report from the president which included the state of the tent rep shows from the beginnings of unionization until the tent rep actors disappeared from the union roster.
[22] Letter, September 23, 1965.
[23] Letter, April 15, 1967.
[24] June 23, 1938.
[25] December 16, 1937.
[26] *Bill Bruno's Bulletin*, June 13, 1940.
[27] *The Billboard*, April 19, 1952.
[28] April 5, 1952.
[29] Abilene, Texas, *Reporter-News*, October 15, 1954.
[30] *Bill Bruno's Bulletin*, July 3, 1930.
[31] *The Billboard*, July 26, 1947.

APPENDIX NOTES

[1] Mrs. Barrick, various letters.
[2] *Ibid.*
[3] *The Billboard*, November 30, 1940.
[4] From Fred Wilson's official application for federal government employment, November 23, 1942, lent by Mrs. Barrick.

INTERVIEWS
(Place of interview and date)

Ethan Allen, Mt. Pleasant, Iowa, September 5, 1970.
Addison Aulger, La Plata, Missouri, July 13, 1965.
Mrs. Ethel Bennett, Canton, Illinois, April 16, 1965.
Mrs. Chick Boyes, Hebron, Nebraska, August 6, 1964, August 12, 1966.
* H. R. Brandt, Kansas City, Missouri, July 27, 1965.
Ralph Blackwell, New Virginia, Iowa, July 16, 1965.
* Lawrence (Boob) Brasfield, New Fulton, Tennessee, August 11, 1964.
* Mr. and Mrs. Wallace Bruce, Hutchinson, Kansas, March 9, 1965.
Billy Choate, New Fulton, Tennessee, August 11, 1964.
* Lodema Corey, Kansas City, Missouri, March 24, 1965.
Emile T. Conley, Monango, North Dakota, August 16, 1965.
Mrs. Margery Dare, Chicago, Illinois, September 16, 1964.
Mr. and Mrs. James V. Davis, Enroute with the Schaffner Players; July 6,
    1963, Carthage, Illinois; July 3, 4, 1964, Quincy, Illinois; July 12, 13, 1965,
    La Plata, Missouri; July 6, 1966, Quincy, Illinois; August 8, 1966, Edina,
    Missouri; September 3, 4, 5, 1967, Mt. Pleasant, Iowa; June 2, 1968,
    Wapello, Iowa; September 5, 6, 7, 1970, Mt. Pleasant, Iowa.
Bert Dexter, En route with Schaffner show, on dates given.
Mr. and Mrs. Crawford Eagle, July 6, 1963, Carthage, Illinois; September 5, 1970,
    Mt. Pleasant, Iowa.
Edward Ewing, February 12, 1965, Decatur, Illinois.
Johnny Finch, Olney, Ill., November 29, 1974.
Mr. and Mrs. Robert LaThey Johnson, March 9, 1965, Texarkana, Texas.
Mr. and Mrs. Erman Gray, September 5, 1970, Mt. Pleasant, Iowa.
Beatrix Maskew, March 23, 1965, Kansas City, Missouri.
Monte Montrose, July 23, 1965, Shenandoah, Iowa.
Christy Obrecht, September 4, 1967, Mt. Pleasant, Iowa.
Mr. and Mrs. LeRoy Overstreet, March 30, 1965, Mallard, Iowa.
Mr. and Mrs. Alex Pitcaithley, Carlsbad, New Mexico, March 13, 14, 15, 1965.
Mrs. Tracy Sherman Rath, Chicago, Illinois, April 25, 1965.
Mrs. Amber Rebein, Great Bend, Kansas, March 10, 11, 1965.
Rogers Tent and Awning Co. (Staff), Fremont, Nebraska, March 29, 1965.
Mrs. Walter Savidge, Wayne, Nebraska, March 29, 1965.
Karl Simpson, Chicago, Illinois, March 4, 1965.
Lucille Spooner, Centerville, Iowa, July 15, 1965.
Mr. and Mrs. Jess Sund, New Virginia, Iowa, July 16, 1965.
* Hilliard Wight, Great Bend, Kansas, March 10, 11, 1965.
Mason Wilkes, Mt. Pleasant, Iowa, September 4, 1967.
L. H. Wight, Chicago, Illinois, April 22, 1965.
Charles Worthan, Perry, Oklahoma, March 20, 21, 1965.
Henry Wodetzki, Danville, Illinois, February 14, 1967.

* deceased.

CORRESPONDENCE

Mrs. Evelyn Wilson Barrick, Portland, Oregon, April 8, 16, 20, 27, May 21, July 4, 9, 20, October 8, 1965.

Mrs. Gladys Feagin Baxter, Tucson, Arizona, May 21, 1965.

Ralph Blackwell, Belmont, North Carolina, February 19, 1965.

H. R. Brandt, Kansas City, Missouri, January 19, October 7, 1966.

Henry L. Brunk, Wichita, Kansas, January 25, 1965.

H. L. Carlstrom, Los Angeles, California, April 30, May 11, 31, 1965.

William Chagnon, Montreal, Quebec, May 25, 1965.

Jack Collier, Farmer City, Illinois, February 11, 1965.

Mrs. Margery Dare, Chicago, Illinois, September 13, 1964.

Mr. and Mrs. Crawford Eagle, Los Angeles, California, November 11, 1970.

Ray Evans, Hutchinson, Minnesota, February 8, 1965.

Hal Fontinelle, Joplin, Missouri, February 7, 1965.

Lucelia Frazier, Los Angeles, California, May 30, 1965.

Madge Kinsey Graf, Delray Beach, Florida, December 1, 1965.

Mrs. Dorothy Gerall, Rochester, Minnesota, July 10, 1965.

Harry Harvey, Sr., Los Angeles, California, May 18, 1965.

Mrs. Mabel Mason Harvey, Los Angeles, California, May 18, 1965.

Lee Harrison, Saginaw, Michigan, June 2, 1965.

Audra Hardesty, Broughton, Illinois, January 23, 1965.

Ward Hatcher, Mountain Grove, Missouri, February 9, 1965.

Otto Imig, Fostoria, Ohio, October 8, 1965.

Monte Montrose, Shenandoah, Iowa, August 24, 1965.

Horace Murphy, Los Angeles, California, April 8, 1965.

William L. Oliver, St. Louis, Missouri, August 16, 1965.

James Parsons, Philadelphia, Pennsylvania, August 27, September 1, 10, 14, 23, October 14, 22, 1965, March 7, 1966.

Chic Pellete, Lake Helen, Florida, April 21, 1965.

Lee Reinhardt, Portland, Oregon, April 18, 1965.

Harold Rosier, Jackson, Michigan, November 21, 1966, March 22, 1967.

Dr. William Slout, Los Angeles, California, April 8, September 28, November 24, 1965, June 8, 1966, June 6, 1967.

Sid Snider, Dixon, Missouri, January 28, 1965.

H. C. Somerville, Mission, Kansas, April 29, 1965.

Mr. and Mrs. M. H. Tilton, St. Petersburg, Florida, February 12, 1965.

B. E. Walton, Los Angeles, California, May 11, 1965.

Al. C. Wilson, Kansas City, Missouri, February 8, 1965.

In addition to these I have had the privilege of constant correspondence with Alex Pitcaithley of Carlsbad, New Mexico from 1965 until the present (1974). Some of these letters are used as references in the text.

PLAYS

Play title, author, copyright and source of play in that order; if author is not given but known, his name is put in parentheses; any other information about play known but not in script in writer's collection is also in parentheses.

§ Indicates writer produced play at Monticello, Illinois in 1967.

† Indicates writer produced play at Millikin University, Decatur, Illinois, in 1966.

All That Glitters by Thomas and J. M. Morton; New York, 1899, Harold Roorbach.
    —William L. Slout
Awakening of John Slater by (Charles Harrison) (copyright 1914).
    —William L. Slout
Best Laid Plans by Hilliard Wight.   —Amber Rebein
Call of the Woods by (W. C. Herman) (copyright 1912).
    —Mrs. Tracy Sherman Rath
Chicken Preferred by Robert J. Sherman; copyright 1931.   —Billy Choate
Clouds and Sunshine by W. C. Herman; copyright 1911 by Alex Byers. § †
    —Hilliard Wight
Dr. Jekyll and Mr. Hyde by Nelson Compston; copyright 1910 by Alex Byers. §
    —Mrs. Rath
Gossip by Robert J. Sherman; (no copyright given but a return on front cover to Robert J. Sherman, 648 N. Dearborn St., Chicago.)   —Slout
The Hoodlum (sometimes called Rags); (no author or cpyright given). §
    —Mrs. Chick Boyes
Holy Sinners, or The Devil's Gossip; (no author) (no copyright).
    —Mrs. Chick Boyes
Lena Rivers (Nelson Compston) (1909).   —Mrs. Chick Boyes
The Only Road (Charles Harrison) (no copyright).   —Slout
Out of the Fold (original version by Langdon McCormick) (copyright 1904) tab (cut) version.   —Mrs. Rath
Over the Hills to the Poorhouse or Sent to the Poor Farm (Robert L. Sherman, *Drama Cyclopedia*, p. 416 cites two plays *Over the Hill* etc. by J. L. Polk and *Over the Hills* etc. by A. O. Miller, both copyrighted in 1889, the first with first production in Syracuse, New York, and the second with first production in Blissfield, Michigan. Which version the writer has, he does not know.)   —Mrs. Boyes
The Push (on flyleaf alternative title, *Tamed and How!*) by Glenn Harrison, copyright by author n. d. §   —Slout
Retribution, or The Italian's Revenge by W. C. Herman; copyright 1915 by Alex Byers.   —Mrs. Rath
Rip Van Winkle §
Rodeo Dance (no author but apparently a version of Sputters) (no copyright).
    —Slout
The Right Road by L. Verne Slout; (no copyright but on flyleaf "return to Bennett's Dramatic Exchange 36 W. Randolph, Chicago, A. Milo Bennett").
    —Slout
Saintly Hypocrites and Honest Sinners by (Charles Harrison); (copyright 1915). §
    —Mrs. Boyes

Spooks by Robert J. Sherman publisher, Samuel French, Inc.; New York, copyrighted.

Sputters by (George Crawley); (1916).   —Mrs. Rath

Sweethearts Again (no author) (no copyright).   —Mrs. Boyes

Talk of the Talkies or She Made Him Do It by L. Verne Slout; (no copyright). —Slout

Ten Nights in a Barroom by William Pratt; (no copyright). Version used by L. Verne Slout Players. §   —Slout

Ten Nights in a Barroom by William Pratt.

Tildy Ann by (Robert J. Sherman); (no copyright).   —Slout

The It Girl by Edmund L. Paul; copyright, 1929. (From E. L. Paul Play Co., Gladstone Hotel Bldg., Kansas City, Missouri.)   —Mrs. Boyes

Toby, the Yankee Doodle Dandy by L. Verne Slout; (no copyright).   —Slout

Thorns and Orange Blossoms (no author); (no copyright).   —Hilliard Wight

Tropical Love by (E. L. Paul); (no copyright).   —Mrs. Boyes

Uncle Tom's Cabin. New York, n. d. French's Standard Drama # CCVIII.

Wandering Spooks: A Novelty Mystery Comedy by L. Verne Slout; (no copyright date; exclusive agent Hoffman-Maxwell Play Co., 830 Market Street, San Francisco, California).   —Slout

Won by Waiting by Nelson Compston and W. C. Herman; copyright 1912 by Alexander Byers. §   —Mrs. Rath

BIBLIOGRAPHY

Books

Gertrude Andrews, *The Life of Corse Payton* (New York, 1901).

Zachary Ball (Kelly Masters), *Tent Show* (New York, 1964).

T. Allston Brown, *History of the American Stage* (New York, 1870).

—— *A History of the New York Stage from the First Performance in 1732 to 1901.* 3 vols. (New York, 1903).

Alfred Bernheim, *The Business of the Theatre* (New York, 1964).

Margarete Bieber, *The History of the Greek and Roman Theatre* (London, 1961).

Daniel Blum, *A Pictorial History of the American Theatre* (New York, 1950).

Lilly B. Campbell, *Scenes and Machines on the English Stage During the Renaissance* (New York, 1960).

Earnest Elmo Calkins, *They Broke the Prairie* (New York, 1937).

William G. B. Carson, *Managers in Distress* (St. Louis, 1949).

—— *The Theatre on the Frontier: the Early Years of the St. Louis Stage* (Chicago, 1932).

Earnest Chandler, *Awnings and Tents: Construction and Design* (New York, 1914).

Oral Sumner Coad and Edwin Mims, Jr., *The American Stage:* v. 14 *The Pageant of America* (New Haven, 1929).

Luke Cosgrave, *Theatre Tonight* (Hollywood, 1952).

Clarence Darrow, *The Story of My Life* (New York, 1934).

Peggy Dern, *Tent Show* (New York, 1944).

Maurice Dolbier, *Benjy Boone* (New York, 1967).

C. B. Glasscock, *Then Came Oil* (Indianapolis and New York, 1938).

Henry C. Hadkell, Jr., and Richard B. Fowler, *City of the Future: A Narrative History of Kansas City* (Kansas City, Missouri, 1950).

Francis Hodge, *Yankee Theatre: The Image of America on the Stage, 1825-1850* (Austin, 1964).

Harlo R. Hoyt, *Town Hall Tonight* (New York, 1965).

Joseph Jefferson, *The Autobiography of Joseph Jefferson* (New York, 1889).

M. F. Ketchum, *Born to be an Actor* (Newton, Iowa, n. d.).

Susanne K. Langer, *Feeling and Form* (New York, 1953).

Noah Ludlow, *Dramatic Life as I Found It* (St. Louis, 1880).

Gay MacLaren, *Morally We Roll Along* (New York, 1938).

Marian McKennon, *Tent Show* (New York, 1964).

Albert F. McLean, Jr., *American Vaudeville as Ritual* (Lexington, Kentucky, 1965).

J. H. McVicker, *The Theatre; Its Early Days in Chicago* (Chicago, 1884).

John Robinson, *Old Wagon Show Days* (Cincinnati, 1925).

Neil E. Schaffner with Vance Johnson, *The Fabulous Toby and Me* (Englewood Cliffs, New Jersey, 1968).

Joseph S. Schick, *The Early Theater in Eastern Iowa* (Chicago, 1939).

Ernest Jack Sharp (Sharpsteen), *One Life* (Grand Rapids, Michigan, 1950).

Robert L. Sherman, *Actors and Authors* (Chicago, 1951).

—— *Drama Cyclopedia* (Chicago, 1944).

—— *Chicago Stage: Its Record and Achievement* (Chicago, 1948).

Cornelia Otis Skinner, *Madame Sarah* (New York 1968).

Sol Smith, *Theatrical Management in the West and South for Thirty Years* (New York, 1869; reprint 1968).

William Lawrence Slout, *Theatre in a Tent* (Bowling Green, Ohio, 1972).

Louis Verneuil, *La Vie Merveilleuse de Sarah Bernhardt* (New York, 1942; also trans. by Ernest Boyd, New York, 1942).

Townsend Walsh, *The Career of Dion Boucicault* (New York, 1915).

Herbert Walters (Channell) with Velma E. Lowry, edited by Miron A. Morrill, *Fifty Years Under Canvas: The Autobiography of Herbert Walters* (Hugo, Oklahoma, 1962).

William S. Walker, *The Chicago Stage* (Chicago, 1871).

Writers Project of Illinois, *Stories from the Stage in Chicago* (Chicago, 1941).

Harlan Ware and James Prindl, *Rag Opera* (Indianapolis, 1929).

William Allen White, *Autobiography* (New York, 1946).

Magazines, Newspapers and Specific Magazine and Newspaper Articles

Abilene, Texas, *Reporter-News*, October 15, 1954.

The Billboard, 1894-1960 *passim*.

Bill Bruno's Bulletin, 1929-1930, 1935-40, *passim*.

Centerville, Iowa, *Iowegian*, fall and spring 1903-04, and February 3, 1930.

Chicago *Sun-Times*, "Theatre Trunk Firm Locks Up After 92 Years," April 25, 1951.

Christian Science Monitor, Interview with Bessie Robbins, January 15, 1951.

Dolores Dorn Heft, "Toby: The Twilight of a Tradition," *Theatre Arts*, XLII (August, 1958).

Equity Magazine, 1921-37 *passim*.

Alice Henson Ernst, "Tent Shows," Sunday Magazine Section, Portland *Oregonian*, December 21, 1952.

D. C. Gillette, "Tent Shows," New York *Times*, October 16, 1927, IX, 2:1.

Elmer Hinton, "Along the Sawdust Trail," Nashville *Tennesseean* Sunday Magazine, July 6, 1958.

Vance Johnson, "Hits in the Tall Corn," *Colliers*, August 20, 1949.

The Kinsey's 60 Years of Show Business 1888-1938, Brochure from the Kinsey Co., 1938.

Bill Ladd, "Bill Ladd's Almanac," Louisville, Kentucky, *Courier - Journal*.

Lansing, Michigan, *The State Journal*, "The Rep Show Travels On," November 29, 1936.

Eugene Lockhart, "The Sign Business Evolved from Scenery Painting, *"Signs of the Times*, March, 1957.

Louisville, Kentucky, *Courier - Journal* interview with Ward Hatcher, October 28, 1948.

Earle Chapin May, "Our Canvas Broadway," *Country Gentleman*, May, 1931.

Carlton Miles, "Doubling in Brass," *Theatre Arts*, X October, 1926.

New York Times, April 25, 1954, Sec. 2, p. 3.

New York Clipper, December 30, 1865, p. 298; February 17, 1872, p. 364. Courtesy of Dr. William Slout.

Oskaloosa, Iowa, *Daily Herald*, review of Schaffner Co., June 10, 1958.

Omar Raney, "Forever Toby," *Theatre Arts*, XXXV August, 1951.

Arthur Stringer, "Gun Play," *Golden Book Magazine*, July, 1927, pp. 88-99.

Sabula, Iowa, *Gazette*, Article on Jack and Maude Brooks, September 16, 1948.

Saturday Evening Post, Sept. 17, 1955, p. 62, "Corniest Show on Earth."

Tennessee Folklore Society Bulletin, Carol Pennepacker, "A Surviving Toby Show: Bisbee's Comedians," XXX:2 June, 1964.

210

Variety, April 11, 1962, "Last Tent Show Ending Forever." May 16, 1962, "Folding of Last of Toby Tents" (Robert Downing).

Vermontville, Michigan, *Echo*, special supplement devoted to the L. Verne Slout Co., May 2, 1929.

K. C. Young, "Tent Shows," *New York Times*, April 21, 1927, IV, p. 18.

Unpublished Materials

Robert Dean Klassen, *The Tent-Repertoire Theatre: A Rural American Institution* (Michigan State University Dissertation, 1970).

Trudy Trousdale Latchaw, *The Trousdale Brothers Theatrical Companies from 1898 to 1915* (Master's Thesis, University of Minnesota, 1948).

Autobiography of Alex Pitcaithley, Carlsbad, New Mexico.

Wallace Bruce, Notes collected and written down for a projected book never published for Frank Luther; done at Hutchinson, Kansas.

Larry Dale Clark, *Toby Shows: A Form of American Popular Theater* (University of Illinois Dissertation, 1963).

William Lawrence Slout, *The Repertoire Tent Show from its Beginnings to 1920.* Published as *Theatre in a Tent*, The Popular Press, Bowling Green, Ohio (University of California, Los Angeles, Dissertation, 1970).

Lucille Spooner, written speech and memorabilia of the Payton and Spooner families.

Mrs. Ethel Bennett, Memorabilia of A. Milo Bennett, famous Chicago theatrical agent, Canton, Illinois.

GLOSSARY

airdome

An open air theater. It usually consisted of an area surrounded by a temporary wall of canvas, metal or wood without any roof covering, with the ground for the floor where the seats were placed. The stage at the back was a covered area along with off-stage areas and the dressing rooms all of which were masked from the audience, usually with canvas.

bail-ring

A ring of iron about a foot in diameter.

bail-ring tent

A tent constructed for use when the spread of canvas necessary for the show was so heavy that the pushpole type of tent could not carry it. A bail-ring tent was used with such large circuses as Ringling Brothers, and with a few tent shows such as Sarah Bernhardt's and Billy Wehle's Bilroy's Comedians, the one successful tent show of the late thirties. The center poles are erected first with the iron bail-ring at the bottom or butt end of the pole. From the top of the center pole hangs a pulley system. There is a bail-ring at the bottom of each center pole.

The sections of canvas of each separate part of the tent are laced together and tied to the bail-ring. From the top a rope attached to the pulley system hangs.

First the side-poles are put in place, then the next higher poles, called quarter-poles; after that the bail-rings are hoisted, by man power, or, as on a circus, by elephant power, which makes the hoist of the canvas roof very easy.

A bail-ring tent is necessary for any tent over 50 feet wide; Bilroy's Comedians, which reached its greatest success as a motorized one-nighter musical show with a line of girls in the late 30s, had a tent 100 feet wide, 225 feet long, seating 4200 people, and requiring six bail-rings and center poles to support the canvas. Mrs. Marian McKennon in her book *Tent Show* describes vividly the raising of a bail-ring tent (pp. 83-87), the last show to take to the road after World War II, and a show which used a bail-ring tent.

This information comes chiefly from Johnny Finch, Olney, Illinois who spent almost a decade as juvenile comedian and public relations man with Bilroy's Comedians.

ballyhoo

A synonym for any kind of show business advertising gimmick.

barker

We would call him an announcer. He would stand in front of the tent, airdome or sideshow and try to attract an audience by shouting the merits of the attraction through a megaphone, the old-time equivalent of a microphone.

battens

Properly spelled *baton* from the French word meaning *stick*. A strip of wood or length of pipe measuring a little more than the width of a stage (28 feet more or less), placed at the top and bottom of a drop curtain. At the top it

212

held the curtain the proper height from the stage floor, at the bottom it stretched the curtain into a smooth, unwrinkled surface.

bill, bills
> Synonym for play or program offered, *e. g., Smilin' Through* is the bill for this week; or Glotz's Comedians is presenting a great vaudeville bill this week.

billing
> Synonym for advertising, especially display sheets.

blowdown
> The destruction of a tent by storm.

blue comedy
> Dirty jokes.

blues
> Bleachers at the back of the tent used for general admission seats in contrast to the reserved section.

bunchlights
> A set of lights with receptacles set close together in any kind of container such as a tin dishpan which would reflect the lights onto the stage from off stage at the side. They are a crude and home-manufactured form of the old-fashioned flood-light.

business
> The activities of the actor while playing a part for the audience, his movements about the stage and his use of cigarette lighters, fans, handkerchiefs, cigars, cigarettes, etc., appropriate to the playing of the part.

calliope
> A mechanical musical instrument in the earlier days operated by steam, later by forced air, whose sound tried to give the effect of an organ. Comparable to a player piano. It was almost always in use during the operation of a carousel or merry-go-round.

candy pitch
> Sale of candy during the course of the show. Pitch means sale.

canvas men
> The crew of men who did the mechanical part of the show, such as setting up the tent, and, after the engagement was over, taking it down, packing it, and loading it on truck or train or whatever means of transportation was used. These men also did all the menial tasks connected with the show.

circle stock
> Playing the same play for a stated period, such as a week, first in one town and then in another. The same towns would be played the next week with a change in play. The McOwen Company in 1928 played two days in Kearney, two days in Grand Island, and two days in Hastings, all towns close together in Nebraska, then played the same towns the next week with a different play.

commonwealth basis

A business arrangement whereby the manager and the members of the company agreed to share equally in the expenses and profits of the show. It was often used in the later days of the rep shows when definite salaries were hard to pay. It was also difficult to work the arrangement out so that it was accepted by all as fair.

diamond dye scenery

The scene painter, instead of using conventional scene paint which tends to crack and flake, especially if taken down and rolled up, uses the old-fashioned dyes available in any drugstore under the trade name Diamond Dyes. The process was invented by Jesse Cox of Estherville, Iowa.

doubling in brass

The actor is required to play a musical instrument and also usually to present a specialty or variety act. This became very common in the later days of the rep companies.

dramatic end tent

A type of tent that makes audience viewing of the stage complete by the elimination of the last centerpole of the conventional tent which always blocked the view of the stage. This was done by substituting two masts at either side of the stage opening for the last center pole. A cable was stretched between the masts in the center of which was a block and tackle for lifting the canvas at a point midway between the two masts. Most dramatic end tents, however, were made with two quarter poles at either side of the stage opening which supported the upper part of this end of the tent. In any case, the "dramatic end" is really a separate addition to the tent just as the marquee or front entrance is at the front. The conventional tent is simply not used where the dramatic end begins, and a more unobstructed view of the stage is provided.

drop curtains

A common name for any painted curtain which provided the completion of the set at the back of the stage. In city theaters they were hung on battens and pulled up into the stage house (second story of back stage) when not in use. In the opera house or tent which had no room above stage they were simply left in place or rolled up in the fashion described in Section II chapter 3.

flat

A frame covered with light material, preferably canvas or heavy muslin, and painted as part of a set of scenery. They are light and easy to take down and put up, but are difficult to carry in traveling unless they are crated. They were always used in city theaters. They were invented in the late 1840s by Madame Vestris in London and are chiefly useful in making a stage set look like a real room.

found

A term used as a synonym for food.

French leave

A term in general use meaning to leave any job without giving notice and almost always secretly.

front and back, timber and town

A term which, according to Mrs. Neil Schaffner, is used to describe the backdrops which a company could expect to be furnished in any small-town theater. Translated, the terms mean, parlour, kitchen, woods, and street. Mrs. Schaffner has presented a wonderful collection of these backdrops to the Theater Museum at Mt. Pleasant, Iowa.

gelatine

A colored, transparent piece of material something like a clear celluloid used to make the lights for the show less glaring. Nowadays they are made of plastic usually. They are generally known as 'gels'. A gel of the shade called Surprise Pink could make a sallow complexion look young from the stage.

Go gilley

To motorize a show.

grand drapes — see proscenium

grouchbag

A small container, usually of chamois skin sewed together in the form of a pouch. It was fastened to the actor's underwear or in some fashion to the part of his body not generally viewed by the public or his fellow actors. Money saved for emergencies was put in this packet.

G-string comedian

Garrulous, foolish, old men comics such as Doc Quackenbush in *Call of the Woods*. These characters were something like the Yankee character of the early 19th century but they were always old men. The writer has been unable to find out the origin of this term as applied to these characters, but it certainly has no relationship at all to the term as used at the present day describing a strip-tease artist's smallest piece of body covering.

ghost show effects

Some arrangement of mirrors to achieve the sudden and apparently magical appearance of a character such as Mephiste in *Faust* or the ghost of Banquo in *Macbeth*. How to achieve these effects must have been a well-kept secret for this writer's research has so far yielded no information on the subject.

"Hey Rube"

A riot, usually in a southern or southwestern area like Texas. Someone offended at something in the show, or even for sheer mischief, would shout the phrase which was a signal for a general attack on the people connected with the show and anybody else in the crowd spoiling for a fight.

house, houses

Synonym for theater.

ingenue

A young woman very sweet and innocent. Sometimes these parts were played by older women who had forgotten how they had aged. Johnny Finch tells how he broke up at one time after he had played opposite a woman playing an ingenue whose real age was 54. He suddenly broke into laughter and spoiled the scene.

jacks and stringers

Supports for the stage, orchestra, and candy prize platform floors. The jacks are supports made something like sawhorses. Across them in parallel lines a few feet apart run two by fours, the stringers which fit into notches on the jacks. The platform boards are then laid in numbered order across the stringers.

legs

Narrow pieces of cloth cut to hang from a batten on either side of the stage. They were painted to resemble tree trunks, part of a wall of a house interior, side of building, etc. They were meant to cover the view of the area backstage from the audience.

lighting

As used in this book, illumination for the stage or theater auditorium.

Since most theatrical activity since the 16th century has taken place inside an enclosed room with no windows permitting outside light to enter, some device has always been necessary to light the interior, especially the stage area to make the action visible to the audience. Up to the middle of the 18th century candles had to suffice. Sometimes a big chandelier was used to light the auditorium as well as the stage. Gas light introduced in the 18th century was a great improvement although very dangerous. Its intensity on the stage was controllable as were the colors used, but its use resulted in innumerable theater fires. Up to the invention of the electric lamp in the 1880s the lack of adequate lighting resulted in the development of very detailed scene painting. Kerosene lamps were also used before and after the invention of the electric lamp; kerosene footlights and overhead lamps were equally as dangerous as gas fixtures.

Stage lighting today has developed instruments capable of effects undreamed of even as short a time ago as 1925 when the first electronic lighting system was installed in the Goodman Theater in Chicago.

makeup

Actors have always needed something to make their faces look alive in the intense light focused on them or to help them change their faces to look more like the character played. A rather homely young woman can be made to look glamorous and beautiful on the stage with the right makeup on her face, just as she can in real life. Greasepaint of various colors has been used as the basic medium of makeup on the stage for a long time, with the use of an appropriate face powder to keep the paint from shining. Recently, a different kind of makeup called pancake has been invented, consisting of somewhat solidified powder rubbed off on a thin puff and then applied to the face.

marquee

The front entrance to a show tent. It is actually an addition to the main tent itself, attached to it by ties, and contains the box office, perhaps pictures of the cast and show and is often decorated gaily.

masking

Any curtain or screen used to cover an area on the stage not supposed to be seen by the audience.

216

medicine shows

Old-fashioned small shows which traveled about the country from town to town giving a free performance of vaudeville or drama. During intermissions and before and after the show the "doctor" and his troupe peddled medicines supposed to cure any ailment, usually some sweet syrup mixed up with water and a little alcohol. Several medicine shows were huge organizations such as Doc Rucker's which played the big cities of the midwest; he carried a large troupe of actors who knew the parts in most of the current shows. Every night Doc would ask the audience which show they wanted to see. The show which carried the most votes was prepared during the following day. The medicine usually sold for a dollar a bottle. Charles Worthan's original show, the Parker Carnival Co., was a medicine show. Charlie was a great dancer so his contribution to the entertainment was fitting.

minstrel show

The one original invention of the American theater, minstrel shows originated from the entertainments of singing and dancing that the enslaved black people evolved during any holidays on the old plantations before the Civil War. Black people, who were first accepted as equals in the theater, made up the first minstrel show troupes which traveled about the country, soon to be imitated by whites using the same format and burnt cork as makeup. These shows were immensely popular from 1870 to World War I but disappeared in the 1920s. The show was not dramatic, but consisted of singing, dancing, and clever repartee.

olio

A curtain hung about three or four feet behind the front curtain, used to hide the stage during a change of scene between acts while a vaudeville or specialty act was going on in front of it.

Also used to indicate the act itself.

one-nighters

Shows which traveled by train and presented one play and stayed only one-night in each town they played.

opera house

Synonym for theater.

pitchman

A sidewalk salesman offering novelties and even useful articles to passers-by. They were usually operating in large cities. A pitchman means a salesman and a pitch is an attempt to sell something. The Billboard used to have a column called "Pipes from Pitchmen."

possum belly

A man-sized receptacle in the bottom of a baggage car which was covered by a top made to match the floor. If a show wanted to carry an extra crew man, one more than the railroad would allow a free ride, he was often concealed in the possum belly. What it's railroad use was, I have not discovered.

preacher plays

Plays such as *Saintly Hypocrites* and *Clouds and Sunshine* in which the leading man is a minister, or a play with a strong moral and religious message.

Charles Harrison was famous for writing preacher plays. They were an attempt to divert church criticism from the shows.

props

Articles in use on the stage. There are two kinds: stage props, which are generally furniture, and hand props which are articles used by the actors in projecting characterization or plot, such as handkerchiefs, fans, guns, cigarette lighters, etc.

proscenium

The frame for the stage. The stage as finally perfected in the Renaissance was built so that the stage end was surrounded by a picture frame. This complex separated it completely from the audience. It could have a grand drape, a lavishly decorated piece of material, hung above it and helping to frame the sides; it could also have a teaser which was a movable curtain at the top of the stage opening which could lower or raise the height of the stage opening. The Obrecht show was unusual among the tent shows for having an elaborate proscenium complex. Most tent shows did not. If they had anything at the top of the stage opening, it was a short, immovable, pleated curtain like a valance on household window draperies. All permanent city theaters were equipped with elaborately designed upper and side curtains of this type. They helped mask the part of the stage the producer did not want the audience to see.

pushpole

A pushpole tent is of the type usually made for smaller entertainments and assemblies than the bail-ring of the circus tents. Its area was adequate for a width of 50 feet or less. This was the type of tent usually used by the tent rep companies.

The process of raising and lowering it was exactly the opposite of that used with the bail-ring tent. The whole tent is put in place on the ground before any poles are used. With the bail-ring the center poles, each with its accompanying bail-ring and the guy wires are set up before the tent sections are raised. In both cases the bags with the canvas sections rolled in them are set in their approximate places. On each kind of tent stakes have been driven around the tent to hold guy ropes and wires.

Next on a pushpole tent the sections of the tent are laid out on the ground, the front or marquee end first, and laced up. The lacing must be carefully done because not a hole can be missed. After this has been done, the side poles, about 9 feet in height, are put in place, starting at the back or dramatic end. The side poles are slid under the canvas and raised up. The three quarter poles holding the dramatic end are raised next. When all the quarterpoles are in place, the center poles are put in place and raised beginning at the stage end of the tent. A dolly wagon is used to straighten the poles that cannot be straightened by hand. After the auditorium and dramatic end are completely up with the ropes sufficiently taut to the stakes, the stage, lighting equipment and chairs are put into place.

rep.shows

Short term for the repertory companies. Sometimes the members of the company were called repsters.

218

repertoire

Playing a series of plays during one engagement. Usually the tent shows played an engagement of a week, changing the play every night. The same people usually played in every show. Conventional small companies usually employed five men and three women. Plays were written with this type of cast in mind.

rigging

The stage machinery back stage used to hang, draw up and let down scenery. In the city theaters it was a very elaborate system of weights and counterweights, ropes and "sheaves" or wheels in the extreme height of the stage loft put there to make the raising and lowering of the curtains easier. This sort of thing was almost non-existent in the tent theater.

It can also be applied to any system of ropes, or wires, used to hold up anything within the tent or the tent itself.

roll-up curtains

The sketch in the chapter on the old opera house describes the construction and working of this type of curtain. It was used in these theaters in place of the curtain that could be drawn up into the stage loft in the city theaters. The front curtain in an opera house was almost always a roll-up curtain. One can observe excellent examples of these in the old opera house at Shelbina, Mo., or the old theater at Findlay, Illinois, now host to a Country O'pry every Saturday night. This latter curtain is a very fine piece of construction.

roundtop tent

The conventional type of tent with both front end and back end exactly the same. A roundtop tent was often used for dramatic entertainments in the old days. The chief difficulty these presented was the last center pole in front of the stage area obscuring the view of all of the audience. The invention of the dramatic end tent eliminated this difficulty.

side, sides

A set of pages, halves of an ordinary 8½ x 11 inch sheet of paper, containing the lines and cues of a characters part. Plays were usually a long time reaching publication, often not until the copyright ran out (cf. Charley's Aunt) and were available only as sides to the actors with a complete typewritten copy only for the director. Hence the Chicago Manuscript Play Company. With the coming of play publishers such as Samuel French of New York and the proliferation of amateur performances of standard plays after they were released for use by the general public, the use of sides has been discontinued except in the production of new plays and stock company performances.

show print

Advertising for the show. Also, the printing company doing the printing of these sheets.

Stage Right, Stage Left, Downstage, Upstage

Usually written SR, SL, DS, US. Stage Right is the actor's right as he looks at the audience, SL the actor's left in the same position. DS is the front of the stage, US, the back. These last terms arise from the fact that the early 19th

219

century stage was raked, slanting from at least a foot higher in the back to the front level. US was a great place to be seen from and to present a great speech. Nowadays we would consider it too far away from the audience to be an effective position.

tab show

A shortened version of a popular musical comedy featuring a line of girls (dancers), usually in connection with a motion picture. Joe Marion ran one of these successfully in a circle stock in central Nebraska in 1930-31, later moving to the Moon Theater in Omaha.

teaser

See Proscenium

Three-sheeting

Showing off. Advertising sheets were conventionally 28 x 42 inches. The smallest size was called the one-sheet. Everything larger was made in multiples of a one-sheet. A three-sheet was a strip of considerable size. An actor was said to be three-sheeting when he dressed up, wore his best jewelry, and made an appearance at the post office at mail-time, carrying an air of great importance. This was supposed to impress the towners with his greatness.

The size of the sheets went up as high as a 24-sheet. So did the actions of the actors in their attempts to call attention to themselves in public.

Toby

The silly kid or light comedy role.

Tom show

A show playing *Uncle Tom's Cabin* and that play only.

towners

The inhabitants of the town being played as contrasted with the show people.

troupers

Members of the company of traveling players; actors.

vaudeville

Variety acts, such as singing, dancing, acrobatics, comic dialogues, any kind of very brief form of entertainment. In big-time vaudeville, one-act plays, such as "War Brides" starring the great actress Nazimova, were often used. Such movie stars as Theodore Roberts, Clara Kimball Young and Henry B. Walthall often toured the vaudeville circuits.

Vaudeville was the big money-maker of show business between 1900 and 1930. It evolved from the singing, dancing, comic and other kinds of acts presented in the old-time honky-tonks, places of entertainment generally associated with saloons and considered not quite respectable. Big-time vaudeville was the glamour business of showbiz in the first thirty years of this century, corresponding very closely to the TV shows of today. On a big-time show eight acts were conventional. They took about two hours. Small-time vaudeville was anything from six acts down plus a motion picture as part of the program. Albert F. McLean Jr.'s book *American Vaudeville as Ritual* gives a wonderfully appreciative appraisal of this form of entertainment.

220

wings

As pieces of scenery, two-fold screens painted to represent outdoors, or indoors, and placed at an angle from the back to the front of the stage. The backdrop completed the set of scenery. The wing and drop type of set was developed by the 18th century and continued in general use until the invention of the box set by Madame Vestris in the 1840s. Even so it remained a conventional type of set outside of the metropolises up to as late as 1930. Its last use was probably in schools and colleges which had been supplied with such by the old commercial scenic supply houses which went out of business with the disappearance of theater in the smaller cities.

Term can also be applied to the area off-stage just out of sight of the audience,. An actor caught by the audience standing in the wings, waiting for a cue, has raised hilarity in the audience in this writers's experience as late as 1973.

INDEX

Robinson, Bill — 40
Robinson, Gil — 37
Robinson, Yankee — 16-17, 146
Robbins, Bessie — 110
Robbins, Clint — 65, 68
Robbins, Clint and Bessie — 29, 74
Rogers Tent and Awning Co. — 54
Rosier, Harold — 189-190
Rotnour, J. B. — 19, 92, 131
round-top tents — 54
Ruble-Kreyer Theater Co. — 52, 114
Russell, Genevieve — 20, 184

Sadler, Harley — 60, 73, 80-81, 94, 132,
   153, 185, 187
St. Elmo — 149
St. Louis — 43
Saintly Hypocrites and Honest Sinners
   — 8, 66
salaries, actors' — 104
Salt House — 43
Savidge, Walter — 39, 107, 182
Savidge, Mrs. Walter — 29, 107
Schaffner, Neil — 67, 68, 149, 153
Schaffner, Neil and Caroline — 29, 186
Schick, Joseph — 12, 43
Secret; or a Hole in the Wall, A — 16
Seven Cairns Brothers — 61, 62
Seymoure, Schnitz; — 89, 182
Sharp, Ernest Jack — 37
Sheriff Jim's Daughter — 65
Sherman, Robert J. — 67, 159
Sherman, Robert L. — 8, 11, 16
show print — 57
Shubert, Sam and Lee — 19
Simpson, Mrs. Agnes — 182
Simpson, Karl — 67, 88-89
Slout Players, L. Verne — 56, 58, 62,
   153, 155, 182, 185-186
Slout, Dr. William — 149, 157
Smith, Sol — 12, 15, 16
Somerville, H. C. — 54
Sparks, Ted and Leon Hahn — 88
specialties — 71-74
Spider and the Fly, The — 67
Spooks — 67
Spooner, Lucille — 48
Sputters — 66, 150
Squawman, The — 67
Stone, Milburn — 189
Street, Doc Franklin — 183

Strong, Elwin — 29, 59, 64, 104, 175,
   182
Strongheart — 67
Sund, Dot and Jess — 186
Swain, Col. W. I. — 28, 56, 87, 107,
   177
Switchell, Sample — 146

talking pictures — 14, 162, 164, 165,
   166, 167
Taylor Players — 163
Taylor Trunk Co. — 40
Teeters, Tol — 89
Ten Nights in a Barroom — 13, 146
Tent Rep Managers Protective
   Association — 32, 176, 177
They Broke the Prairie — 12
Three in a Bed — 65
Tildy Ann — 67, 75
Tilton-Guthrie Players — 101
Tilton, M. H. (Mid) — 101, 186
Tobe Haxton — 147
Toby — 8, 68, 77, 132, 145, 160, 179
Toby Goes to Hollywood — 159
Toby's News — 59
Toby Tompkins — 149
tornadoes — 126
towners — 109-115
Tracy, Spencer — 189
Trilby — 65
Trousdale, Boyd — 24, 89
Trousdale Brothers — 23-26
Trousdale, Winn — 24-25
Tucker, Sophie — 40
Turn to the Right — 68, 130
Tuscola, Illinois — 61

Uncle Tom's Cabin — 12, 13, 16, 186
Union Concession Co. — 82
Union station, Kansas City — 88
United States Tent and Awning Co.
   — 54
Universal Theatres Concession
   Company — 81, 82

Variety — 71
Varney, Vivien — 112
Vitaphone — 161

Wagon Shows — 36-37
Walters, Herb — 37, 183

225